The Office Relocation Sourcebook

The Office Relocation Sourcebook

A Guide to Managing Staff
Throughout the Move

Dennis A. Attwood

JOHN WILEY & SONS, INC.
New York ♦ Chichester ♦ Brisbane ♦ Toronto ♦ Singapore ♦ Weinheim

Library of Congress Cataloging-in-Publication Data:
Attwood, Dennis A.
    The office relocation sourcebook: a guide to managing staff
  throughout the move / Dennis A. Attwood.
        p.   cm.
    Includes index.
    ISBN 0-471-13016-8 (alk. paper)
    1. Business relocation—Handbooks, manuals, etc.   I. Title.
  HD58.A85   1996
    658.2′1—dc20   96-13424

Printed in the United States of America

10 9 8 7 6 5 4 3 2 1

To my daughter Cathy and my sons Gord and Sean, and especially to my wife and partner Pam for her encouragement and understanding

Contents

Preface

═══════

This book is about the human factor in office staff relocation. It is written for the people who constitute the team that makes the relocation happen and those on the periphery who, if they have been involved in relocation in the past, dread the disruption that the relocation causes—the managers and supervisors that are deluged with complaints by employees who resist relocating and the building services staff who endure the agony of dealing with project staff and contractors while, at the same time, trying to do their normal job.

The relocation of a workforce is not just about moving furniture, equipment, and office workers from one place to the next. It's not just about reconstructing the office space or purchasing new carpeting. *A relocation project is a people project.* It's about real-life office workers who are affected by every decision that corporate management and the relocation team make. It's about respecting their needs.

The relocation project is also about the project team—those who have to make it happen, often with impossible deadlines, too little help, and an inadequate budget. As is usually the case, many team members are chosen from the office staff and have no prior relocation experience. These are the one-time movers who will never again do anything as traumatic, chaotic, stressful, exciting, exhilarating, and self-satisfying in their working careers.

The book is not intended to be another text about visual display terminal (VDT) ergonomics, though the ergonomic design of the office will figure prominently in several chapters. Neither is the book intended to make the members of the project team "experts" in all aspects of relocation. It is intended to provide the team with the information that they need to "pull off" the relocation. It is not intended to replace the experts, but to provide the laypersons on the team with the information that they need to direct and manage the experts. To accomplish this, the book is written, for the most part, as a series of short ideas punctuated by "how-to" lists and easy to use tools that the team members will need to "jump-start" the project.

No relocation can be accomplished without some amount of office reconstruction. Thus while the book is targeted at the relocation of office staff, tips on design and reconstruction will inevitably be sprinkled throughout each chapter.

Dennis A. Attwood, P.Eng., Ph.D., CPE

Acknowledgments

═══════════════════

The experiences that I have shared with the many people with whom I have dealt over the years gave me the incentive to write this book. But four colleagues—Ted Walker, Ed Green, Siep Nyholt, and Terry Moynihan—stand out as the source of many of the ideas that I was able to capture and put into print. I shall be ever grateful to Debby Hudgins at Exxon, Inc. Biomedical Sciences Inc. and to Grant Parker at Imperial Oil Limited who were instrumental in giving this book its life. I also want to thank Mary Danz-Reece, Joe Deeb, Bill Diana, Lisa Garrison, and Bob Moritz, my colleagues at Exxon Biomedical-Sciences, Inc. who reviewed the manuscript.

Finally, I am indebted to son Sean who typed the draft manuscript. I couldn't have made it without him.

Chapter One

Introduction

═══════════

Office workers relocate in response to a corporate need, which may be the result of:

- Reorganization or downsizing
- Merger with another company
- Product development project
- Expiration of a lease

It's important for those who have been given the responsibility for implementing the relocation to know why it is taking place and what the objectives are. As this book unfolds, the relocation team will come to appreciate how the goals of the relocation can affect their choices among the alternative courses of action that are available to them.

Corporate management is responsible for making the decision to relocate staff, for deciding when the relocation must be completed, and for deciding how much money to spend on it. The relocation team acts as management's consultants, providing information and counsel on which the decisions are made. Once the decisions are final, how-ever, the team's responsibility is to carry them out no matter how little time, money, and help are available. While the pressures to complete the project on-time and on-budget seem enormous, the team will ultimately be judged on how well they handled the people they were charged with relocating.

This book is about the human factors involved with the relocation of office staff. It deals with all aspects of designing for human use—from the best way to put together the relocation team to the best location for building signs. It introduces the project team to diverse concepts that they should consider, such as the extent of employee participation and when to implement alternative workplace strategies, and to the issues that they *must* plan for, such as communications to employees and barrier-free facilities.

Every project consists of at least four phases:

1. Planning
2. Design
3. Implementation
4. Follow-up

This book is divided into sections that reflect this project sequence. However, since planning and design are often accomplished simultaneously during a relocation project, they are combined to form the largest section of the book, Chapters 1 to 8. Implementation and follow-up are presented as stand-alone chapters (Chapters 9 and 10).

1.1   PLANNING AND DESIGN

Planning the relocation project is considered by most practitioners to be the most critical phase of relocation. Too often, however, relocation teams under pressure to show visible progress don't devote enough time and effort to the planning process. As a result, the teams continue to struggle with planning decisions while the project is underway. The outcome can be catastrophic as policies are decided on the fly and decisions are inconsistent, creating an imbalance in what one group gets over another.

1.1.1   Planning the Relocation

If the company relocation is associated with the planning and construction of a new building, the building schedule drives the program. Since construction projects typically require months to complete, adequate time is available to plan the relocation. In most cases, however, relocations are driven by sudden changes in a company that require immediate changes to the way people work and who they work for and with. Consequently, relocations are put on a fast track.

Chapter 2 deals with planning the strategy for relocating and about organizing the team that will make it happen. Several team organization models are provided to help you decide how to proceed. Team positions, such as "relocation coordinator," are described, and the responsibilities that are normally assigned to each position are listed. Tables are provided as templates for you to customize once you decide who should be responsible for what activities.

1.1.2   Social Issues in Office Relocation

People naturally resist change, and office relocation is about change. Thus people naturally resist relocating. The challenge to the project team is turning the employees' resistance into acceptance.

Chapter 3 is about the initial resistance to relocation that occurs among office workers and the stress that accompanies the change. It helps you understand why workers resist change and design ways of overcoming the resistance. It shows how the company can intervene to help the workers accept change and what the workers can do to help themselves.

1.1.3 Communications

Most experts in relocation agree that the manner in which the organization communicates its intentions and plans to its office staff, suppliers, customers, and the community determines the success or failure of the relocation. Effective communication is a two-way process—both from the company to the people who are affected and from the people to the company. Feedback from employees is especially important.

Chapter 4 addresses the types of communications that are required:

- During planning, design, and premove stages
- During the move
- After the move has been completed

Each of the recommendations are in list form or in the form of tables and figures that can be copied for your own use.

1.1.4 Environmental Concerns of the Office Worker

The advent of computers in the late 1970's and early 1980's underscored the importance of the office environment to the health and efficiency of the office worker. Glare, for example, from artificial and natural light sources has always been a problem in the office, but until glare was linked to productivity losses and errors in visual display terminal (VDT) use, it did not receive the attention that it does today.

Chapter 5 examines four environmental variables that concern employees:

1. Lighting
2. Office acoustics
3. Temperature and relative humidity
4. Air quality

It examines the effects of each variable on the worker, provides design guidance for each, and recommends ways of identifying problems and solving them. Most of the guidance and recommendations are in the form of how-to lists or tables that you can modify to suit your own plans.

1.1.5 Office Planning

Recent advances in computer and telecommunications technology have redefined the office and office work. It is no longer necessary to physically be located in the office in order to "be at work." Traditional workplaces have been replaced by virtual workplaces as office workers conduct activities from their homes, their cars, or anywhere else that provides power for their equipment and voice and data connections.

Chapter 6 is about planning offices to meet organizational objectives and worker needs. It revisits the concept of traditional offices and provides alternative office concepts.

Quite apart from alternative officing, the chapter also addresses the planning and design of the traditional office. Both open-plan and closed-office concepts are considered, and guidance is provided for selecting and designing each.

1.1.6 Workspace Design

The bread and butter issue in any relocation is how the resulting workspace supports the office worker's job. Hence during the course of every relocation, the project team will inevitably be faced with decisions on the selection and layout of furniture, seating, and accessories in the worker's office, decisions that should support the technology with which the worker is provided.

Over the past 10 years, the health of the individual has become an issue for many organizations. As office automation invades the worklives of all office workers, it carries with it a new threat to their well-being—cumulative trauma disorders (CTDs). These are injuries caused by frequent microtraumas of the soft tissues of the body. The microtraumas are caused by prolonged work using improper postures. The immediate and obvious cause of the poor postures is the design of the physical workstation and its associated lighting. The reason for prolonged work without recuperative breaks may be traced to poor work processes.

Chapter 7 addresses the design and layout of the physical workspace. The chapter is dedicated to four major objectives in workspace design:

1. Prevent the occurrence of acute injuries and illnesses as well as those caused by repeated trauma to soft tissue (CTDs)
2. Increase productivity of office workers
3. Match the design of the workstation and layout of the office to the work functions
4. Increase the comfort of office workers and their ability to access the tools they need to do their jobs

As with other chapters, Chapter 7 provides many visual examples that you can learn from and a number or guidelines and tables that can be customized for use in your own relocation effort.

1.1.7 Special Areas and Services

In large relocations, almost every area of the building receives the attention of the project team. In small relocations, building services areas such as shipping and receiving are not part of the relocation team's responsibility. This book targets the office systems that need to be addressed in most relocations. Granted, not all experts will agree that the services and specialized areas that are treated in Chapter 8 are the most important. But, all would agree that they need to be addressed.

Chapter 8 provides guidance on the design of two architectural systems and two nonoffice areas:

- Wayfinding and signage
- Designing for the disabled worker
- Meeting rooms
- Restrooms

Checklists are provided for use in evaluating wayfinding systems and the design of restrooms. Guidance is provided for planning a barrier-free facility and for the design of and furniture selection for meeting rooms.

1.2   IMPLEMENTATION

The physical relocation is the most disruptive phase of the project. Employees don't want or need to be subjected to the hassle of a prolonged move. Nor should they have to endure more than one move before they arrive at their final destination. Their furniture and belongings should arrive with them, and the time required to come up to speed in the new location should be minimized. If the move is not conducted effectively, the repercussions can hurt the company, alienate the employees, and severely damage the reputation of the relocation team. So, this is where the planning finally pays off.

Chapter 9 deals with all aspects of the physical move, from gathering information in preparation for the move to the activities required in the postmove follow-up. It contains many checklists that your team can customize for use in their own relocation. A highlight of the chapter is the provision of a project scheduling database that updates the individual schedules of each of the team members and employees automatically. The use of this scheduling system can greatly reduce scheduling errors that commonly occur when so many people are involved in the move at the same time.

1.3   POST-PROJECT EVALUATION

If you don't measure how well the project was conducted, its unlikely that the process will ever improve. We measure project success by talking to the people who were involved—the office workers, the project team members, and the external consultants and contractors.

Chapter 10 provides guidance on how to evaluate your relocation project and gives some tools that you can use to complete the evaluation.

1.4   COMPUTER FILES OF TOOLS DEVELOPED

This book is intended to be not only a source of knowledge for the project team but also a source of guidance and of tools to help the team get a quick start in the process. To this end, each chapter contains tables, figures, how-to lists, and checklists that are available for the project team members to use on their own projects.

To make copying and customization easier, each of the tables and lists that can be customized for use on other projects has been gathered in the Appendices and has also been copied onto a computer disk that is provided with this book. The files are written in Microsoft® Word® version 6.0. Each table and figure that is copied onto disk is identified in the book by a disk icon. Also on disk is a working copy of the project scheduling database that is discussed in Chapter 9. The database is written in Microsoft® Access® version 2.0 and instructions on its use are provided in Appendix 3.

1.5   SUPPORTING DOCUMENTATION

The book also contains a glossary of terms used in the chapters, extensive lists of references in office relocation, and a subject index.

Chapter Two

Organizing the Relocation Project Team

―――――――

2.1 INTRODUCTION

Too often, relocations are driven by sudden changes in a company that are brought about by mergers, reorganizations, or new product development. The redirection requires immediate response including the movement of workers in a short period of time to satisfy short-term corporate objectives.

No matter how short the period might be to relocate, time must be devoted to developing the plan that will orchestrate the move. Knee-jerk reactions to corporate decisions will ultimately result in disaster, often at the expense of the career of the person in charge of the relocation.

This chapter is about planning the move by developing:

- A strategic plan for the relocation and associated construction
- A team that will implement the plan

It would be a mistake to believe that planning is frivolous or time wasting. True, planning does require time because of the people involved, and larger, more complex relocations require more time. The planning process, however, does not have to be ponderous. The objective of this chapter is to provide you with the building blocks necessary to quickly create the draft plan, which can then be reviewed and finalized with the organization.

The information provided in this chapter will, hopefully, reduce the planning time required. The strategic plan will be developed in a hierarchical format, which will make it easy to identify those issues that are pertinent to your specific relocation. Team development and member responsibilities are presented in a matrix format that is keyed to the planning schedule.

2.2   THE STRATEGIC PLAN

The strategic plan is the road map for the relocation. It defines the goals and objectives of the relocation, and specifies the organization and decision making process. It provides the common thread to which every person involved in or affected by the relocation is expected to adhere. By doing so, it reduces uncertainty and the potential for misinterpretation.

The strategic plan usually addresses the following key factors, objectives, and rationales:

- Guiding principles
- Design of the relocation organization
- Project phases and timing
- Cost estimation

2.2.1   Objectives and Rationales for the Relocation

The project objective specifies what the project is to accomplish. For example, it may be specific:

- Relocate 85 employees in the marketing department to new facilities on the fifth floor.

On the other hand, it may be directional:

- Optimize use of space and funds to satisfy business and employee needs for the reorganization of the corporation.

Often, in the latter case, the objective is followed by a statement that specifies the scope of the project. For example:

- 2000 management and staff will be relocated within three buildings in the downtown core.

The rationale for the relocation is often contained in the objectives statement, but it may be addressed separately. For example, the rationale for the first objective above may be:

- The marketing department is to be relocated adjacent to sales to improve one-on-one interaction between workers in each department, and to take advantage of the synergies that exist between the two departments, to reduce the time and effort involved in information transfer.

2.2.2   Guiding Principles

The guiding principles set the tone of the project by stating:

- How the project will be managed
- How managers and employees will be integrated into the project

The principles usually reflect the culture of the organization, and the organizational culture is usually defined by senior management, especially the President or Chief Executive Officer (CEO).

Examples of guiding principles include:

- *Space assignment:* Building/floor assignments must be based on functional needs and group affinities.
- *Priorities:* First priority is the relocation of information services staff and equipment.
- *Employee treatment:* No employee should move more than twice during the relocation.
- *Relocation/construction process*: Construction during relocation should be minimal.
- *Move process:*
  —Move people, not furniture.
  —All moves are to be coordinated by the project team.
- *Furniture*: Maximum use is to be made of existing furniture.
- *Office equipment*:
  —Existing technology must move with employee.
  —Upgrades in technology are by exception only.
- *Planning*: Interaction wastes time. Decisions are to be made quickly and approved in writing at the appropriate level.

In many cases, the principles can be considered "loaded guns," requiring their own implementation system. A case in point is the office equipment example: "Upgrades in technology are by exception only." Who handles the exceptions? How are they to be heard? Has a budget been established?

2.2.3   Design of the Relocation Organization

At the highest levels of the company, the design of the relocation organization is very simple and is guided by the project objectives, principles, and decision processes. Many organizational models have been proposed (Himes, 1991; IFMA, 1991; Rayfield, 1994), and each is a variation on the basic theme shown in Figure 2.1.

The project manager (PM) is the focal point in the project. In most cases, the PM carries the full responsibility for the success of the project and has the delegated authority of the company executives. The responsibility is enormous and can have serious career consequences. Stern and Gordon (1989) report that two-thirds of all people who handle the relocation process for their company are in a less responsible position or out of a job after the move. Furthermore, while the project team will interact on a day-to-day basis with the organization and consultants, it is the PM who will ensure that the timely decisions are made to facilitate the project and satisfy the stakeholders.

In the next section, the makeup of the project team and the roles and responsibilities of the team members and of office workers and managers are discussed.

IFMA (1991) suggests that the authority of the PM can be affected by the reporting structure of the organization. The structure diagrammed in Figure 2.1 provides the PM with the most authority, since it is designed with the PM in an intervening position. The PM's authority would be weakened under a structure that had the project executive in direct contact with the departments and the PM with his or her organization in a staff relationship with the executive. This staff structure is shown in Figure 2.2.

Another major consideration in the design of the project organization is the role taken by the building services function. In most cases their day-to-day activities are directly linked to every aspect of the relocation. Thus if the building services department is not in charge of the project, and often they are not, it is important that the reporting relationship between the PM and building services be established early.

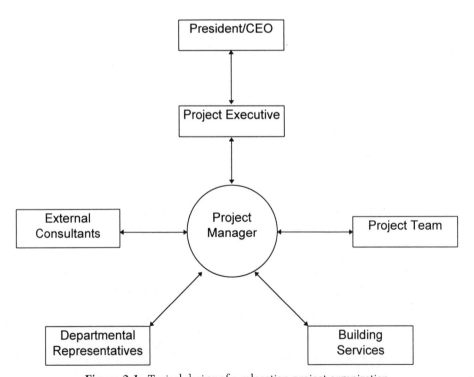

Figure 2.1. Typical design of a relocation project organization.

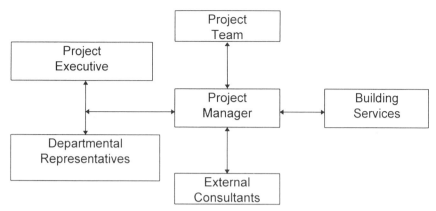

Figure 2.2. Design of a "staff" reporting project organization.

2.2.4   Process Phases and Timing

At the outset of the project, it is important for each of the stakeholders to know how the project will be implemented and approximately how long it will take. Most projects have a definite beginning and end, and are comprised of the same generic sequences of activities. At the same time, each project has quirks that are defined by the needs of the internal organization. Figure 2.3 represents the generic relocation process in the form of a Gantt chart.

In practice, depending on the size of the project, several of the processes diagrammed in Figure 2.3 could be running in parallel, and phases of one subprocess could be interacting with phases of another. For example, the start of one phase may be dependent on the completion of another, or two phases may share the same contractor.

For the purposes of communicating the project to the company, it may only be necessary to briefly define each phase of the project and provide a simple overall time line. Figure 2.4 represents a time line of major activities that might be conducted during each phase of the project.

In more complicated projects, it may be necessary to relocate critical functions first, before relocating the rest of the organization, and additional temporary space, termed "swing" space, may be required to house employees in order to make a "hole" in company buildings to begin the relocation process. Whatever the plan becomes, it's important to describe it to the employees and prepare them for their relocation.

2.2.5   Cost Estimation

Most organizations recognize the difficulty in accurately forecasting the cost of a relocation/reconstruction project. Even so, there is pressure to be as accurate as possible as soon as possible.

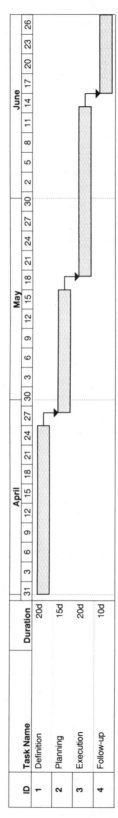

Figure 2.3. Generic relocation project phases.

12

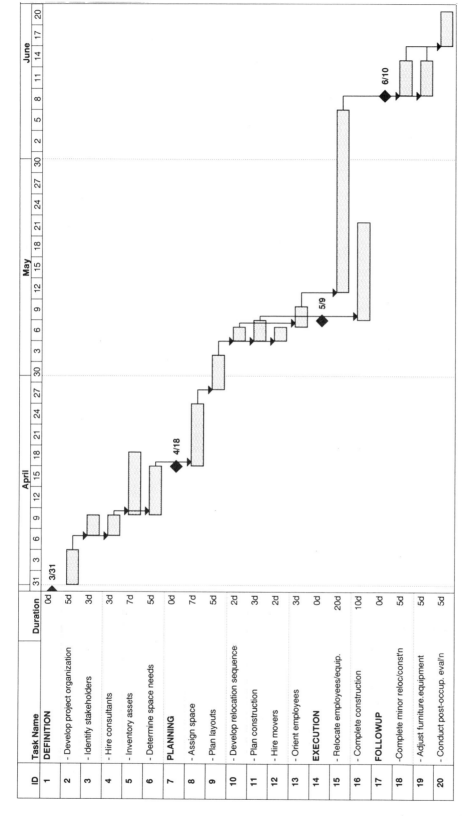

Figure 2.4. Project schedule of activities that might be associated with each phase of a relocation project.

Many organizations have developed classes of forecasting accuracy and the rules that accompany them. Figure 2.5 is an example of the types of accuracy that are typical in the industry.

Initial estimates are expected to be inaccurate. They are based on rules of thumb such as:

- Relocation cost per person
- Cost per unit of service (e.g., telephone line, carpeting)

However, as the project becomes better defined in terms of number of people being moved by location, management expects the estimates to become more accurate, with final estimates to be accurate to within a few percentage points. North American readers who are interested in learning more about cost estimating are referred to courses sponsored by professional organizations such as the International Facilities Management Association (IFMA) and the Building Operators and Managers Association (BOMA). Cost estimating information may also be found in Owen (1993), Rayfield (1994), and Shaheen (1987). Finally, PMs need to be realistic about the budget and the schedule. You won't do yourself a favor by being overly optimistic.

2.3 CREATING THE PROJECT TEAM

Every author who writes about staff relocation or facilities reconstruction has a different view about the makeup of the project team. This section provides general information about the formation of the team, the use of internal and external team members, and the roles and responsibilities of each member. You are encouraged to apply these concepts to your own project design. The goal of this section is to help you create the first pass team design as a basis for discussion and subsequent tailoring to your own organization.

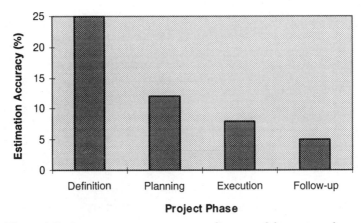

Figure 2.5. Cost estimation accuracy as a function of the project phases.

In review, Figure 2.1 proposes a generic organization design that shows the PM at a focal position. Figure 2.2 shows an alternative design with the PM and the project team in an advisory role for the senior management committees. As an advisor, the PM has reduced authority. Moreover, experience suggests that the project will not move as quickly if the minute-by-minute decisions cannot be made by the project team.

Depending on the size of the project, the number of groups, external contractors, and team members could vary considerably. For large relocations involving several buildings and several hundred employees, the project team may have the representation shown in Figure 2.6.

Building services involvement is likely both within the core team and at each individual location.

2.3.1 Team Members

The selection of core team members and their participation in the project will again depend on the scope of the project. For a large project, as defined above, the core team will likely represent the following functions:

Core Team's Functions
- Project Management
- Relocation coordination
- Project scheduling
- Construction coordination

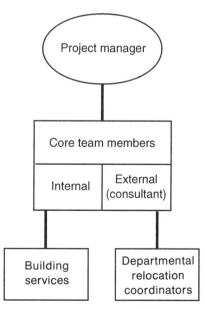

Figure 2.6. Project team organization model for a large relocation project.

- Space planning
- Furniture coordination
- Art coordination
- Telecommunications coordination (voice and data)
- Purchasing
- Information management coordination
- Personnel coordination

External Contractors' and Consultants' Functions
- Moving
- Interior design
- General contracting

The roles and responsibilities of each function can vary from project to project, and can overlap considerably. Nevertheless, the basic roles are explained in the following subsections.

2.3.1.1   *Responsibilities of Core Team Members*

Project Manager (PM). This is the key position in the project team. In most relocations the PM is totally responsible for the success or failure of the project, and is provided with the authority to make decisions on project activities and spending within an approved budget. The PM should be a senior level appointment, though often the PM's level is lower than the Departmental managers that he or she is directing. This situation can be disastrous unless the corporate executive advises senior management about the role, responsibilities, and authority that have been conferred on the PM.

The PM must have very good people skills, be confident, and be an excellent communicator. He or she will have a good understanding of the culture of the organization. Technical expertise is certainly an asset, but is not essential to success. The PM must gain the confidence of the technical experts early, and rely on them to provide him or her with the correct information. Last, but not least, the PM must have the confidence of the executives involved in the project, and the respect of senior management. Even though the PM may have been given the authority to run the project, he or she cannot afford to make enemies of senior management.

The responsibilities of the PM cover every aspect of the project. Even so, there are certain activities that the PM must perform:

- Review the project schedule, costs, and concerns with the project executive team.
- Chair all meetings of the core project team. (These will likely be convened frequently on a prearranged schedule.)
- Communicate project design and status to functional senior management.
- Intervene to make key decisions on project plans, schedules, staffing, contractors, and expenditures.

Relocation Coordinator (RC). Next to the project manager, the RC has the most pivotal role in the relocation team. The RC is a juggler of people and time. His or her responsibilities include:

- Serve as primary contact with outside movers.
- Plan, implement, and coordinate moves according to dates provided by the *project scheduler* and in coordination with the PM.
- Ensure that client contacts are aware of the timing of moves.
- Chair move coordination meetings (usually weekly).
- Coordinate follow-up deficiency activities between building services personnel and other members of the core team.

Project Scheduler (PS). The PS must fulfill these responsibilities:
- Maintain the overall schedule of project activities.
- Work with RC and construction coordinators to ensure that project remains on schedule.

Construction Coordinator (CC): Depending on the scope of the project, this job may require a full time practitioner or its duties may be spread among other members of the core team such as space planning, furniture coordination, and relocation coordination. Most likely, the duties will be taken over by the interior designer or building services site coordinators. The CC's duties are:

- Define the construction-related activities required for the project, such as painting, carpeting, and interior reconstruction and wiring.
- Manage all construction-related activities, including the direction of the general contractor.
- Estimate the cost of construction.
- Estimate the time required to perform each activity.
- Maintain standards for office lighting, noise, and air quality.

Space Planner (SP). The person in this position must:
- Obtain data on space requirements and affinities.
- Maintain and implement office standards.
- Direct the activities of the interior design consultant.
- Be responsible for "blocking" and "stacking" each building.
- Estimate the cost of space used by each business group.

Furniture Coordinator (FC). The FC is the person who must:
- Identify, tag, and inventory all office furniture and equipment.
- Track the movement of furniture and equipment between office location and temporary storage.
- In coordination with the SP, develop standards for furniture and equipment.
- Specify the design of new furniture and equipment.

- Dispose of excess furniture and equipment.
- Direct furniture restoration and refurbishment.

Art Coordinator. The Art Coordinator's responsibilities are to:
- Identify, tag, and inventory corporate art.
- Determine placement of corporate art in buildings.
- Direct and track the movement of corporate art between locations.
- Direct the removal and, later, replacement of art when relocation or construction activities may damage it.
- Manage short- and long-term storage of corporate art.

Telecommunications Coordinator. This team member must:
- Define Telecommunications requirements for the relocation (switches, lines, etc.).
- Estimate costs for telecommunications.
- Direct the disconnecting and reconnecting of phones, faxes, and so on during the relocation.
- Order and install new telephones, cables, and switching equipment.
- Serve as first line contact with providers of Telecommunications equipment and services.

Purchasing Coordinator (PC). The functions of this position are to:
- Manage the building and contracting process for all materials and services purchased for the relocation.
- Develop guidelines for the disposal of furniture and equipment.
- Track project costs through purchases and payments to contractors.

Personnel Coordinator (PCoor). This job includes these responsibilities:
- Learn of impending personnel changes that could affect the relocation.
- Track business reorganizations and advise appropriate members.
- Meet with individuals and groups to determine needs and hear complaints.
- Provide stress counseling as required.

Computer Services Coordinator (CCS). This team member must:
- Coordinate all mainframe connects and requests for access.
- Provide mainframe terminals in new locations.
- Update asset management system.
- Ensure that personal computers (PCs) are prepared for movement.
- Disconnect PCs and local area networks (LANs).
- Reconnect on the other end.
- Manage contractors who are hired to supplement staff.

2.3.1.2   *Responsibilities of Noncore Team Members*

Records Coordinator Manager. This person should advise employees on what can be:

- Discarded
- Archived

Departmental Move Coordinators. They will:
- Orient employees to their new areas (layouts).
- Arrange communication meetings between project team and office work-ers.
- Assist RC to obtain space requirement data.
- Assist IM coordinator to determine system needs.
- Ensure that office workers are prepared to move on time.
- Communicate relocation policies to office workers.
- Arrange archiving and the disposal of files.
- Ensure that office workers unpack as quickly as possible and return pack-ing materials.
- List postrelocation deficiencies and attend deficiency meetings.
- Obtain sign-offs for space plans.

Building Services Staff. These people should:
- Plan and implement installation of voice and data lines.
- Assist move coordinators.
- Manage keys and security for new employees.
- Orient new employees to building.
- Assist move coordinators to correct postmove deficiencies.
- Arrange for building cleanup after move-out or move-in.
- Manage security during the relocation.

2.3.1.3   Responsibilities of External Contractors and Consultants
It is important to understand at all times that external contractors and consul-tants are not part of the company. They do not have their future riding on the success of the project to the extent that company employees do. Moreover, external contractors are, from a legal standpoint, in an adversarial relationship with the company (Owen, 1993). Their allegiance to the project is defined by their contract with the company.

Having said this, I must now point out that external contractors and consul-tants can provide an essential expertise that is not available in-house. The roles of each of the major contractors and consultants are outlined below.

Moving company. The moving company hired should:
- Provide the personnel and equipment necessary to relocate office furniture and equipment.
- Often provide the expertise to assist the internal project team expedite individual moves.
- Provide warehouse space for the interim storage of furniture and office equipment until it is required.

General Contractor. This person should:
- Provide the personnel, equipment, and materials to perform the construction necessary to accompany the relocation.
- For small jobs, provide mechanical, electrical, and wiring support.

Interior Designer/Architect. The functions of this job might include:
- Provide space planning and layout.
- Assist with the selection of interior design materials, including fabrics for wall surfaces and materials for ceiling surfaces and window coverings.
- Help specify new furniture requirements.
- Provide space planning services
- Provide layout of floors and individual offices that meet the company's office standards.

Interior designers are experts in building and workplace design (Follett, 1991). They tend to judge success in purely aesthetic terms, however, not on the criteria that help organizations achieve business goals or the employees achieve a sense of community. Interior designers are not human factors specialists. They know very little about the human-system interface.

2.4   SUMMARY

The point to remember from this chapter is that the activities necessary to plan for and implement the relocation are being identified. How the activities are divided between team members will depend on many factors, including:

- The guidelines on furniture replacement
- The number of computers and how they are networked
- The complexity of the move
- The need for upgraded systems like LANs or telephone switches

 Perhaps the most important determinant of who does what will be the relocation process and schedule. One way to determine a fair distribution of effort among project team members is to calculate which activities are tied to each of the project phases. The matrix in Table 2.1 can be used to match team members against functions during each phase of the relocation.

REFERENCES

Follett, I. (1991). Facility management and corporate culture. Proceedings, Canadian Facility Management Conference, Toronto, ON, April.
Himes, P. E. (1991). Effectively managing complex renovation projects within occupied conditions. Proceedings, Canadian Facility Management Conference, Toronto, ON, April.

Table 2.1. Assigning Project Activities to Project Team Members

Project Phases*

TEAM MEMBER	DEFINITION					PLANNING					EXECUTION		FOLLOW-UP		
	1.	2.	3.	4.	5.	6.	7.	8.	9.	10.	11.	12.	13.	14.	15.
Project Manager															
Relocation Coordinator															
Project Scheduler															
Construction Coordinator															
Space Planner															
Art Coordinator															
Telecom Coordinator															
Materials & Contracting Coordinator															
Human Resources Coordinator															
Information Management Coordinator															

*Where column headings are functions defined as follows:

1. Develop the project organization and strategic plan
2. Identify stakeholders and their special needs
3. Inventory assets
4. Obtain space needs requirements
5. Block and stack floors by Department

6. Assign space to individuals
7. Lay out offices
8. Obtain external support
9. Develop relocation sequence and timing
10. Client orientation to new buildings

11. Relocate employees and equipment
12. Complete associated construction
13. Complete minor relocations and construction
14. Adjust furniture and equipment
15. Conduct postoccupancy evaluations

21

Owen, D. D. (1993). Facilities planning and relocation. Kingston, MA: R. S. Means.

IFMA (1991). "Managing facilities projects: Notes and readings." Training course provided by the International Facilities Management Association, Montreal, Quebec. Facilitated by D. Horowitz.

Rayfield, J. K. (1994). The office interior design guide: An introduction for facilities managers and designers. New York: Wiley.

Shaheen, S. K. (1987). Practical project management. New York: Wiley.

Stern, R. M. and B. Gordon (1989). Making a move that won't mean your job. IFMA Journal, February, pp. 20–31.

ADDITIONAL READINGS

Andrews, C. F. (1987) Finishing a project—Organizing components of a major move. Proceedings, Eighth International Facility Management Conference and Exposition, Dallas, November.

Becker, F. (1987). Managing an office relocation. Report prepared for the International Facility Management Association, November.

Carstairs, E. (1987). The corporate relocation game. Corporate Design and Realty, January/February, p. 33.

Dennis, H. and D. A. Brown (1992). Merging and moving at Comerica Bank: Putting people first in a complex relocation plan. FM Journal, May/June, pp. 42–45.

De Siena, R. (1990). The corporate move—Who is responsible? BOMA New York: Building Operators and Managers Association.

Engel, P. (1987). Corporate moves: Managing the confusion. Facilities Design and Management, April, pp. 64–67.

Farren, C. E. (1988). Planning and managing interior projects. Facilities Design and Management, May, pp. 80–82.

Farren, C. E. (1989). Streamlined project management. Tutorial, T-1, International Facilities Management Association '89 Conference, Seattle, WA, November 1.

McDonald, J. H. and T. Huckfeldt (1988). Staff relocation: Reducing the hidden costs. Bank Administration, November.

Sanders, M. (1990). Planning for a smooth move. The Construction Specifier, May, pp. 161–162.

Snyder, A. (1992). Are you sitting on a gold mine? Asset management can save your bottom line. Facilities Management Journal, September/October, pp. 35–38.

Tuttens, N. (1990). Site selection and relocation: Making a move—Step by step. Canadian Facility Management, May/June, pp. 13–16.

Chapter Three

Planning: Social Issues in Office Relocation

===========

3.1 INTRODUCTION

Office relocation is about change: change in your co-workers, change in your office environment, change in your relationship to other groups, change in your job, and change in your location. It is well known that people resist some types of change but not others (Becker, 1990). They change their jobs, their hobbies, their houses, their friends, and at times their spouses. The obvious question is what kinds of change do people accept and what kinds do people resist?

This chapter is about resistance that almost always occurs among workers during an office relocation and about the stress that can accompany the relocation if it is not handled properly. Mostly, however, this chapter is about ways to help the project team deal with the resistance to a relocation and help the workers deal with the stress that will inevitably occur.

The cost of not overcoming the resistance to the relocation can be enormous. It can include:

- Increased absenteeism
- Substantial reductions in productivity
- Low morale and a poor attitude toward the company that may persist for months and years
- An increase in work errors
- The loss of experienced, hardworking people
- Even attempts to sabotage the move

3.2   WHY OFFICE WORKERS RESIST RELOCATION

Office workers resist relocating across the country, across the city, next door, to the next floor, or to the next office. The reasons are many and varied, and may be based on a lack of communication, information, and employee involvement.

Workers may perceive that the new location does not have the amenities of the old, or they may know that their new offices will be smaller than their old ones. Whatever the reasons, resistance to change is often due to a lack of information about:

- Why the relocation is happening
- When it will happen
- Where the new offices will be
- What will happen to the workers' jobs and relationships
- How the company plans to deal with the relocation

Workers may also resist a relocation because they are not involved in the planning. They see the move as something that management is doing *to* them without their consent. Individual and group participation in the planning and implementation of the move is an essential element for success. Without it, workers will not take ownership of their new surroundings. The space will be management's, not theirs. Subsequent sections of this chapter deal with many aspects of individual and group participation in the relocation.

New bosses, new jobs, new workmates, or a new corporate culture can trigger resistance. Workers with many years of service in one location may be moved away from workmates to work with colleagues who may be new to the corporation. It may become apparent in premove meetings and surveys that the attitude of valuable employees could be soured by the move unless something is done to ease the transition.

A company move may disrupt families and friends. Moves across the country place an enormous stress on families who must decide whether to stay with the company and leave their homes or to leave their jobs to maintain their home, their family, and their friends. Even moves across town can disrupt the workers and their families. The move will almost certainly affect commuting patterns and, often, methods of transportation. Consider, for example, a husband and wife, with long service, who may be split by a relocation. Before the move, they may have lived centrally within walking distance of their office and amenities. The new location could require a car and increased commuting time. In this situation, living and working downtown may be valued more than working for the company. One spouse may quit the company rather than commute. Thus the relocation could cost the company a valuable employee, not to mention the cost of rehiring and retraining a new worker.

Finally, the company move may disrupt its own business associations and could put local suppliers out of business.

People do not generally resist relocation if it will improve their commute, or their standard of living. They will view a relocation positively if a promotion accompanies the move, or if their working environment improves. Clearly, knowledge of what the effects of the relocation will probably be, on each individual involved or even on key individuals who wield influence with their colleagues, would be valuable information. The next section explores ways that the project team can, at best, overcome resistance to the relocation and, at worst, help the employees to cope with it.

Becker (1987) offers these suggestions for those implementing a relocation:

- Do not assume that every employee will resist change.
- Management can take steps to overcome the resistance to a move.
- Do not assume that information available to senior management will trickle down to employees.
- Take time to find out what employees want.

3.3 OVERCOMING RESISTANCE TO CHANGE

Employees resist change for many reasons, but as the previous sections noted, the main reasons for resistance are:

- *Lack of communication.* Management should consult with employees to tell them who is moving, why they are moving, when they are moving, and what the move will mean.
- *Nonparticipation.* Employees should be invited to be part of planning the relocation and implementing the move.
- *Nonintervention.* The company should survey the needs of individuals and determine what their concerns are. A survey is like a contract with the employees that promises follow-up.

This section addresses each of the above in more detail and provides examples of ways that other companies have dealt with these issues.

Inevitably, not every office worker can be satisfied by the interventions made by the company. Some will be disappointed because the company could not or would not solve their particular problems. In this event stress will build and resistance may occur. Section 3.4 examines ways in which employees can learn to cope with their stress.

3.3.1 Communication

It is generally agreed by facilities specialists that effective communication can help reduce the stress of a relocation. Communication to employees can be addressed separately in each of the three phases of the project:

1. Prior to the move
2. During the move
3. After the move

When the move is announced, employees are most concerned with the details of the move and the plans that will affect them personally. More specifically, they want to know:

- Why the relocation is happening
- Who it will affect
- Where the new space will be located
- When the move will take place
- How the new space will affect them

Office workers will not stand for deception. Therefore the communications must be honest and must clearly give a balanced position. Learning both the positive and negative outcomes of the move helps reduce stress. As these outcomes become apparent during the planning stage, employees become concerned with how the relocation will affect them personally:

- Who will move with them
- With whom they will work
- What their new job will be
- How their working space will be designed
- How they will commute to work

During the implementation stage employees are more interested in how the process of the move affects them. For example:

- How many interim moves they must make
- Whether the move will be completed in time
- What changes have taken place in the plan

After the move employees want to know what did not happen as intended and how it affects them.

Each of the above questions has been answered in a myriad of novel ways. Examples of how others have effectively handled communications are presented in Chapter 7.

3.3.2   Participation

Every successful relocation owes its success to the people involved, both in and outside of the corporation, but there is no one right answer to who should be involved in the project. History tells us that the odds of delivering a project on-time and on-budget depend on the cooperation of everyone affected by the relocation, and science tells us that the probability of securing and maintaining employee cooperation will improve with their level of involvement in the project.

This section is about participation of the office workers in the relocation project. While at first blush, the idea of involving inexperienced people in the relocation process may appear ludicrous to some, and at the very least inefficient to others, experience tells us that, on balance, it may be a very smart thing for the project team to consider.

Worker participation in the relocation process works for the following reasons.

- It takes advantage of the knowledge skills and experience available from the multifaceted working population to produce a better result. Using knowledgeable workers in the project recognizes and makes legitimate the background and experience that they bring to the project. The success of participative groups and individuals depends, in part, on how they are selected. More is said about individual and group selection later.
- Participation also takes advantage of the effort (person-days) of many workers to produce results faster and less expensively than exclusive reliance on a few specialists or outside consultants could.
- Participation by workers from inside the company increases their knowledge and experience for use in future projects. Consultants are hired to solve "a problem." The solution may not generalize to other problems or to future problems. Workers learn techniques from consultants that can be generalized to other issues.
- Worker "ownership" of an objective enhances the likelihood of success. The motivation that is often engendered by participation increases a worker's sense of commitment and responsibility to the activities that he or she is assigned.

The advantages of worker participation in the relocation are not all in the company's favor. Workers also gain from participation in the relocation in ways that are both self-satisfying and self-aggrandizing:

- Information is power. Workers who participate are often privy to information about the relocation, the people, or the company that can give them influence with their peers.
- Today's workers expect more from their work than "hygiene" factors such as pay, benefits, and a safe place to work (Noro and Imada, 1991). They also need to:
  —Participate in meaningful decisions
  —Celebrate success (Kouzes and Posner, 1987)
- Participation shows commitment and responsibility. These are considered excellent characteristics for promotion within the organization.
- Workers want to exercise control. In participation, they find an important source of gratification.

- A person who "participates" can make decisions, and may affect policy, in ways that are consistent with his or her own self-interest (Tannenbaum, 1966).
- Participation is often intrinsically satisfying. The worker may participate in group meetings, discuss interesting topics, visit vendors and consultants, all of which removes him/her periodically from day-to-day activities.

With all the advantages to worker participation in the relocation project cited above, downsides still exist and must be dealt with by the project team. For example, management in some organizations operates in an autocratic, top-down manner. They may resist worker participation or give it only perfunctory support because:

- Their management style does not recognize worker responsibilities or initiative.
- Their experience supports a traditional autocratic style. The traditional approach, for example, may produce immediate results, even though the psychosocial atmosphere is poor.
- They fear that workers are inherently opposed to management principles, philosophies, and goals. They believe that giving workers control of anything will threaten their own power and lead to chaos (Tannenbaum, 1966).
- They believe that workers cannot do their regular jobs while, at the same time, participating in other activities.

The project team needs to convince management that worker participation is a net plus both to the project and to future operations, and that management's authority will not be diminished.

Having said the above, I must point out that there are situations to avoid when workers are participating in the project. Table 3.1 lists the situations to avoid and gives some advice on how to avoid them.

The structure and organization of participation groups is vitally important to the success of the group. The following is some advice for the project team:

- Ensure that some of the members have some experience in the problem area assigned. For example, if the group's job is to develop principles for mail-room design, one or two of the members should have knowledge of how a mail room operates. However, avoid the situation when all members of the team are mail-room employees; it will likely perpetuate the status quo.
- All teams should be facilitated by a member of the relocation project team.
- The team should be comprised of members who represent all functions and levels, the so-called "diagonal slice" through the organization.
- Ensure that the team is oriented to produce a deliverable.
- Ensure that each member of the team is willing to put in the time required to solve the problem.

Table 3.1. Situations to Avoid when Workers Are Participating in a Project and Corresponding Techniques for Avoiding Them

Situation	Avoidance Techniques
1. Individuals or groups whose recommendations have been rejected may feel alienated.	1.1 Agree with the team/individual on groundrules, e.g. cost or time to implement. 1.2 Keep problems small, so even bad solutions may be bearable.
2. Participation may lead to an anti-management bias.	2.1 Create groups from a diagonal slice through the organization.
3. Participation on the relocation may set up expectations of continued participation beyond the project.	3.1 This may be a good thing, but, even so, ensure that everybody knows, up-front, that this is a one-time event.
4. Participation is time-consuming and may be frustrating to those involved.	4.1 Set groundrules. 4.2 Set deadlines. 4.3 Make it easy for people to leave groups.

- Set project ground rules, for example, timing, cost, and project principles.
- Train the team to be highly effective. Periodically measure how well they are performing.
- Measure the cognitive styles of each member of the team, that is how adaptive or innovative their problem solving styles are (Kirton, 1994). Use that information to help the team perform to its maximum extent.
- Reward the team members for their time. Rewards may be intrinsic—visit by the CEO—or extrinsic—theater tickets—or both—dinner with the CEO.

3.3.2.1   Potential Team Projects in the Relocation

The number of teams formed and the variety of tasks that can be assigned depend on the scope of the project.

The simplest relocation is little more than regular churn. Groups, for example, may be consolidated on the same floor after a reorganization. There is no new furniture or accessories. Everyone changes location and computers; chairs and specialized furniture go with the individual. In this situation, the relocation team may be responsible for:

- Working with the mover (schedules, staging space, moving boxes)
- Redesigning, in cooperation with the facilities management group, the layout of the panels to reduce noise
- Setting move sequences and schedules
- Scheduling voice and data disconnects and reconnects

Larger moves between buildings where reconstruction may be involved may require substantial team effort in the following areas:

- Employee communication over weeks and months
- Group move coordination
- Furniture selection
- Chair selection and testing
- Design of specialty areas:
  —Cafeteria
  —Meeting rooms
  —Receiving areas
  —Mail room
  —Coffee areas
- Design of communication areas:
  —Fax
  —Copiers
  —Mail drops
- Interior color selections
- Working with the mover
- Building welcoming committees
- Committees to relieve the stress of the moves
- Telecommunications:
  —Selection of equipment
  —Group training on the use of equipment

3.3.3   Company Intervention

Company intervention to reduce the stress of and resistance to change must be well-planned and executed; a typical planning sequence is shown in Figure 3.1.

Preplanning surveys provide a wealth of information to the project team on how to alleviate employee concerns.

The types of concerns that are voiced by preplanning surveys usually fall into categories that can be classed as hygiene or survival factors:

- Job concerns
- Changes in building standards
- Commuting concerns
- Leaving friends and co-workers
- Leaving the "neighborhood"

The project team can seldom influence the job changes and reorganizations that accompany a relocation. In fact, most relocations are conducted as fallout from reorganizations.

However, the project team can affect some of the other concerns above. The remainder of this section deals with each of the above issues.

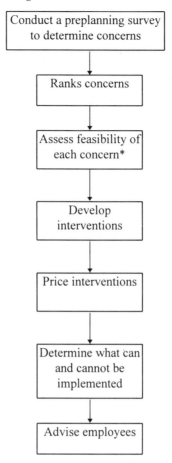

* Feasibility may be assessed using the following decision matrix

	High impact	Low impact
Easy to implement		
Difficult to implement		

Figure 3.1. Planning for intervention.

3.3.3.1   New Standards

The relocation is an opportunity for the company to meet two needs at the same time:

1 To move the organization to new office standards
2. To use the opportunity of moving to new standards to overcome resistance to change

The 1990's ushered in a new philosophy of how an office should function. During the late 1970's and early 1980's the introduction of computers created visions of paperless offices and 30-hour work weeks, visions that were never realized. The systems that supported computerization and computer-based work were never able to keep pace with the rapid growth of automation. For example:

- Building services such as cabling could not keep pace with demand because the cable space was never designed to be large enough to cope with the load.
- Air conditioning was not sized to cope with the heat load produced by automation.

Although facilities organizations responded admirably to the test, responses take time. Furthermore, it was not until the advent of new buildings, innovative retrofit support equipment, and massive renovations that a balance was seen between automation and its support structures. In my experience, that balance did not occur until the late 1980's and early 1990's. Even today, the systems are changing faster than facilities people can cope. Fortunately, many of the changes are designed to take the load off the facility; such changes include:

- Low-energy computers
- Fiber optics and wireless connectors
- Stand-alone computers and Local Area Networks (LANs) with few between-floor connections

This respite will be short-lived as fax, external, digital, and voice communications increase.

The effects on the support systems are profound and beg for the establishment of new rules, principles, and philosophies of workplace design to keep the potential of chaos in check.

The point is that standards can work for the people or against them. During a relocation, when the potential for stress is high already, standards that negatively affect the office workers should be avoided if possible. Instead, companies should be using the new positive standards to reduce the stress of and resistance to the move. For example:

- New furniture and seating standards can go a long way to improving acceptance of the relocation.
- New color schemes for wall, floor, and ceiling coverings can seem to brighten the offices.
- Improved lighting, particularly personal (task) lighting, will be well accepted.

3.3.3.2   Commuting Concerns

There are four possible changes in the commuting patterns of employees when they relocate, as shown in Table 3.2. Depending on the degree of change, each of these pattern changes can be an issue to the employees. Urban locations generally mean:

- Good public transportation
- Close to shopping
- Parking charges
- Traffic tie-ups

Suburban locations, on the other hand, generally mean:

- No public transportation to the workplace
- Limited shopping, if any
- Free parking
- Fewer traffic stoppages

Consider, for example, a case where office workers are being transferred out of a downtown location, close to public transportation, excellent dining, theaters, and good daytime shopping, to a suburban location with good bus service but very few amenities. A preplanning survey might quickly identify the commute as a major concern for all workers, regardless of where they live.

Formal Intervention. A consulting organization might be hired to determine how serious the dislocation would be to the people affected, and if alternate assignments of groups to buildings could reduce the dislocation effects.

Consulting companies have developed software that evaluates the trip times for driving or commuting between workers' homes and each of the office buildings being considered. Input to the computer consists of the workers' names and addresses, current work location, current method of commuting, new work location, and what times they normally leave home and work.

Output from the program is the travel time that each worker experiences if he or she drives or uses public transit. This time can then be compared with the commute time that is currently required. The result can be reported as:

Table 3.2. Possible Changes in Commuting Patterns

From Location	To Location
Urban	Urban
Suburban	Urban
Urban	Suburban
Suburban	Suburban

- Frequency histograms plotting the number of employees experiencing changes in travel times, to the nearest 15-minute interval.
- Frequency histograms plotting the number of employees experiencing travel time differences under different building location scenarios and methods of commute.
- Travel time changes for each individual employee.

Figures 3.2 and 3.3 demonstrate the results of a hypothetical analysis of 108 employees who are being considered for relocation from downtown to a suburban location. The data in Figure 3.2 indicate that if all employees *drove* to the suburban location, 61% would experience a decrease in travel time; 27% would experience no change, and the remaining 12% would experience an increase. Alternatively, if all employees who were relocated used *public transit* (Figure 3.3), 13% would experience a decrease in travel time; 29% would experience no change, and 58% would have a greater travel time.

In addition to the group analyses, individual results could be made available for each of the office workers.

Informal Intervention. Resistance to a relocation can manifest in commuting issues. Employees, for example, might conduct their own informal survey to determine:

- The proportion of employees who would or would not want to change buildings
- The changes in commute times and methods of commute that a change would require

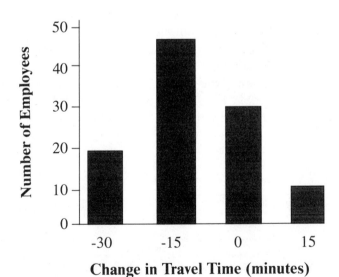

Figure 3.2. Change in travel time to a suburban location if all employees drove.

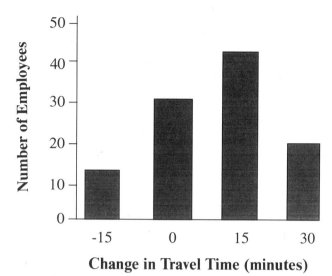

Figure 3.3. Change in travel time to a suburban location if all employees took public transportation.

• Options that the employees would consider if they had to move

 A survey that could be used by employees to collect the above data is reproduced in Table 3.3.

With very few questions, employees could provide the relocation team with their opinions to a number of issues, including:

• General concerns about the move, for example, access to subway, time with family
• Which working locations are preferred
• Which locations would be acceptable and which would be unacceptable
• How workers would cope if they were asked to move to the unacceptable locations

The caution with this type of informal survey is that the responses are often based on emotion, not on fact. Hence the results may not compare well with objective data about the commuting times, building locations, or amenities. The results of a worker survey may be more realistic if the workers are provided with objective data from, for example, a trip time analysis, and available transit options, before they complete their survey.

You can learn a valuable lesson from the above example:

• As soon as workers learn of an impending relocation, they will begin to consider how it will impact them. If they expect that the impact will be negative, they will react in resourceful ways.

Table 3.3. Office Location Survey

Please complete the following questions to help us understand what impact moving to a new location would have on you.

- What are your general concerns with a new office location?

- Given a choice, which of the office locations, listed below, would be most suitable to you?

Location	Location Preferences			Reason for concern (be as specific as possible)
	Preferred	O.K	Not wanted	
Building 'A'				
Building 'B'				
Building 'C'				

- How would you cope with a move to the "Not wanted" location? (e.g. buy a car, move, consider resigning, ask for a transfer, etc.)

- What suggestions can you offer as alternatives for you moving to a new location or ideas to lessen the impact on you and your co-workers?

Name (optional): _____ **Date:** _____

PLEASE RETURN COMPLETED SURVEY TO: [Insert name here]

- Plan, as much as possible, to respond to workers' concerns before they learn about the relocation. In the case above, it should not have been necessary to have the trip time and building data before the relocation announcement, but it would have been necessary to preempt the workers' informal survey by announcing that you had identified commuting as an issue and that you would work with them to find the best solution.

3.4   DEALING WITH THE STRESS OF RELOCATION

The previous sections deal with organizational interventions that can reduce the adverse impact of the relocation on employees. Each intervention has a price to the organization. The use of outside consultants, for example, costs money. Even the interventions that are employee driven, such as producing the relocation newsletter or participating in groups, require effort that can affect productivity. Some companies will invest in more interventions than others, but all companies will draw the line at some point.

The purpose of this section is to review ways in which the employee can deal with the stresses of relocation that the company is not able to support. Management in most organizations knows the effect that stress can have on productivity and are willing to support individual stress-reduction programs. In fact, most senior managers encourage employees to develop their own strategies because it takes the pressure off them to change organizational processes.

The title of this section is "dealing" with the stress of relocation rather than "coping" with it. While the two words have similar meanings, coping often suggests passiveness . . . . strategies that focus on alleviating the symptoms of the stress such as exercise or relaxation techniques.

The modern stress literature recommends dealing actively with the stressful situation by one of two methods:

1. Prevent the stress from occurring
2. Or deal with the cause of the stress

3.4.1   Preventing the Stress from Occurring

Stress prevention implies gaining as much control as possible over the work situation and turning it to your advantage. It requires a "take charge" attitude that recognizes:

- The organization will not hold your hand.
- You have to manage your own response to the situation.

Some preventive recommendations for dealing with organizational or personal change that may accompany a relocation include:

- Work smarter, not harder:
  —Find out what the new organization wants and adjust to these expectations.
  —Prioritize your activities and focus on the ones that will make your job more rewarding.
  —Get rid of the administrative or "make work" tasks that do not contribute to the organization's goals or your happiness at work.
  —Increase your efficiency by improving the way you do your work.

- Look for opportunities to improve the way the organization does business. Try to improve the work processes in ways that will make your job more valuable, fulfilling, and interesting.
- Try to avoid being pushed into the future. Create your own future by identifying business opportunities, and pull the organization along.
- Stay current. Take courses and take on new assignments to give you new skills and experience.

3.4.2   Dealing with the Causes of Stress

Stress programs that deal with causes of the stress appear to be much more effective at alleviating stress than those that teach strategies for coping with the symptoms.

The approach for dealing with causes includes the following sequence of activities:

1. Help workers identify the cause of the stress.
2. Show them how to analyze why they are reacting adversely to their stress.
3. Train workers to think differently about the stressor.
4. Assist workers to develop options for dealing with the stress.

3.4.3   Implementing a Stress Management Program

It is estimated that, in the United States, there are over 500 different stress management consultants and programs that companies can contract with when potentially stressful situations, such as staff relocations, occur.

Stress management consultants may offer approaches to stress reduction other than the preventive and cause identification approaches described above. Quite apart from the approach, it seems clear that every stress management program needs to be able to:

- Measure the success of the program:
  —Either with anecdotal techniques, such as self reports or unobtrusive observation
  —Or with objective techniques, such as the use of a questionnaire or survey
- Deal with the cause, not the symptom.
- Make use of commonly accepted coping strategies to help create the environment for dealing with causal factors. These may include:
  —Physical improvement strategies, such as exercise, diet, and getting enough sleep
  —Mental improvement strategies, such as relaxation techniques or meditation
  —Social strategies, such as peer support groups

REFERENCES

Becker, F. (1987). Managing an office relocation. Report prepared for the International Facility Management Association, November.

Becker, F. (1990). The total workplace: Facilities management and the elastic organization. New York: Van Nostrand Reinhold.

Kirton, M. (1994). Adaptors and innovators: Styles of creativity and problem solving. Routledge, London.

Kouzes, J. M. and B.G. Posner (1987). The leadership challenge: How to get extraordinary things done in organizations. San Francisco: Josey-Bass.

Noro, K. and A. Imada (1991). Participatory ergonomics. London: Taylor and Francis.

Tannenbaum, A. S. (1966). Social psychology of the work organization. Belmont, CA: Wadsworth.

ADDITIONAL READINGS

Adams, J. (1987). Creating and maintaining comprehensive stress management training. Chapter 5 in L. R. Murphy and T. F. Schoenborn, Stress management in work situations. Washington, DC: U.S. Department of Health and Human Services, Washington, May.

Beehr, T. A. and K. O'Hara (1987). Methodological designs for the evaluation of occupational stress interventions. Chapter 4 in S. V. Kasi and C. L. Cooper (Eds.), Stress and health: Issues in research methodology. New York: Wiley.

Cohen, F. (1987). Measurement of coping. Chapter 10 in S. V. Kasi and C. L. Cooper (Eds.), Stress and health: Issues in research methodology. New York: Wiley.

Fisher, C. and J. B., Shaw (1994). Relocation attitudes and adjustment: A longitudinal study. Journal of Organizational Behavior, May, pp. 209–224.

Gjessing, C. C., T. F. Schoenborn, and A. Cohen, A. (1994). Participatory ergonomic interventions in meatpacking plants. Washington, DC: U.S. Department of Health and Human Services, National Institute for Occupational Safety and Health.

Hurrell, J. J. and L. R. Murphy, (1992). Psychological job stress. Chapter 52 in W. N. Rom (Ed.), Environmental and occupational medicine. Boston: Little Brown and Company.

Pritchett, P. and R. Pound, (1994). A survival guide to the stress of organizational change. Dallas: Pritchett and Associates.

Waldsmith, L. (1993) Balance stress for healthy harmony. Corporate Detroit Magazine, March.

Chapter Four

Planning: Communications

4.1 INTRODUCTION

Communication can be defined as the transmission and reception of a message that travels between two or more points (Preston and Zimmerer, 1978). It is fundamental to the operation of a society and is essential to the operation of an organization. In times of change, communication determines success or failure. Relocation is a change process that will succeed only if communication is planned and executed as well as any other element in the process. Becker (1990) notes that "how the project team will handle communications should be treated as a design problem in its own right."

This chapter is devoted to all aspects of communication that are required in the relocation process. Considering the social issues dealt with in the previous chapter, one facilities manager noted (Anonymous, 1989) that every relocation must include ". . . an aggressive, comprehensive communication plan that enables an employee to ask 'What is going to happen to me?" But communication plans are not just for employees. In any relocation there are stakeholders that need to know:

- The status of the project in terms of cost and timing
- Whether the business is being affected
- Whether clients and customers are being affected
- How the employees are accepting the changes
- How the contractors are performing

If communications are not properly managed, the consequences can be very serious. Employees, not knowing what the future holds, may assume the worst and resent the organization, which could lead to loss of productivity and an unwillingness to help with the move. Contractors who are not properly briefed may work inefficiently. Furthermore, if outside communications are not handled properly, customers and clients may become concerned about the quality of goods or services that they are receiving.

Communication is the flow of information between two or more parties. It is not a one-way process. Communication must flow down and up the organization. Employees must not only be informed of the relocation plans, but they must be able to respond to them. Often their responses will not be what some managers want to hear, so it can be expected that some proportion of management will not want feedback from employees.

This chapter explores the types of communications that are essential during a relocation. It describes communication methods and provides examples that have been used successfully in other projects.

There are many ways of communicating. For this reason, the methods are organized by communication categories that follow the project sequence:

1. Planning and premove
2. During the move
3. After the move has been completed

The methods are listed in a tablular format to make it easy for you to copy them for use in your own planning process.

Meetings will figure prominently in all phases of the project. It is essential that each formal meeting be documented completely. Other features of meetings that should be considered include (Becker, 1990):

- Whom to include in the meeting
- Whom to copy
- Where to hold the meetings (turf issues)
- When and how agendas are set
- What materials are distributed in advance

4.2   COMMUNICATIONS DURING PROJECT PLANNING AND PRIOR TO THE MOVE

Under this heading, the communication methods can be further subdivided by the groups with whom the project team communicates, including:

- Senior management who are responsible for the successful outcome of the project
- Consultants and contractors who are part of the planning process
- Employee groups, managers, and supervisors who are affected by the relocation

- Employees who are not affected by the relocation
- Customers, suppliers, and the community.
- Building services and facility groups within the organization

4.2.1 Senior Management

Communications with this group will include:

- Meetings to lay out the project and obtain approvals
- Regular progress updates, which may be in the form of review meetings that are scheduled regularly, scheduled to correspond to project milestones, or held as required

4.2.2 Consultants and Contractors Who Are Part of the Planning Process

In addition to day-to-day contact between individual contractors and individual members of the project team, formal review meetings among project team and contractors should be scheduled frequently, e.g., weekly or biweekly, to ensure that work is proceeding satisfactorily.

4.2.3 Employee Groups, Managers, and Supervisors Who Are Affected by the Relocation

According to Himes (1991), if the project team does not properly communicate with employees "their lives will be miserable." In most companies, the organization already exists to provide excellent communications with employees. The methods that may be used for communicating the status of the relocation are listed in Table 4.1.

Of particular importance is the establishment of a relocation newsletter to provide the opportunity to report progress in the project, events that will affect employees in the near future, and policy decisions such as the use of coffee makers, the provision of new office accessories, or the care of personal items like plants during the move. Newsletters may be distributed informally and mailed to the employees' homes. Figure 4.1 shows an example of relocation newsletter.

For each of these methods of communication, it is important to provide the names and telephone numbers of project team members whom office workers can contact.

4.2.4 Customers, Suppliers, and the Community

The relocation has the potential of affecting customers, suppliers, and the surrounding community, so the company has an obligation to advise these groups about their plans. Table 4.2 outlines some of the ways that this can be done.

Table 4.1. Methods of Communicating the Status of the Relocation Project to Employees

- *Relocation newsletter*. Is used to update employees on the progress of the project and to advise them about future activities.
- *Videos*. Can be used by senior management to announce the relocation, why it is occurring, and how senior management are committed to making it as painless as possible.
- *Large meetings/forums*. Intended to be more personal than videos by bringing senior management to the office workers. Members of the relocation team are usually present to answer questions about the move.
- *Electronic mail and electronic bulletin boards*. Provide continuous updates on the relocation that employees can access at their convenience. Moreover, they provide a channel for dialogue with management and the relocation team. This "hot line" concept can serve to defuse issues quickly if questions are answered openly and honestly.
- *Roving communicator/listener*. Can act as the ears of the relocation team and a pipeline to employees. The role of this person is to promote dialogue with employees and determine the true feelings of the rank and file that would never be heard through formal communications. This person must be well respected by the employees and credible to each of the parties involved with the move. Conversations with the listener must be held in confidence if employees request confidentiality. This listener may also be provided with a "hot-line" number, an electronic mail address, a beeper, or a cellular phone so office workers can contact him or her directly
- Desk drops (i.e., circulars placed on the employees' desks) are one of the fastest methods to distribute written information throughout the corporation. The cooperation of the mail department is essential.

MOVING ON
The Relocation Newsletter

This package of information has been developed to update employees on the status of the office relocations that are beginning at our Corporate Head Office. The Newsletter will be published biweekly until the relocation is complete. It will include answers to the most frequently asked questions concerning the move and a list of all the members of the Building Relocation Team, who will be pleased to answer individual questions.

The Plan

The relocation involves the entire head office building. About 100,000 square feet of space and about 250 employees will be affected by the relocation. A major challenge for the Relocation Team is to ensure that the design process, any interior reconstruction, and the actual moves to consolidate departments and related func-

Figure 4.1. An example of a relocation newsletter.

tions all take place as soon as possible and with the least disruption to employees and the day-to-day business.

Here's how its going to be done:

- Leasing "swing space" in an adjacent building to relocate a group of employees and create vacancies in the main building.
- Starting to consolidate departments and related work groups within the building—through moves from one floor to another.
- Finally, Moving employees occupying the swing space to their final destinations within the head office building.

A Progress Report

About 10,000 square feet of "swing space" has been leased at 100 Main Street to house staff for an interim period in order to create some vacancies within the head office building. Since the head office is now fully occupied, creating vacancies will allow the Relocation Team to begin moving designated groups to their final home.

About 40 employees will move into the swing space. They'll continue to work out of 100 Main street for about three months until their final office space is available.

Stacking Up

"Stacking plans"—who will occupy what floors—have been completed for the head office building. They are shown in the attached Building Model.

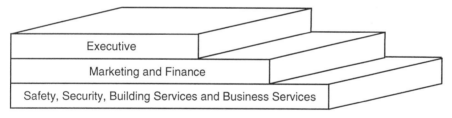

Model of the head office building.

Relocation Team

The Building Relocation Team has been formed to implement the moves. Team members are listed in the following Table along with their office and extension numbers. Also listed are the names of the volunteer Division Move Coordinators. If you have a question or concern about your own office relocation, please contact your Division Move Coordinator.

Name	Position	Room	Extension
R. Jones	Relo. Coord.	217	6555
J. Black	Space Plan	233	5666
G. Pearson	Move Coord. Business Services	156	7373
M. Hardon	Move Coord. Marketing	206	6611

Figure 4.1. (Continued)

Table 4.2. Methods for Advising Customers, Suppliers, and the Community About Relocation Plans

---

- *Articles and advertising space.* Such listings in the business sections of major newspapers and trade magazines will advise customers and suppliers.
- *Flyers.* Material distributed to the surrounding community will advise them of abnormal activity such as temporary road blockages or high truck traffic and abnormal work times for moving and furniture delivery companies.
- *Town hall meetings.* These can answer the community's questions and allay their concerns.

4.2.5   Building Services and Facilities Management Personnel

Business continues while the relocation takes place. Building services are provided, the building is maintained, and equipment is installed in the midst of the relocation. Since operations and relocation are so intertwined, it is essential that daily informal communications be maintained. It would be uncommon for building services or facilities management groups not to be part of the relocation effort, but if they are not intimately involved they must be constantly updated with:

- Formal meetings,
- Copies of correspondence to contractors and designers

4.3   COMMUNICATIONS DURING THE RELOCATION

The same types of communication methods are used during the relocation as before it, but the messages will likely be different. Table 4.3 explains how each of the communication techniques can be used during the relocation.

4.4   COMMUNICATIONS AFTER THE MOVE IS COMPLETE

When employees first enter their new facilities, they will require orientation to the facility and an opportunity to communicate with building services staff, moving contractors, and the relocation team.

Chapter 9 provides detailed tables that outline the information that the employee requires prior to the move, during the move, and for the first few days after the move is complete. Chapter 10 describes, in some detail, the design of postoccupancy evaluations and other types of debriefing techniques. This section highlights the information that is presented in detail in Chapters 9 and 10 to make employees comfortable on their first day of work at the new location:

Table 4.3. Methods of Communicating During the Relocation

- *Video tapes.* They can describe the employees' role in the physical move and can provide information about:
  —Packing
  —Purging files and discarding trash
  Dennis and Brown (1992) reported that such a tape developed around a friendly funny theme helped reduce the content of files moved by 68%. Videos can also be developed to show weekly progress. They can be played continuously in lobbies or cafeterias.
- *Relocation newsletters.* These can now be used to record progress and advise employees of impending activities. The illustration below, for example, shows employees the progress of the relocation. The shaded areas on the stacking diagram demonstrate completed moves.

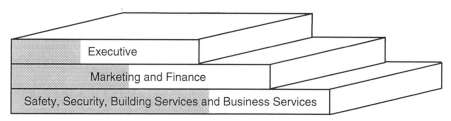

Model of the head office building showing the progress of the relocation.

- *Orientation programs.* These are one of the most effective methods of advising employees about their new facilities and the surrounding communities. Depending on the physical distance to the new location, employees can be bussed to the new building and given a tour of the community, or shown a video tape of the new location and the amenities. Becker (1987) cites the results of a post move survey of one successful relocation program. The "open-house" to the new facility was the single most effective communication program provided before the move. The orientation program can be tailored to specific groups within the organization, depending on their needs or the issues that develop.
- *Meetings.* Meetings between key personnel in the move take on a new flavor during the move, as opposed to during the planning session. Much more time is spent between the relocation team, contractors, and consultants, debriefing on the recent past in order to continuously improve the process.

- Desk drop in the form of a card and a small chocolate or a momento can welcome the new employee (Figure 4.2).
- Orientation packages provide the employee with information about the services available. Materials can be included to advise employees about routine activities that they must complete to obtain services such as parking passes or to obtain site access.
- Welcome meetings are held for groups or divisions or for the occupants of specific floors. These are informal meetings facilitated by building services

```
        Welcome to your new home

   We know how disruptive a move can be and

         how it can leave a sour taste.

   So, please accept this sweet as a symbol of a

         fresh start in your new home, and

   Our thanks for making our job a little easier.
               The Relocation Team
```

Figure 4.2. A "Welcome" card for the newly relocated employee.

staff to review the material in the welcome packages and to answer any questions that employees may have. Snacks and refreshments reinforce the informal atmosphere and make attendees more comfortable.

- Welcome meetings hosted by supervisors and managers provide detailed information on the procedures and policies that are in place and on the unique physical properties and equipment within their workspace.

REFERENCES

Anonymous (1989). Corporate roundtable: Executives discuss how they keep employees productive during group moves. Expansion, July/August, pp. 33–35.

Becker, F. (1987). Managing an office relocation. Report prepared for the International Facility Management Association, November.

Becker, F. (1990). The total workplace: Facilities management and the elastic organization. New York: Van Nostrand Reinhold.

Dennis, H. and D. A. Brown (1992). Merging and moving at Comerica Bank: Putting people first in a complex relocation plan. FM Journal, May/June, pp. 42–44.

Himes, P. E. (1991). Effectively managing complex renovation projects within occupied conditions. Proceedings, Canadian Facilities Management Conference, Toronto, ON, April.

Preston, P. R. and W. Zimmerer, (1978). Management for Supervisors. Englewood Cliffs, NJ: Pentice-Hall, Inc.

ADDITIONAL READINGS

Cheikin, L. (1991) Moving the facility—What's it all about? Proceedings, 12th International Facility Management Conference and Exposition, November, San Diego, CA.

Devlin, H. J., L. Howell and D. H. Morton, (1992). A moving experience. Proceedings, 13th Annual International Facility Management Conference and Exposition, New Orleans, LA, October 4–7.

Engel, P. (1987). Corporate moves: Managing the confusion. Facilities Design and Management, April, pp. 64–67.

Krigsman, N. and R. Krigsman, (1994). Relocation: How to move an organization successfully. Personnel Journal, May, pp. 14–16.

Tuttens, N. (1990). Site selection and relocation: Making a move—Step by step. Canadian Facility Management, May/June, pp. 13–16.

Chapter Five

Planning: Environmental Concerns of Office Workers

A poor office environment can affect worker health, morale, and productivity. An office that's too cold can interfere with work. One that's too hot can make workers drowsy. Too much noise can be annoying, and poor lighting can cause eye fatigue and short-term near-sightedness. Relocation provides an excellent opportunity to improve the environmental conditions in which office workers work. During most moves, offices are empty or vacated for short periods of time, and during such periods, without people or furniture occupying a space, it is easier to modify the facilities.

This chapter reviews the four environmental issues that are of most concern to office workers and building managers:

1. Lighting
2. Acoustics
3. Temperature and relative humidity
4. Air quality and air movement

In keeping with this book's underlying principles, each section will be written to accomplish three objectives:

1. Provide some background on each area so the team will understand why the issues are identified.
2. Identify the issues.
3. Recommend positions to take with your consultants.

5.1 LIGHTING ISSUES

5.1.1 Introduction

The relocation team should be sensitive to the types of visual adaptation situations that can be created during a move. Many situations cannot be identified in design and need to be identified during the postrelocation audit.

Beginning in the late 1980's, the Steelcase Corporation employed Louis Harris and Associates, Inc. to survey office workers to determine what they believed were:

- The most important environmental variables in the design of their offices
- Of those variables, which require the most improvement

The results from the 1991 survey (Steelcase, 1991), which was conducted among American, Canadian, European, and Japanese office workers, are summarized in Table 5.1. The survey found that the environmental variable considered most important among office workers in the four survey areas was "proper" lighting, followed closely by air conditioning.

The results also identified workers' opinions about the quality of current lighting and HVAC systems. The gaps (Δ) can be considered as the differences

Table 5.1. Percentage of Respondents, by Country, Reporting the Importance of Lighting and HVAC (Very Important) and the Percentage of Offices Where Each Has Been Adequately Considered (Very True)

Country		Lighting		HVAC	
		%	Δ%	%	Δ%
USA	Very important	92	28	85	40
	Very true	64		45	
Canada	Very important	90	28	84	47
	Very true	62		37	
Japan	Very important	87	33	82	38
	Very true	55		44	
EEC	Very important	81	31	72	45
	Very true	50		37	

Where:
  Δ% = The difference in percentage between "very important" responses and "very true" responses.

Source: Adapted from the Steelcase Worldwide Office Environmental Index 1991, © Steelcase.

between the quality that the workers wanted and the quality that they felt they were provided with. For lighting, the gaps averaged about 30%, indicating the need for improved lighting.

Table 5.2 compares the responses received from Canadian and American office workers about lighting with those received from Canadian and American facilities managers and designers. The results show that office workers and designers in both countries, and facility managers in Canada, agreed that lighting quality was not as good as it could be at the time that the survey was taken.

In addition to identifying the importance of lighting, workers in each of the countries surveyed identified eyestrain as another serious office hazard. These results compare favorably with those reported by Kupsh and Jones (1991). A survey of employees in an airline computer center in Singapore found that 94% of the data entry workers and 79% of the workers who alternated between the VDT and hard copy reported visual problems. These data were compared to 44% of office workers performing non-VDT tasks who reported visual problems. The reader will appreciate the importance of lighting on eyestrain as this section unfolds.

This section addresses the following issues in lighting:

• The effect of the visual environment on visual tasks
• Factors affecting the visual environment
• The advantages and disadvantages of different types of lighting systems
• Methods to estimate lighting issues before the lights are installed

Table 5.2. *Comparsion of the Opinions of Office Workers, Facilities Managers, and Designers About the Importance of Office Lighting and the Adequacy of the Lighting in Today's Buildings*

Worker Category	Statement	Canada		USA	
		%	Δ%	%	Δ%
Office workers	Very important	90	28	92	30
	Very true	62		62	
Facilities Managers	Very important	90	28	85	5
	Very true	62		80	
Designers	Very important	81	49	83	39
	Very true	38		44	

Where:

Δ% = The difference in percentage between "very important" responses and "very true" responses.

Source: Adapted from the Steelcase Worldwide Office Environmental Index 1991, © Steelcase.

5.1.2   The Effect of the Visual Environment on Visual Tasks

Most information processed by office workers is visual, so proper design of the visual environment is essential to the optimal performance, health, and well-being of office workers. The major visual office tasks include:

- Filing and storage
- Hard copy, reading and writing
- Computer use
- Moving between office locations (wayfinding)

Features of the visual environment that can affect the health and well-being of the workers and the performance of their tasks include:

- Color of surroundings
- Brightness of surroundings
- Quality of the visual environment

Section 5.1.3 addresses the relationship between human visual needs and the design of the visual environment. The objective of this review is to sensitize the reader to the complexity of this relationship and of the effects on one factor of changing another.

5.1.3   Human Factors Affecting the Visual Environment

The characteristics of the human visual system dictate the design of the visual environment and the factors that influence it. It's important for members of the project team to appreciate those features of the system that can be influenced by a poor environment.

5.1.3.1   Acuity

Acuity is the ability of the eye to resolve detail such as alphanumeric characters on a VDT or a printed page. Our ability to resolve detail depends on three factors:

1. The size of the object being resolved,
2. The contrast between the object and the background
3. The brightness of the visual field

The relationships between these factors were established quantitatively by Blackwell during the 1940's (Blackwell, 1952). In the simplest terms, the relationships can be explained as follows:

- The bigger an object is, the easier it is to see. "Bigness" in this context is the visual angle the object subtends at the eye. As Figure 5.1 indicates, "big-

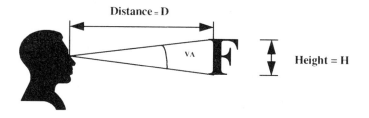

VA = Visual Angle = 2 x VA/2

$$= 2 \times Tan^{-1} \frac{H}{2D}$$

For small angles (< 1 degree or 60 minutes of arc)

$$VA \sim 3438 \times \frac{H}{D} \quad \text{(minutes of arc)}$$

Note: H and D are dimensions with the same units (e.g. inches, meters)

Figure 5.1. Illustration of "visual angle" (VA), the angle subtended at the eye by the object being viewed.

ness" depends not only on how high the object is, but also on how close it is to the eye.

- The more contrast between the object and its background, the easier it is to see. White letters against a black background, for example, are easier to see than brown letters would be against the same background. Research shows us which combinations of object and background, shown in Table 5.3, are easier to see.
- The brighter the object and background, the easier the object is to see. Thus printed material is easier to see in a bright office than in a dark one.

Each of the above factors is related to the others. For example, as the contrast decreases, objects must be made larger to have the same visibility. Reduced contrast alphanumeric characters can be made more visible by making them larger. Hence if one factor must be compromised, the visual task can be made easier by improving the other two. This is important to remember in subsequent sections.

5.1.3.2   *Accommodation*

Accommodation is the ability of the eye to focus on objects at different distances. For those with normal uncorrected vision, accommodation is achieved by adjusting the shape of the lens in each eye. The process is illustrated in Figure 5.2.

Table 5.3. Acceptability of Combinations of Object and Background Colors

Legend: ■ Unacceptable   ▨ Marginally Acceptable   □ Acceptable

Color (reflectance)	Black	Dark Blue	Dark Red	Pink (30)	Light Orange	Lime Green	Cyan	Yellow	White
Black (3)	■	■	■	▨	□	□	□	□	□
Dark Blue (10)	■	■	■	■	▨	▨	□	□	□
Dark Red (20)	■	■	■	■	■	▨	□	□	□
Pink (30)	▨	■	■	■	■	■	■	□	▨
Light Orange (40)	□	▨	■	■	■	■	■	■	□
Lime Green (50)	□	▨	▨	■	■	■	■	■	■
Cyan (60)	□	□	▨	■	■	■	■	■	■
Yellow (70)	□	□	▨	■	■	■	■	■	■
White (98)	□	□	□	▨	■	■	■	■	■

When we look at a distant object, the lens flattens (Figure 5.2*a*). When we look at a near object, the lens bulges (Figure 5.2*b*). Some individuals are unable to accommodate to far and/or near objects. Those who cannot accommodate to far objects are termed nearsighted (Figure 5.2*c*), and those unable to accommodate to near objects are termed farsighted (Figure 5.2*d*). Each of these conditions can be corrected optically with glasses or contact lenses. Many workers require glasses that offer the choice between corrected and uncorrected vision or even two different corrections in the same lens. These are termed bifocal lenses. Glasses with three corrections in the same lens are termed trifocals.

The far distance correction usually occupies the top half of a bifocal lens, while the near distance correction occupies the bottom half. Hence users often need to tilt their heads up or down to view what they want to see or read. If head tilt is excessive, users can suffer discomfort in the upper body. The issue of head posture will be addressed in the section dealing with workspace design.

Another design issue that is relevant to accommodation is the distance to the visual object. Typically, the reading distance to hard copy is about 35 cm, and VDTs are designed to be read at about 50 cm. For many tasks the office worker must continually alternate his or her focus between hard copy and the VDT. If the difference between the reading distances is excessive, the eye muscles controlling the shape of the lens can fatigue, causing eyestrain. In the 1991 Steelcase survey of office workers that was introduced above, respondents cited eyestrain as the most serious office hazard. So, as a rule, all objects to be viewed in one task should be placed at the same distance from the eyes to minimize eye fatigue and discomfort.

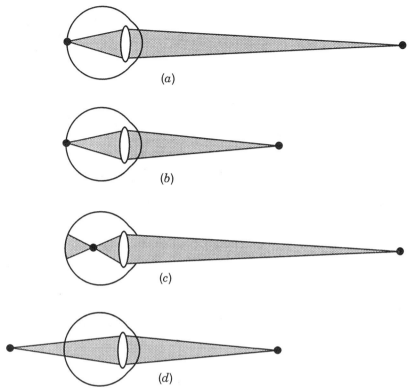

Figure 5.2. Illustration of accommodation. (*a*) Normal far vision, light focused on retina. (*b*) Normal near vision, light focused on retina. (*c*) Nearsightedness, light focused in front of retina for far objects. (*d*) Farsightedness, light focused behind retina for near objects. From M. Sanders and E. McCormick, *Human Factors in Engineering and Design,* Fifth Edition (1982). New York: McGraw-Hill. Reproduced with permission of The McGraw-Hill Companies.

5.1.3.3   Age

When we age, our vision deteriorates in several ways including:

- Lenses in the eye lose elasticity, requiring visual correction.
- The fluid inside our eyes clouds, thus scattering the light entering our eyes and reducing the light falling on our retinas where the image is sensed. The result is:
—An increased sensitivity to glare
—The need for increased illumination

5.1.3.4   Adaptation

Adaptation refers to the ability of our eyes to adapt to changes in the luminance (brightness) of our surroundings. Adapting to brighter or less bright surroundings involves several complex mechanisms in the eye. Each takes time to complete, although we adapt to an increase in brightness much faster than we adapt to a decrease in brightness.

While we are adapting to a brighter visual scene, our eyes are under the stress of being overexposed. Our pupils contract to reduce the light entering our eyes, but until the electrochemical response of our eyes is complete, we squint and our eyes tear. During this adjustment period, we can see to work, but are distracted.

While we adapt to a less bright environment, our ability to resolve detail can be affected. In the extreme—for example, when entering a movie theater from the sunlight—the adaptation process could take 20 minutes to complete and our ability to see in the darkened environment could be severely affected for several minutes.

A computerized office presents a wide range in potentially different brightness situations. The window is often the brightest light source and the VDT screen the least bright. The window can be 1000 times as bright as the VDT. Moreover, the items that are illuminated with natural light, for example, paper, could also be very bright.

The problem of adaptation in a computerized office is the frequency with which we look at a bright, then a less bright, surface. When typing, for example, the eye could move every few seconds from one surface to the other. This movement has prompted the development of a rule of thumb for office work based on the concepts of "luminance ratio" and "optimal visual field":

> No object in the optimal visual field should be more than 10
> times as bright as any other object.

The optimal visual field is shown in Figure 5.3a and 5.3b. It is the visual area bounded by +/– 45 degrees either side of the line of sight to the object of interest, for example, the VDT, and the area bounded by the horizontal line of site and 45 degrees below the horizontal.

Identifying "bright" and "dark" objects in an office can be difficult without the aid of illumination meters. Our eyes are not good judges of illumination because they adapt so well. In addition, some poor luminance situations are not obvious.

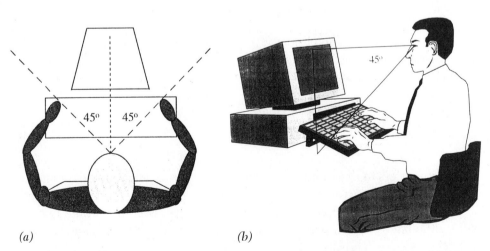

(a)   *(b)*

Figure 5.3. (*a*) Top view of the optimal visual field. (*b*) Side view of the optimal visual field.

Figures 5.4 and 5.5, for example, illustrate a situation in which the occupant suffered visual fatigue. On closer examination, it was determined that the reflected light from the hard copy resting on the window sill was over 200 times brighter than the user's VDT. Even though his windows were covered with horizontal blinds, the blinds were adjusted downward (Figure 5.4), allowing the sun to shine on the paper. By merely reversing the blinds (Figure 5.5), the incident sunlight was blocked and the luminance ratio reduced from about 200:1 to about 20:1.

Figure 5.4. Photo illustrating an unacceptably high luminance ratio between the hard copy and the VDT screen. Published with permission of Imperial Oil Limited, Toronto, ON.

Figure 5.5. Photo illustrating an acceptable luminance ratio between hard copy and the VDT screen. Published with permission of Imperial Oil Limited, Toronto, ON.

5.1.3.5   *Glare*

Glare is defined as "a sensation caused by light within the visual field that is brighter than the level of light to which the eyes are adapted" (Steelcase, 1994). Glare can cause discomfort, which leads to squinting or tearing of the eyes. More importantly, glare can mask the visual task, thus affecting our ability to function effectively. There are two types of glare:

- Indirect or reflective glare, in which light bounces from a highly reflective surface, such as a glossy desktop, or from the screen of a VDT (Figure 5.6)
- Direct glare, when bright lights shine directly into the eyes (Figure 5.7)

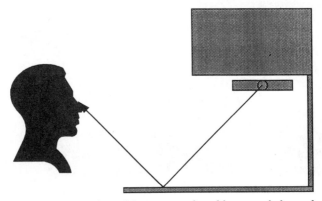

Figure 5.6. Specular refelections produced by a poorly located light source.

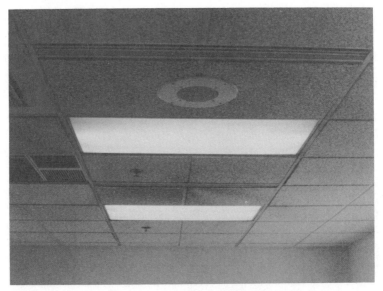

Figure 5.7. Direct glare produced by ceiling mounted light sources.

Glare can be reduced by the appropriate design of the workstation and lighting system. Each is addressed in following sections.

5.1.4   Other Factors Affecting the Visual Environment

Most of what we see is illuminated by natural or artificial light. The brightness of illuminated objects depends on the brightness of the incident light and how much of the light the object reflects. The relationship between reflectance, illumination, and brightness can be expressed by equation 5.1:

$$\text{Brightness } (B) = \text{Incident illumination } (I) \times \text{Reflectance factor } (R) \quad [5.1]$$

Dark objects have a lower reflectance factor, so they reflect less light than light objects. Other objects, such as VDTs, are self-illuminating. The brightness of self-illuminating objects depends on the intensity of their light source.

For the most efficient use of natural or artificial light, as much light as possible should be reflected from walls and ceilings. Thus office walls and ceiling coverings should have high values of R. Studies have shown that the reflectance of office surfaces should increase with height, as shown in Figure 5.8. The figure illustrates that reflectance on the floor and lower wall levels should be low to keep brightness levels low thus maintaining an optimal luminance ratio. Surfaces surrounding VDTs should be about as bright as the VDT. If the back-

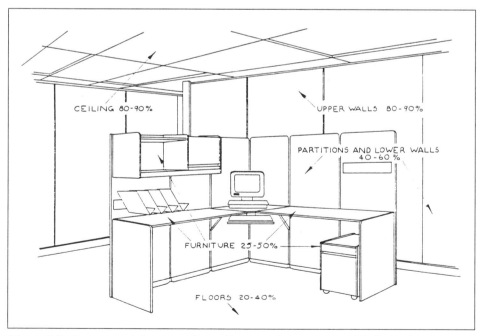

Figure **5.8.** Recommended room surface reflectances for VDT use. Published with permission of Imperial Oil Limited, Toronto, ON.

ground surface and the VDT are equally bright, the eyes will not have to adapt as they move from one to another.

Typical reflectance factors for common colors are given in Table 5.4.

Most manufacturers will provide reflectance factors of their materials. Often, however, the reflectance of the surface is unknown. A quick way to estimate reflectance is demonstrated in Figure 5.9. The reflectance of the vertical surface is the ratio of the illuminance measured with the photometer pointing at the surface divided by the illuminance measured with the photometer pointing away from the surface.

The reader should note that the reflectance factor calculated in Figure 5.9 is only a rough estimate (+/− 10%) of actual. To increase the accuracy of the estimate, the illumination meter should be held as close to the wall as possible without casting a shadow on it. In most cases the proper distance is about 15 cm (6 inches).

Color rendering is defined as the effect of a light source on the color appearance of objects, compared with the effect produced by a reference light source of the same color temperature (Gordon and Nuckolls, 1995). The color rendering index (CRI) is a number between 0 and 100. A light source with a CRI between 80 and 100 provides excellent color rendering. A source with a CRI between 60 and 80 provides good color rendering, and sources with CRIs <50 provide poor color rendering. Color rendering is generally best for light that contains a wide spectrum of colors. Natural daylight, with a CRI = 100, is considered to provide the most natural color rendition. The CRIs of office lighting are discussed in the following sections.

5.1.5   Lighting Systems

The objective of every office lighting system is to provide the proper *quantity* of good *quality* light and place the light *where* it is needed.

Table 5.5 lists the illumination levels (quantity of light) required for tasks performed in typical offices.

In noncomputerized offices, illumination levels are selected to satisfy the visual tasks that are performed. As a general rule, the level of illumination required in a visual task should increase as (Grandjean, 1987):

Table 5.4. Reflectance Factors for Common Colors

Category	Reflectance factor	Example Colors
White	.85 - 1.0	--
Light	.65 - .75	Ivory, gray, lemon, yellow cream.
Medium-light	.55 - .65	Deep yellow, light green, pastel blue, buff.
Medium-dark	.40 - .55	Lime green, pale wood.
Wood Finish	.30 - .40	Maple, sandalwood, English oak, walnut, mahogany.

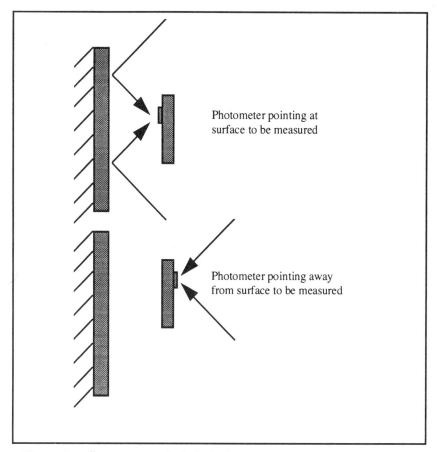

Figure 5.9. Illustrating a method of calculating approximate surface reflectances.

- The size of the visual objects viewed decreases
- The contrast of the objects and their backgrounds decreases
- The speed of perception required increases
- The complexity of the task increases (e.g., interpreting handwriting)

For example, the recommended illumination levels for the drawing task on Table 5.5 is much higher than that required for negotiating stairs and corridors. For most office tasks, the level of illumination on the worksurface provided by general lighting systems should not exceed 1000 lux. Above 1000 lux, the risk of producing glare from reflections outweighs any benefits gained from improved visual ability

Table 5.5 illustrates that recommended illumination levels in a computerized office are typically lower than those for noncomputerized offices. As illumination levels fall, the brightness of objects do as well. As discussed in Section 5.1.3.3, one principle of lighting is to ensure that nothing in the user's visual field is brighter than 10 times as bright as the least bright object. The ratio of the

Table 5.5. Recommended Illuminance Levels by Office Task or Location

Type of interior task or activity	Acceptable range of Illuminance (LUX)	Recommended Illuminance (LUX)
Corridors	50-150	100
Stairs	100-200	150
Cloak Rooms, Lavatories[1]	100-200	150
Offices: **Low range** (tasks requiring VDT use - supplemental task lighting is available)	200-400	300
Middle range (tasks requiring VDT use - no supplemental task lighting available)	300-500	400
High range (tasks not requiring VDTs; or fine details, such as in manual drafting, are required)	500-900	700
Conference rooms[2]	300-750	500
Drawing offices	500-1000	750

NOTES:
[1] Supplementary lighting should be considered.
[2] Conference room lighting should be adjustable.

Source: Published with permission of Imperial Oil Limited, Toronto, ON.

brightest to the least bright object in the visual field is termed the luminance ratio. In computerized offices, the proper quantity of light is a trade-off between two distinct requirements. Because VDTs are self-illuminated, they don't require ambient lighting to read them. In fact, high levels of ambient illumination can produce veiling luminance on the screen, which reduces the contrast between the screen characters and backgrounds, making the characters difficult to read. Generally a *uniform* level of illumination at the work surface of about 300 lux is sufficient. However, 300 lux illumination is not enough to let us comfortably read from printed or handwritten text, so additional light sources, called task lights, are required to increase the illumination on the paper and pencil tasks. These sources are directed away from the VDT so they will not cause glare or veiling luminance.

5.1.6   Artificial Lighting Systems

Types of Lighting sources for office lighting systems are:

- Fluorescent
- Incandescent
- High intensity discharge [HID]

Each light source is produced in a number of different variations and is packaged in many different ways. For example, fluorescent light sources can be manufactured using a wide variety of phosphors, which changes the fluorescent's color properties, efficiency, and cost. Moreover, the luminaires in which the sources are packaged can be designed to decrease direct and reflected glare and the efficiency with which they deliver light to the work surface. This section provides an overview of the most commonly used lighting systems and a sense of the relative advantages of each. For more detailed treatment, the reader is referred to Gordon and Nuckolls (1995).

Lighting systems can be classified by the way they direct light to the work-surfaces:

- Down, or direct, lighting systems direct the light from the luminaire downward to the worksurfaces below.
- Up, or indirect, lighting systems throw the light from the luminaire onto the ceiling where it is reflected down to the worksurfaces. Indirect light fixtures can be designed to hang 30–45 cm below the ceiling, to be free-standing on the office floor, or can be integrated into the office furniture.
- Task-ambient fixtures are a combination of direct and indirect systems. They shine a portion of the light up to the ceiling and the remainder down to the worksurfaces.

Table 5.6 illustrates some of the advantages and disadvantages of each type of lighting system.

Figure 5.10a and 5.10b are photographs of offices equipped with indirect lighting systems. Figure 5.10a compares the brightness of the reflection of a covered window and that of a ceiling illuminated by indirect lighting on the reflections from the screen of a VDT. Figure 5.10b compares the brightness of a fluorescent direct-lighting luminaire with that of a ceiling illuminated by an

Table 5.6. Advantages of Direct and Indirect Lighting Systems

	Direct	Indirect
Advantages	• Less expensive to install • Efficiency: More light can be produced for the same power	• More uniform illumination which eliminates harsh shadows and reduces glare. • Can use HID light sources for improved efficiency
Disadvantages	• Indirect glare is produced by all types of luminaires • Luminance levels are reduced by parabolic louvers.	• Clearance necessary to provide a good spread of light requires higher ceilings than are required by direct lighting systems • Lights reflect heat into the workspace rather than into the ceiling plenum.

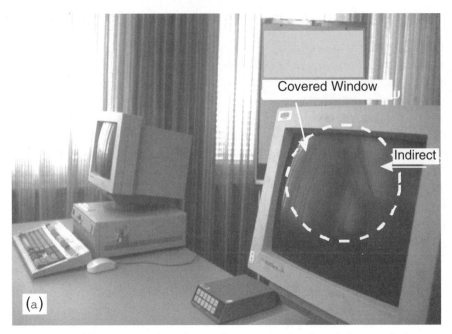

Figure 5.10. (*a*) Comparing the reflection from overhead indirect lighting with that from the natural light from the window.

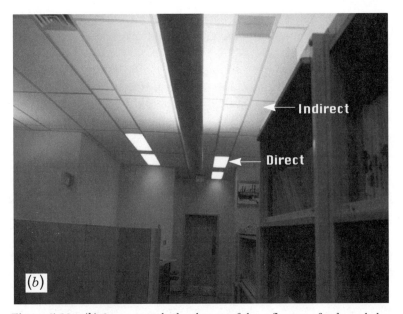

Figure 5.10. (*b*) Comparing the brightness of the reflection of indirect lighting with that of ceiling mounting luminaires. Published with permission of Imperial Oil Limited, Toronto, ON.

indirect lighting system. Note that in both photos, the brightness of the indirect system is less intense. Figure 5.10*b* also illustrates a general principle in light production. As the light is spread over the ceiling creating a large light source, the source does not have to be as bright to produce the same amount of illumination at the worksurface. Hence the goal of an indirect lighting system is to spread the light as uniformly as possible across the ceiling. Unfortunately this has its drawbacks. Most indirect fixtures are limited in their ability to spread light, so to increase the spread, they have to be positioned further away from the ceiling. In offices with ceilings lower than 9 feet, this can mean that the fixtures are mounted so low that they interfere with normal office functions. New fixture designs are reducing the fixture-to-ceiling distances required.

The cost of installing and operating lighting systems varies widely depending on the light source used and the fixture that the source is mounted in. Figure 5.11, for example, illustrates the efficacy of three major light sources. Efficacy is a measure of how effectively the electrical energy provided to the lamp is converted to light. It is calculated by dividing the light output (lumens) by its energy input (watts). The efficacy of incandescent lamps is only about 25% of that of fluorescent or metal halide HIDs.

Table 5.7 illustrates the effect that different combinations of light source and lighting fixture can have on capital and operating costs. The data compare the costs among several different alternative fluorescent fixture systems for a new building application. You should note several important comparisons between the three lighting system in Table 5.7:

- Annual operating and maintenance costs of each system are two to three times more than the annualized capital costs of each system.
- Parabolic louvers add about 15% to the annual costs of the least expensive direct lighting fixture.

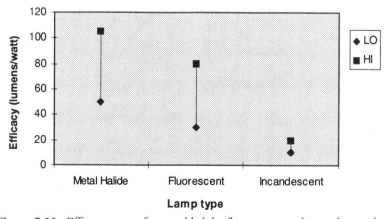

Figure 5.11. Efficacy ranges for metal halide, fluorescent, and incandescent lamps.

Table 5.7. Approximate Relative Operating and Maintenance Costs, per Square Foot of Floor Space, for Three Types of Luminaires

Cost Category	System 1 Direct Lighting -- Acrylic Lens	System 2 Direct Lighting -- Parabolic Louver	System 3 Indirect lighting System
Capital Costs[1]	1.0	1.42	1.64
Annual Capital Cost[2] (Assumes 20-year life)	0.05	0.071	0.082
Annual operating and maintenance costs	0.14	0.145	0.183
Total Annual Cost	0.19	0.226	0.275

Notes
[1] All cost data are normalized relative to the capital cost of System 1.
[2] The annual capital cost does not take into account the present value of the capital outlay over 20 years.

- Indirect lighting systems are about 40% more expensive to purchase and operate on an annual per square foot basis than the least expensive direct lighting system. Compared to a parabolic system, indirect lighting is about 20% more to purchase and operate.

The color rendering index also varies widely among light sources. Figure 5.12 illustrates the range of CRIs for each of the common light sources used in an office. Incandescent sources provide the best color rendering. The CRI of fluorescent lamps varies considerably, depending on the phosphor coating used. Table 5.8 lists the CRIs of the common tubes.

Cool white lamps, the most common and least expensive fluorescent lamps, have a CRI of 62. Cool white deluxe and some triphosphor lamps have CRIs greater than 80. Typically, the high CRI fluorescent lamps are much more

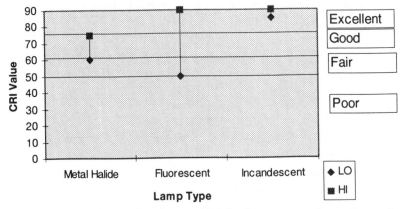

Figure 5.12. Range of CRI values for metal halide, fluorescent, and incandescent lamps.

Table 5.8. CRIs of Common Types of Fluorescent Lamps

Lamp Type	Color Rendering Index
Warm white	52
Warm white deluxe	73
Cool white	62
Cool white deluxe	89
Tri-phosphor	80-83

Source: Adapted from Gordon and Nuckolls (1995). Reprinted by permission of John Wiley and Sons, Inc., New York.

expensive than cool whites, but the price could become more competitive as the demand for better color rendering increases.

5.1.7   Natural Lighting

Natural light generally enters the office through windows and skylights, though there are systems that "pipe" natural light throughout offices from central gathering points. In most design situations, we do not include illumination from natural sources in our lighting calculations, so when measuring the ambient illumination in an office area, it is important to measure at night when there is no natural light to increase the illumination level.

The sun is an intense light source. Even on cloudy days the outside illuminance can be several thousand lux. Hence natural light can cause glare in an office and can increase luminance ratios the same way as artificial light. It must, therefore, be controlled just as artificial light is controlled.

In the northern hemisphere, the sun is most glaring on south facing windows and must be controlled with some form of window treatment. Window treatments come in several designs including:

- Vertical blinds
- Horizontal blinds
- Curtains
- Roller blinds

Each of these treatments can be made of material that transmits some or none of the incident light. The choice of material depends on the use. For example, the window treatments chosen for meeting rooms should include an opaque blind or curtain that can be pulled over the windows when visual aids are used.

5.1.8   Task Lighting

Task lighting is artificial lighting that illuminates a particular area of the workstation. When first mentioned in Section 5.1.5, task lights were recommended as supplemental lights that provided additional illumination to supplement existing ambient lighting systems.

Task lights are also used as "fill-in" lights in dark corners or under shelves or overhead storage units, to fill in shadows that may be produced by ambient lighting. A task light can be a desk lamp, a fluorescent strip light that is mounted under an overhead storage cabinet, or a narrow beam spot lamp that is mounted in a ceiling fixture or on an adjustable track.

Task lighting has advantages and disadvantages like all other lighting systems. These are listed in Table 5.9.

The major advantage to a task light can also be its major downfall. Individual freestanding task lamps can be located almost anywhere. Those equipped with weighted bases can be placed on almost any horizontal surface. Because freestanding task lights can be moved, they can be placed in locations that cause problems of both indirect and direct glare.

Kohn (1990) defines an offending zone as a location from which a light source causes veiling reflections (direct or indirect glare). Light sources should not be positioned directly in front of the work area, as shown in Figure 5.13. Most of

Table 5.9. Advantages and Disadvantages of Task Lights

Advantages	Disadvantages
• Portable: Can be moved to or installed in a variety of locations. • Inexpensive alternative to modifying the general lighting system. • Reduces energy consumption when combined with low level ambient lighting.	• Expensive to purchase when compared with ambient fixtures. • Can be a glare source if not installed properly.

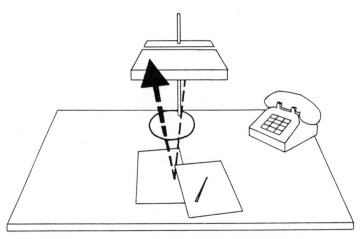

Figure 5.13. Improperly positioned task light. Published with permission of Imperial Oil Limited, Toronto, ON.

the incident illumination will bounce off of reflective material into the user's eyes. Instead, task lights should be located as shown in Figure 5.14. Most of the incident light reflects across the worksurface.

The indirect glare from furniture mounted task lights is more difficult to control. Most workstations are equipped with a strip fluorescent task lamp that is mounted under the overhead storage unit, as shown in Figure 5.15. The fluorescent tube is not directly visible to the user, but the light from the lamp is directed toward the worksurface and is then reflected into the user's eyes. A photograph of the resulting reflection is illustrated in Figure 5.16.

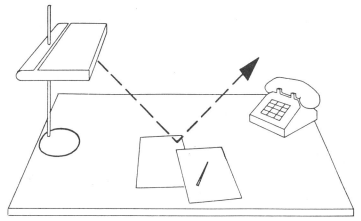

Figure 5.14. Properly positioned task light. Published with permission of Imperial Oil Limited, Toronto, ON.

Figure 5.15. Task light shining on worksurface from beneath overhead storage unit. Published with permission of Imperial Oil Limited, Toronto, ON.

Figure 5.16. Reflected glare from the task light mounted beneath the overhead storage unit. Published with permission of Imperial Oil Limited, Toronto, ON.

There are two solutions to this problem. One is to redirect the light from the undercounter fixture; the other is to diffuse the light. Figure 5.17 shows two task fixtures each equipped with a miniature fluorescent bulb and a lensed hood and mounted on the underside of an overhead cabinet. The fixtures are mounted on either end of the cabinet and oriented so they direct their light *across* the workstation.

Figure 5.18 is a sketch of a hypothetical parabolic diffuser that covers a strip fluorescent. The parabolic diffuser limits the exit angle of the light to +/– 45

Figure 5.17. Directed task lamps mounted beneath overhead storage units. Reproduced with permission of SPI Lighting, Inc., Mequon, WI.

degrees, so that most light is directed onto a matte fabric covering , the "tack-board" surface at the back of the workstation. The light reflecting from the fabric would be diffused and would not create glaring reflections. The problem with such a task lamp is that light would be blocked by the parabolic lens and absorbed by the fabric.

Another problem that can be caused by poor installation of task lights is the overly bright work areas that can be created when the source is mounted too close to the worksurface.

Finally, some task light sources are designed to throw light in all directions as well as onto the worksurfaces, as illustrated in Figure 5.19. The light fixture shown in the figure is well designed to ensure that the brightness of the globe is below the direct glare threshold. Some lights are not so well-designed and create excessive glare.

5.1.9   Illuminance Calculations

It is often necessary for the project team to weigh the costs associated with a project in order to determine the feasibility of continuing. Lighting, as demonstrated in Section 5.1.5, can be a significant cost in projects. Therefore it is important to be able to estimate the number and type of fixtures required and their capital

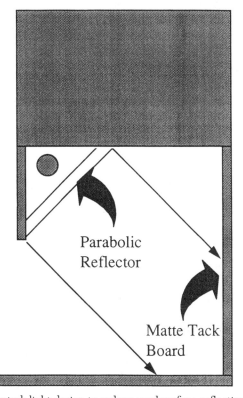

Figure 5.18. Undercounter task light design to reduce worksurface reflections.

Figure 5.19. Task light transmits acceptable level of luminance from the translucent shade. Photograph courtesy of Steelcase Inc., Grand Rapids, MI.

cost. The number of fixtures of a particular type required per square foot of ceiling space is determined by the illuminance produced at the worksurface.

Determining the illuminance level provided by a lighting system at the worksurface is a complex calculation that is typically performed by lighting consultants. However, the project team can estimate approximate costs in two ways.

The most common fluorescent luminaire contains two 32-watt fluorescent lamps and is covered with an acrylic lens. The rule of thumb for standard installations is one fixture for each 25 square feet of floor space, thus providing a gross energy density of about 2.6 watts of light for every square foot of floor space. Assuming standard reflectances and ceiling heights, a power level of 2.6 watts per square foot will provide about 500 lux of illumination at a worksurface that is 75 cm (30 inches) above the floor.

The Illuminating Engineering Society has published methods for estimating average illuminance levels (IES,1984) that are more accurate than the rule of thumb given above. A sample calculation, using the zonal cavity method, is given in Gordon and Nuckolls (1995).

5.2 OFFICE ACOUSTICS

5.2.1 Introduction

The most important function of an office is to communicate (Owen,1993), and humans communicate in two principal ways: visually and auditorilly. Auditory communication is important in an office environment, since face-to-face and telephone speech is the principal method we use to communicate with colleagues and clients.

The objectives of the acoustic environment are threefold:

1. To encourage auditory communication in an office

2. To minimize sound distractions

3. To provide speech privacy

Barkman (1991) claims that office acoustical problems are often overlooked and avoided by facilities managers for several reasons:

- Acoustics is a sophisticated science that is not clearly understood by facilities managers. We tend to avoid those things that we don't understand.
- Most believe that every acoustic problem must be solved by an acoustic specialist, and that the solutions are expensive, time consuming, and disruptive.
- Office workers believe that very little can be done to solve office acoustic problems.
- Acoustical problems are not as critical as nonfunctioning heating, ventillating and air-conditioning (HVAC) systems or a leaking roof.

The purpose of this section is to provide the project team with a basic knowledge of acoustics and acoustic problems in the office and with design solutions that can be implemented without sophisticated knowledge or costly modifications.

5.2.2 Characteristics of Sound

Sound is produced by variations in air pressure that are sensed by the human auditory system.

The primary characteristics of sound are frequency (pitch) and intensity (loudness). Frequency is measured in hertz (Hz), which is equivalent to cycles per second. Intensity is measured as sound pressure level (SPL) with units in decibels (dB); the decibel is a logarithmic measurement. Therefore an increase of 10 dB represents a 10-fold increase in intensity. Similarly, doubling the power of the sound results in an intensity increase of 3 dB.

Most sounds are complex, composed of many frequencies superimposed on each other. The sound at each frequency is typically at a different intensity, so a sound like speech or the noise from a computer is characterized by its intensity (loudness) at various frequency bands within the range of human hearing. The accepted practice is to divide the human audible frequency range into 10 bands with center frequencies at 31.5, 63, 125, 250, 500, 1000, 2000, 4000, 8000, 16 000 Hz.

Intensity or sound pressure is measured by sound pressure level meters. In practice the intensity of most sounds is not measured at each of the 10 frequency bands. Instead, the levels from each frequency are combined into one measure according to the way the human ear weights the loudness of sounds at different frequencies. The most often used weighting scheme for converting sounds to how they are perceived by the human ear is the A-weighted network, which is expressed in dBA.

5.2.2.1   Office Sound Levels

Compared to other working environments, the ambient sound levels in an office are relatively low. Table 5.10 compares the intensity of sounds from a variety of sources. It should be noted that intensities above 80 dBA are regulated in most jurisdictions because of the damage they can cause to the human auditory system.

Sound travels in all directions in an office by reflecting off of some surfaces, and by passing through others. While vertical surfaces like walls and partitions help attenuate sound, they seldom block it totally. If there is a crack in a wall or a pin hole in a barrier, some sound will get through. Sound loses intensity as it passes through the air. Every doubling of the distance from the source results in a 6 dB reduction in intensity (Konz, 1990).

5.2.3   Characteristics of Speech

Human speech spans a wide range of frequencies and intensities, depending on who is speaking and how loud.

Figure 5.20 demonstrates the typical ranges of frequencies and intensities of human speech. As a general comment, the male voice has more dominant components in the lower frequencies and is 3–5 dB louder than the female voice (Sanders and McCormick, 1993).

5.2.4   Noise

Noise is defined simply as unwanted sound. What is noise to one person may be useful sound to another.

The disturbing effects of noise on office workers vary with:

• The physical characteristics of the noise source

Table 5.10. Sound Intensities (dBA) of Some Common Sources

Source	Intensity (dBA)	Comments
Jet engine at takeoff	140	Pain
Shotgun	130	discomfort
Thunder (overhead)	110	deafening
Rockband	100	temporary hearing loss
Heavy street traffic	90	loud, distracting
Typical factory noise	80	8-hour exposure limit
Impact printers	70	annoying
Average loud office	60	distracting, interferes with speech
Busy office	45-60	distracting
Private office	40	comfortable
Quiet conversation	30	requires intent listening
Threshold of hearing	0	

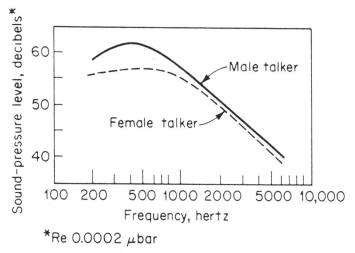

Figure 5.20. The octave-band, longterm average speech spectrum for male and female talkers. From M. Sanders and E. McCormick, *Human Factors in Engineering and Design,* Seventh Edition (1993). New York: McGraw-Hill. Reproduced with permission of The McGraw-Hill Companies.

- The information contained in the noise
- The nature of the task being performed

The degree of noise disturbance depends on these conditions:

- The louder the noise or the higher the frequencies it contains, the more annoying it is. Generally office noise greater than 65–70 dB is considered annoying.
- Unfamiliar, unexpected, or intermittent noises are more disturbing than familiar, expected, or continuous sounds.
- Noises generated by the workers' own activities are more annoying to those around them than to the workers themselves.
- Intelligible speech is more disturbing than meaningless noise. Speech can be equally annoying if it is spoken in a soft or loud voice.
- Occupations that are particularly noise sensitive include those requiring mental work or where understanding speech is important.
- Most office tasks will suffer if there is excessive noise.

The degree to which noise can affect voice communications in an office depends on its frequency and intensity. Noise criteria (NC) curves were developed by Baranek (1957) to help evaluate the communications environment for offices, conference rooms, and factory workplaces. Figure 5.21 plots a family of NC curves as a function of sound intensity for eight major octave bands. While the NC curves have been updated for lower frequencies (Baranek, 1989), the shape and the location remain about the same. The curves illustrate that the

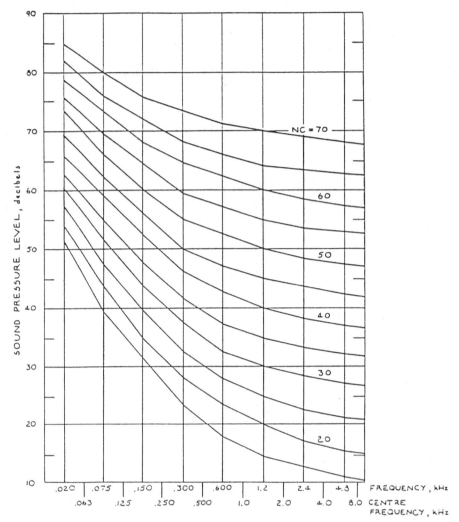

Figure 5.21. NC curves as a function of sound pressure level and frequency. Courtesy of L. L. Beranek, Balanced noise criterion (NCB) curves. Journal of the Acoustical Society of America 86, pp. 650–664, 1989. (See also: American National Standard, Criteria for evaluating room noise. ANSI S12.2–1995. Acoustical Society of America, 120 Wall Street, 32nd Floor, New York, NY 10005-3993.)

higher the NC, the more the sound interferes with voice communication. Note that, for a given NC rating, high frequencies interfere with speech at lower intensity levels than low frequencies.

Figure 5.22 provides an interpretation of the NC curves for tasks that are commonly performed in the office and for levels of annoyance.

To use the curves in Figure 5.21 and the interpretation in Figure 5.22, the following steps should be followed:

1. Measure the sound environment at each center frequency using a sound-presure level meter.

Figure 5.22. NC curves applied to the office environment. Published with permission of Imperial Oil Limited, Toronto, ON.

2. Plot the sound pressure levels (dB) on Figure 5.21.
3. Determine the highest NC curve that is selected by the plot in step 2.
4. Compare the highest NC with the situations in Figure 5.22.
5. If the communication requirements of the space are more restrictive than would be recommended by the NC result, the noise intensity will have to be reduced.

An approximation of the NC values in terms of dBA levels is given in Table 5.11. Use the dBA levels in Table 5.11 to determine whether the space is suitable for the communication task, using the above steps. Figure 5.22 illustrates that high noise levels interfere much more with telephone use than with face-to-face speech. Telephone use is difficult because the listener does not benefit from the visual cues that are present in face-to-face speech, such as body posture and lip movement. Telephone communication can be even more difficult if the conversation is on an unfamiliar topic or if the talker has a heavy foreign accent. NC curves are especially helpful in telephone marketing and switchboard environments.

5.2.4.1   Reducing Noise Levels in an Office
Noise levels can be reduced by taking advantage of the principles of sound transmission and attenuation techniques:

- The intensity of sound reduces as the inverse of the square of the distance from the source.
- Sound is noise to some and information to others.
- Sound can be blocked or absorbed by placing "barriers" between the sound source and the listeners.

The remainder of this section will review techniques that have been developed to take advantage of each of the above principles.

Sound Intensity Decreases with Distance from the Source. The following recommendations increase the distance that sound must travel from the source to the listener:

- Ceiling heights should be 9 feet or higher.
- Plenum spaces (space between the hung ceiling and the slab of the floor above) should be as high as possible.

Table 5.11. dBA Equivalents for NC Curves

Noise Criterion Curve	dBA Equivalent
NC–15	27
NC–20	31
NC–25	36
NC–30	40
NC–35	44
NC–40	50
NC–45	53
NC–50	58
NC–55	62
NC–60	67
NC–65	72

- Arrange open-plan offices so workers in adjacent spaces face away from their colleagues when they speak.

Sound Is Information to Some and Noise to Others. You can take advantage of this effect by using these techniques:

- Design the space to keep compatible groups together.
- Locate "coffee" rooms, meeting rooms, and lobbies away from offices.
- Locate offices where mental work is performed as far away as possible from both external and internal noise sources.

Sound Can Be Reduced by Blocking or Absorbing It. The effectiveness of a sound barrier in blocking the transmission of sound is measured by its sound transmission class (STC). The higher the STC, the more sound is blocked. The ability of a barrier to absorb sound is measured by its noise reduction coefficient (NRC). The NRC is an arithmetic average of the sound absorption characteristics of a material at frequencies of 250, 500, 1000, and 2000 Hz. NRC varies on a scale from 0.1 to 1.0. The higher the NRC, the more sound is absorbed. In summary, STC is a measure of how effectively a material *blocks* or *reflects* sound, while NRC is a measure of how effectively a material *absorbs* sound. Construction materials and office furniture should be chosen for their ability to absorb sound, or to redirect sound into a sound absorbing material, or to take advantage of the inverse square law.

The following recommendations are designed to take advantage of the blocking or absorption characteristics of materials:

- Carpet bare floors. Floors are not effective sound absorbers. A carpeted floor blocks the generation of sound.
- Use intervening rooms for packing and storage to act as buffers between noisy areas and offices.
- Reduce the area of luminaires, air ducts, and other ceiling mounted fixtures that reflect sound rather than absorb it. Parabolic and lensed-indirect luminaires reflect less sound than flat lens diffusers.
- Ceiling tiles should have an NRC of 0.8 or higher (Barkman, 1991) . Ceiling tiles can be very effective in absorbing sound since they first absorb the incident sound, then the sound reflected back from the slab of the floor above the plenum.
- Tackle noise at its source by:
  —Mounting noisy equipment on noise damping materials.
  —Enclosing noisy equipment in suitably designed rooms or noise covers. Many operations locate system printers, fax machines, copying equipment, and coffee stations in enclosed spaces.
- Treat windows with sound absorbing coverings.
- Install acoustical treatments on walls to reduce the sound reflected from hard surfaces. Walls need acoustic treatments only from about 90 cm (36

inches) to about 150 cm (5 ft) above the floor. Sounds striking the wall below 90 cm typically bounce to the floor and are absorbed. Sounds striking above 150 cm are relflected to the ceiling.
- Install high NRC noise baffles from ceilings.
- Select open-plan panels to reduce noise transmission:
   —Panels should have an NRC greater than 0.75, and an STC greater than 20.
   —The larger the panel, the more noise it will absorb. Panels should extend to the floor and be at least 60 inches high.
- Stagger the location of entrances to open plan offices so one entrance is not immediately adjacent to another.
- Place angled panels inside the entrance to open-plan offices to block sound before it reaches the entrance.

There are many ways of constructing walls and ceilings to block or absorb sound. For more detailed recommendations, you are referred to an acoustical specialist or to specialty books in this area.

5.2.4.2   Improving Speech Communications
The acoustic goals of an office environment, which were listed at the beginning of this section, can be restated as follows:

- To minimize speech interference
- To reduce the disturbing and annoying effects of noise
- To promote speech privacy

Previous subsections have dealt with reducing the disturbing effects of unwanted sound and the interference of noise or speech. The more successful the interventions, the quieter the office becomes. Offices can however, be so quiet that it is disconcerting to office workers and, more importantly, so quiet as to reduce the privacy of speech.

It's well known that the best locations for private face-to-face conversations are noisy restaurants or jet aircraft. Ambient noise masks speech when both are at the same intensity. Hence an office that is too quiet will permit speech to travel and be overheard by others at greater distances than an office that has a higher noise level.

The ability to understand speech in a noisy environment is measured subjectively by the articulation index (AI). AI is defined as the percentage of words or sentences that can be understood by a listener. Webster (1985) proposes that speech privacy requirements vary by occupation according to the proprietary nature of conversations and the degree that speech would disturb a random listener. His recommendations are given in Table 5.12.

At one end of the speech privacy spectrum is the manager/supervisor who requires an AI of 0–5%. At the other end are clerical positions that do not require speech privacy.

Table 5.12. Minimum Recommendations for Sentence Intelligibility by Organizational Level

Organizational Level	Recommended Sentence Intelligibility (%)
Manager/supervisor	0 - 5
Professional/Technical	5 - 30
Clerical	90 - 100

Source: Adapted from Webster (1985). Courtesy of Steelcase, Inc., Grand Rapids, MI.

In some offices, the level of ambient noise may not be *high* enough to ensure the privacy of face-to-face speech or meeting conversations. In such cases ambient noise may have to be increased. The situation is illustrated by Webster (1985) in Figure 5.23. The curve labeled *A* represents the sound profile of speech at the speaker's position. The curve labeled *B* represents the speech profile of the speaker at the listener's position (after attenuation by the inverse square distance relationship). The light gray shaded area represents the profile of the ambient noise in the untreated office. Note that the noise level is so low that the speech can carry beyond the listener's position and still be overheard by others. In order to ensure privacy, the ambient noise would have to assume the

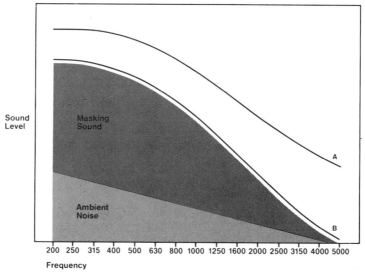

Figure 5.23. Illustrating how noise masking works to improve speech privacy. Reproduced from Webster (1985). Photograph courtesy of Steelcase Inc. Grand Rapids, MI.

shape of the dark gray shaded area. Note that the proposed noise profile is almost identical to the sound profile of the speech at the listener's position, but is a few dB lower in intensity.

Ambient noise in an office environment can be increased artificially by the installation of a noise masking sound system. The masking sound should be designed to match speech sound profile so maximum speech privacy can be obtained with the least amount of total noise.

5.3   TEMPERATURE AND RELATIVE HUMIDITY ISSUES

Strictly speaking, temperature and relative humidity issues are operational issues rather than relocation issues. However, if the new space is not properly designed and equipped to ensure that these issues will be controlled, your hand-off to building services may be difficult indeed. As this section illustrates, not all issues are building related. Specifying the wrong window coverings, for example, may create an excess heat level from south facing windows.

This section briefly reviews the reasons why the control of temperature and relative humidity is important. It also reviews design criteria and recommends steps that the project team can take to ensure that the working space will be comfortable.

5.3.1   Why a Comfortable Climate Is Important

A comfortable climate is essential to promote the well-being of office workers and to maintain their efficiency.

Four factors affect climatic comfort in an office:

1. Air temperature
2. Relative humidity
3. Air movement
4. Temperature of adjacent surfaces

The feeling of thermal comfort is subjective. Research has shown that more than 50% of employees seldom agree on a comfortable room temperature. However, by balancing each of the control factors, most office employees should be thermally comfortable.

5.3.2   Air Temperature

Overheating the office can lead to:

• Weariness
• Sleepiness
• Loss of performance
• Increased errors among office employees

Overcooling an office leads to restlessness, which in turn increases distraction and reduces concentration.

The thermal comfort of an office worker varies, depending on:

- Individual differences. Research has shown that the temperature comfort range for individuals is a relatively narrow 2C to 3C (3F to 6F).
- The amount of clothing worn. In winter the clothing of the average female employee provides only about 60 % of the insulation properties of the clothing of the average male employee. Consequently, women prefer a room temperature that is several degrees higher than that preferred by men.
- Physical work demand. Generally, the more active the worker, the lower is the temperature required for comfort.
- Time of year. Because of the seasonal clothing habits of building occupants, the temperature range for comfort is higher during hot seasons than it is during cool seasons.

Heat is generated by electronic equipment, such as VDTs, printers, copiers, or fax machines. Taken individually, the heat generated by one piece of equipment is too insignificant to affect the thermal load of an office. For example, a common VDT generates about 100 watts, the same as that dissipated by an average person. However, the heat generated by all office equipment can be substantial, and may account for much of the thermal load of an office.

In addition, lights generate heat, especially incandescent lights installed in ceiling fixtures and in task lights. Often the total heat generated by lighting alone is enough to heat a building when the outside temperature is above 5°C. Furthermore, the total heat generated by incandescent task lights can exceed the heat that would have been generated by the overhead fixtures that they replace. Finally, sunlight coming through unfiltered windows radiates a substantial amount of heat inside an office.

5.3.3   Relative Humidity

Relative humidity can have a strong influence on comfort. High relative humidity leads to a feeling of stuffiness. On the other hand, low humidity:

- Irritates the nasal and bronchial passages
- Dries the eye surfaces and gives discomfort to contact lens wearers
- Builds up static charges

5.3.4   Air Movement

The effect of air circulation on comfort depends on:

- Air temperature
- Air velocity

A draft is often felt to be more unpleasant when the temperature is low than when it is high. People are most sensitive to drafts at their feet, neck, and shoulders.

5.3.5 Adjacent Surfaces

Adjacent surfaces that are cold (e.g., outside windows during winter) or hot (e.g., surfaces of office equipment) can decrease the comfort of office workers.

5.3.6 Design Requirements

Table 5.13 shows the minimum requirements to which the project team should be designing. Your mechanical consultants may have additional factors for the team to consider, but they should not affect the design criteria in the table.

5.3.7 Design Guidelines

The following are some guidelines the project team can follow during the planning and design phases to make sure that the thermal comfort issues are being addressed:

- Select electronic equipment that has low thermal emission. Many of today's computers have energy saving "sleep" modes that can also reduce heat load.
- Ensure that equipment is designed and located to direct the heat produced away from the operators. Some computers, for example, expel heat out of the front of the unit onto the operator.
- Check the ventilation capability of individual spaces before permitting several pieces of electronic equipment to be located in one space.
- Do not locate office workers near adjacent surfaces that may become too hot or too cold.
- Ensure that temperatures can be controlled in areas that have more activity (e.g., mail rooms and mail sorting areas).

Table 5.13. Design Requirements for Thermal Comfort

Thermal Comfort Issue	Design requirement

Air Temperature (dry bulb)
         -Winter
 	
         -Summer
	21°C to 24°C
	 (70°F to 75°F)
	 24°C to 26°C
	 (78°F to 79°F)

Relative Humidity	30% to 60%
Average Air Movement	0.2 meters per second
Temperature of adjacent surfaces	Within 2°C to 3°C (3°F to 6°F) of the air temperature

- Install thermal glass, glass film, or window treatments on south, east, and west facing windows (opposite for southern hemisphere).
- Ensure that the location of air vents on equipment does not cause drafts directly on the body, for example, at the ankles or neck.

5.4   AIR QUALITY

Office air quality is a serious concern among about 45% of office workers in the United States, Canada, Japan, and the European Economic Community, second only to eyestrain (about 53%). Air quality is a relatively recent concern for the office environment. Prior to 1970, when energy was inexpensive, buildings and heating systems were not designed to be energy efficient. Hence, the proportion of fresh air in office air was sufficient to maintain a good quality environment.

With the oil crisis of the 1970's, however, and the sudden order of magnitude increase in oil prices, building operators were under pressure to increase operational efficiency. Air leakage in buildings was reduced, and air systems were adjusted to recirculate inside air and reduce the amount of fresh air in the building. As a result, office workers were exposed to more airborne contaminants generated internally. "Sick-building syndrome" exists when contaminants reach the point where 10% of building occupants complain of symptoms such as headache, dizziness, or nausea (Steelcase, 1994). Furthermore, according to Dr. James E. Woods of Virginia Polytechnic Institute and State University, it is possible that 20% of office workers in the United States are exposed to environmental conditions that are manifested as the sick-building syndrome (Steelcase, 1994).

This section provides you with basic information on office air quality and sources of contamination and suggests how to reduce airborne contaminants. The information is intended to make you aware of the issues so you can discuss them with a mechanical consultant. For more detailed information you are referred to Cunningham (1989) and ASHRAE (1989).

5.4.1   Factors Affecting Air Quality

Sources of air contamination in an office building can be loosely classified as follows:

- Solid particulate matter, which is found in dusts, fumes, and smoke
- Liquid particulate matter, found in mists and fogs
- Nonparticulates, such as vapors and gases

Contaminants can be generated internally or can be imported from the outside. Indoor sources of contamination include:

- Tobacco smoke, odors, carbon dioxide, organic contaminants, and even biological organisms from the office occupants
- The building itself, which may produce organic contaminants and odors
- Photocopiers, laser printers, and fax machines, which may produce organic contaminants and ozone

Outside sources of contaminants may include:

- Sulfur dioxide
- Oxides of nitrogen
- Particulates
- Hydrocarbon vapors or mists
- Carbon monoxide
- Carbon dioxide

The quality of the air in an office can be affected by how well the air conditioning equipment can remove the airborne contaminants and how well the sources of contamination can be reduced.

Most buildings today are equipped with systems that filter, wash, and disinfect the indoor air. When the systems are very efficient, the particulate content of indoor air is likely to be lower than that of the "fresh" air from the outside.

5.4.2   Ventilation Rates and Air Quality

Ventilation rates are the flow rates of outside or makeup air that enters the office. The American Society of Heating, Refrigerating and Air-Conditioning Engineers (ASHRAE) standards specify the minimum ventilation rates and indoor air quality that are acceptable for human occupation (e.g., 80% or more of the people exposed do not express dissatisfaction) and that are intended to avoid adverse health effects (ASHRAE, 1989). The carbon dioxide (CO_2) concentration in office air is a surrogate indicator of overall air quality. The maximum allowable concentration of CO_2 in office air is 1000 parts per million (ppm). Most operators work to an 800 ppm standard.

To maintain the minimum CO_2 level, the indoor air is diluted with outside "fresh" air. But even outside air contains CO_2, and the percentage of outside air required for dilution will depend, in part, on its CO_2 concentration. The outside air in many cities today could contain as much as 300 ppm CO_2.

Minimum ventilation rates for different inside areas as calculated by ASHRAE are presented in Table 5.14. The rates specify the minimum percentage of outdoor air that must be mixed with building air before being delivered to the space.

5.4.3   Recommendations to Improve Air Quality

As mentioned above, there are basically only two strategies for improving air quality:

Table 5.14. Outdoor Air Requirements for Indoor Ventilation

Application	Estimated Maximum Occupancy	Outdoor air flow rates cfm/Person (Liters/Sec./Person)
A. Office		
Office span	7	20 (10)
Meeting rooms	50	20 (10)
Auditoriums	150	5 (8)
Cafeterias	100	20 (10)
Reception areas	60	15 (8)
Smoking	70	60 (30)
Lounges		
Restrooms		50 (25)
(cfm/wc or urinal)		
Elevators		1.0 cfm/ft^2
Lobbies	30	15 (8)
Telecom centers and data	60	20 (10)
entry areas		
Duplicating		0.5 cfm/ft^2
B. Miscellaneous		
Bars, cocktail lounges	100	30 (15)
Dining rooms	70	20 (10)
School rooms	50	15 (8)
Laboratories	30	30 (10)

Source: Copyright © 1989 American Society of Heating, Refrigerating and Air-Conditioning Engineers, Inc. Reprinted by permission from ASHRAE Standard 62–1989.

- Reduce the production of airborne contaminants
- Increase the rate of removal of contaminants

5.4.3.1 Reduce Production of Contaminants

Many decisions made by the relocation team can reduce airborne contaminants for months and years after the project has been completed. These include:

- Select office equipment that emits (off-gases) the least amount of volatile organic compounds (VOCs) such as formaldehyde.
- Remove old ballasts that contain polychlorinated biphenols (PCBs).
- Ban aerosol adhesives.
- Improve handling of fiberglass products.
- Regulate the removal of old lead-based paints.
- Replace solvent based paints with water-based (e.g., latex).
- Clean existing carpets to eliminate bacteria and fungi.
- Build smoking areas with dedicated air conditioning systems that are isolated from the building system, that take in outside air exclusively, and that exhaust to the outside.

5.4.3.2   Increase Rate of Removal of Contaminants
In airtight buildings all removal and replacement of airborne contaminants is accomplished by the air conditioning system. The project team should have access to mechanical and industrial hygiene practitioners who can be consulted on the sources of contamination within the air conditioning system and can examine ways to improve the efficiency of the system in removing:

• Particulates
• Biological contaminants

The practitioners should also be consulted on ways to efficiently dilute indoor with outdoor air. For example, most building managers use 100 percent outside air when the ambient outside temperature is between 5° and 20°C (40° and 70°F).

REFERENCES

ASHRAE (1989). Ventilation for acceptable indoor air quality. American Society of Heating, Refrigerating and Air-Conditioning Engineers, Inc., Standard 62-1989.
Baranek, L. L. (1957). Revised criteria for noise in buildings. Noise Control 3(1), pp. 19–27.
Baranek, L. L. (1989). Balanced noise-criterion (NCB) curves. Journal of the Acoustical Society of America 86(2), August, pp. 650–664.
Barkman, A. P. (1991). Common acoustical problems: Their correction and avoidance. Proceedings of the Canadian Association of Facilities Management, Toronto, ON, April.
Blackwell, H. R. (1952). Brightness discrimination data for the specification of quantity of illumination. Illumination Engineering. 65, p. 389.
Cunningham, G. (1989). Air quality. Chapter 2 in N. Ruck (ed.) "Building design and human performance." New York: Van Nostrand Reinhold.
Gordon, G. and J. L. Nuckolls (1995). Interior lighting for designers, 3rd edition. New York: Wiley.
Grandjean, E. (1987). Fitting the task to the man. London: Taylor and Francis.
IES (1984). IES lighting ready reference. New York: Illumination Engineering Society of North America.
Kohn, M. B. (1990). Task lighting. The key to a productive work place. Consulting/Specifying Engineer, November, p. 68.
Konz, S. (1990). Work design: Industrial ergonomics, Third Edition. Publishing Horizons, Inc., Worthington, OH.
Kupsh, J. and C. L. Jones (1991). Ergonomics and the office work environment. Proceedings of the Canadian Association of Facilities Management, Toronto, ON, April.
McCormick, E. J. and M. S. Sanders (1982). Human factors in engineering and design, 5th edition. New York: McGraw-Hill.
Owen, D. D. (1993). Facilities planning and relocation. Kingston, MA: R. S.Means.
Sanders, M. S. and E. J. McCormick (1993). Human factors in engineering and design, 7th edition. New York: McGraw-Hill.
Steelcase (1991). Worldwide office environment index summary report. Steelcase Inc., Grand Rapids, MI.

Steelcase (1994). Workwell: A magazine from Steelcase. Steelcase Inc., Grand Rapids, MI.
Webster, M. P. (1985). Design to be seen and not heard. Acoustical control in the open plan office. Designers West, 32(12).

ADDITIONAL READINGS

Ontario Hydro (1989). Lighting. Ontario Hydro Energy Management Series.
Polgar, S. (1987). When technical standards support design acceptance. Canadian Facility Management, April/May, pp. 56–60.

Chapter Six

Planning: Office Planning

6.1 INTRODUCTION

This chapter deals with the planning of offices to meet organizational objectives and the working requirements of office workers. It demonstrates the importance of strategic planning in the selection of work systems. The concept of the "traditional" office workplace is challenged by alternative work systems that have been developed over the last decade. Final sections discuss the concepts of space planning, furniture configurations, alternative office layouts, and an analytical method for optimizing office layout.

The concept of having an alternative to the traditional office space concept is indeed novel. Alternative workplace strategies (AWS) include many new and varied working paradigms that have only become possible because of recent advances in computers and telecommunications.

Office design, however, is not the only segment of the work system that has changed since the mid-1980's. Work itself has been redefined. According to Harmon-Vaughan (1995), work used to be defined as a 9–5 job that took place in a company office building in an assigned office. Most office workers rarely worked at home. Today, work happens anywhere and anytime.

The company's outlook on office work has also changed since the early 1980's. According to Cook (1993), the 1980's saw rapid growth in the numbers of offices and office workers. Business was upsizing, offices became larger and more opulent. The business focus was on increased employment.

But the 1980's saw several global recessions that affected the organization's outlook, so in the late 1980's and early 1990's, businesses began to downsize. They closed offices and reduced workstaff. Their focus was on profits that could be achieved by reducing office expenses. The theme of much of this chapter is responding to the need to reduce office costs while maintaining or increasing productivity.

There is a growing body of evidence that the planning and design of an office affects:

- Job performance
- Job satisfaction
- Ease and quality of communications

Brill (1991) summarized the research that was conducted during the 1980's to examine the effects of office characteristics (which he calls "design facets") on each of the above indices (which he calls "bottom line measures"). As a result of his studies, conducted at the Buffalo Organization for Social and Technological Innovation (BOSTI), he was able to prioritize the effects of changes in design facets on the bottom line. A number of the facets in Table 6.1 deal with workspace issues. These issues will be revisited in Chapter 7. However, a number of the facets deal with office design including:

- Flexibility
- Communication
- Status
- Windows (i.e., whether an office is located next to a window)

The BOSTI studies also examined the cost of office facilities as a percentage of the total cost of operating an office. They found that people costs were as much as 13 times as great as the total costs of the building, furniture, technology and operations and maintenance. In other words, over a 10-year period, "of all the money spent to achieve the organization's office-based mission, 93% goes for people, 2% goes to maintain and operate the building and workspace and only 5% is the first cost of building it, fully furnishing it and fully equipping each workstation electronically" (Brill, 1989).

On the other hand, enclosure, layout, and furniture resulted in productivity improvements of 2% to 5%. This means that the cost of providing new furniture or technology could be paid back in one year because of increased productivity. The corollary of this finding is that poor office design can reduce the productivity of what might normally be highly productive workers.

6.2   PLANNING STRATEGY

The purpose of an office is to (Brill, 1991):

- Support and enhance the capability of workers and workgroups to perform a variety of tasks
- Help organizations respond to challenges and seize opportunities

Table 6.1. How Design Facets Affect Bottom Line Measures

Design Facet	Environmental Satisfaction	Ease of Communication	Job Satisfaction	Job Performance
Enclosure	■	■		■
Layout	■	■		■
Furniture	■	■	■	
Noise	■	■	■	
Flexibility	■	■	■	
Participation	■		■	
Comfort	■		■	
Communication		[is the same]		
Lighting	■		■	Probably
Temperature/ Air Quality	■		■	
Floor Area		■	■	
Privacy	■	■		
Status	■	■		
Pathfinding	■	■		
Display	■			
Appearance	■			
Windows	Possibly		Possibly	

Where

■ = Positive effect

Source: Reprinted with the permission of Teknion Furniture Systems, Toronto, ON.

- Give structure, clarity, and meaning to the elements of the organization
- Provide an image that articulates and supports the organization's culture

Considering the design of many existing office buildings, it appears doubtful that some organizations are achieving the above goals. In many cases, offices are inflexible and could not be changed quickly. Designs do not provide structure and clarity of purpose. Rather they underscore organizational values of status and power.

Status through space standards is very expensive to maintain and is wasteful of an organization's time and effort (Becker and Steele, 1995). Very few companies today could justify, to their shareholders, new building construction with greater than 300 square feet gross space per employee.

Today, drivers of space design and planning are closely aligned with organizational goals such as:

- Increasing profits by:
  —Reducing space
  —Reducing staff
  —Reducing operating costs
- Flattening organizations so that every worker has the authority to make decisions at some level.

In other words, the office becomes a tool that is a fundamental element of the business (Becker and Steele, 1995; Brill, 1989).

Office space should be planned and designed according to the corporate culture, the corporate vision of the organization's objectives, and how its leaders define the organization.

The design of Steelcase Corporation's Corporate Development Center (CDC) was driven by how its senior managers defined their objectives. In their case study on the design of the CDC, Becker and Steele (1995) presented the objectives that were developed by Steelcase. Some of them are listed below.

- *Decision hierarchies*: Every one should have some decision authority, but different decisions should be made at different levels of the organization.
- *Multiple work areas*: Various work areas should provide variety of character and purpose, and encourage employees to walk around.
- *Mixed neighborhoods*: When people from different disciplines share the same area, employees learn more about the company.
- *Directors clusters*: By locating senior managers in the center of the building, they are made much more accessible.
- *Activity generators*: Town squares, cafeterias, and break areas are designed to promote communication.
- *Comers commons*: Highly flexible multipurpose activity spaces promote team effort and spontaneity.
- *Escalators/stairs*: These increase opportunity for visual contact.
- *Reverse adjacencies*: Areas that would normally be functionally located adjacent to each other are located far away, to encourage interaction.

The point of the above list of objectives is the importance of knowing what type of space or spaces the company wants to achieve in the relocation. Clearly, this phase of space planning needs to be integrated with the overall strategic relocation plan that was developed in Chapter 2.

6.3   WORK SYSTEM PLANNING

6.3.1   Traditional Office Designs

Our experience with designing office workplaces has fostered a set of traditional design principles that ensures:

- Every office worker is assigned a place at work in the office building.
- Workers in the same group work close together.
- Groups that have close interaction are located as close together as the floor plate will permit.
- Workers are located as close as possible to the equipment that they use.

In practice, the process is much more complex than is portrayed above. A more complete description is provided in a future section. Still, the above principles illustrate the point that *traditional office designs are the outgrowth of traditional systems of work*—systems that value:

- Coffee breaks
- Lunch hours at the cafeteria
- The cafeteria
- Low absenteeism
- A chain of command
- The workspace
- The filing room
- Mail delivery and so on.

In the late 1960's and 1970's the traditional workplace began to change under the influence of new management theories and the concept of the "workstation." At the same time new concepts of workspace planning emerged *within* the traditional design.

6.3.1.1   *Neighborhood Concept*
In the neighborhood concept, individual "homes" (private offices or workstations in open plan) belonging to individual workers from one functional workgroup are mixed in with those from other functional workgroups. Most neighborhoods have identifiable boundaries and a center.

Neighborhoods are usually formed when workgroup integrity is not as important as cross-group communication or when people serve in more than one workgroup. The upper limit of a neighborhood is about 60 employees (Brill, 1989).

6.3.1.2   *Team Concept*
The team concept was made popular in the 1980's. The concept is embodied by physically enclosing a group of workers who have a common work objective. The

work objective could range from the design of a new software system to the dashboard of a new car.

The team concept has team member offices (or workstations) in close proximity to shared facilities and includes centralized team areas that are designed to bring the team together.

An example of a team area plan is shown in Figure 6.1. The plan illustrates a number of individual workstations surrounding a central meeting area. The team area could be physically separated from other areas by corridors, high furniture panels, or hard walls. Team areas provide a sense of community among team members and a sense of isolation from other parts of the organization.

6.3.1.3 Flexible Workspace Concept

Flexibility means being able to reconfigure the office space quickly and easily (Reinback, 1994). It is best used in a high churn environment. Flexibility requires:

- Lighting and HVAC designed for small work zones
- Electrical, telecommunications, and computer outlets installed at frequent intervals within the space or easily reached
- Furniture and walls that can be moved easily
- Small number of office configurations (usually two)

Figure 6.1. An example of a team area plan. Photograph courtesy of Steelcase Inc., Grand Rapids, MI.

6.3.2 Alternative Workplace Strategies (AWS)

Companies in the 1990's face several challenges to traditional office building concepts:

- Environmental regulations are making it necessary to reduce commuting to offices.
- Occupancy costs substantially affect profit.
- Changes in labor force demographics can make it difficult to attract the best workers to company offices.

The development of sophisticated telecommunication systems (embodied by cellular phones, faxes, communication networks, and digital switching systems) and the advent of powerful portable computer systems has changed both the way we work and the way we physically support the new worker.

As a consequence, the concept of office has changed. We are no longer tied to one space. Work is now performed wherever the worker happens to be—in the office or a car, on a boat or a plane, at your home or cottage. Even total freedom, however, needs boundaries to maintain order and promote productivity. Thus the new freedom is embodied in what are becoming known as alternative workplace strategies (AWS).

AWS may be thought of as techniques for increasing the number of alternative work locations that can be used by a worker. Locations may include the main office, a satellite office, the client's premises, or the worker's home. The model in Figure 6.2 illustrates the link between company challenges, technology, the flexible workstation, and AWS.

According to Wiener (1994), AWS offer an alternative to the traditional office, which used to be seen as the solution to every workplace situation.

Most AWS share the following principles:

- Reduction in amount of office space per employee in the corporate building (assuming that only a fraction of employees will be in the office at any one time)
- Reduction in the size of the office
- Standardized designs

AWS embody a number of different design concepts, including:

- Nonterritorial offices
- Hoteling (also known as addressable offices)
- Just-in-time
- Telecommuting (also called homework or telework)
- Satellite offices
- Virtual offices

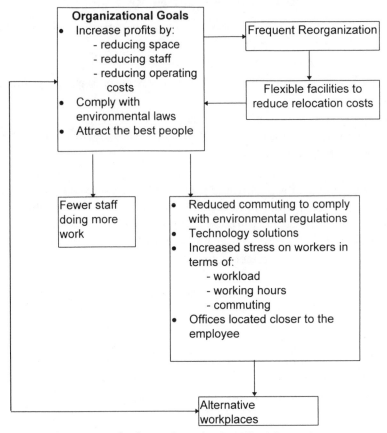

Figure 6.2. The drivers for technology, flexibility, and AWS.

The above concepts can be implemented in two ways:

- Reuse of existing office space to support AWS
- Designing and using facilities outside of the company office

The following subsections describe each of the major concepts, outline their advantages and limitations, and provide recommendations for their use.

AWS provide the relocation team with unique opportunities to save the company space and the cost of relocation and reconstruction. They also provide the team with the opportunity to reduce the stress of office work on the employee.

6.3.2.1   *Reuse of Existing Office Space to Support AWS*

Nonterritorial offices
- Employees call ahead to reserve workstations or private offices.
- This strategy is usually used in organizations where the workforce spends

most of its time on the road or telecommuting between the office and home or a satellite office.

- It allows workers to occupy offices on a first-come, first-served basis and routes telecommunications and computer services to their offices.

Hoteling. A close cousin of the nonterritorial office, hoteling allows the worker to reserve a room for occasions when he or she is between assignments. It is used in consulting organizations where the employee generally works at the client facilities.

Hoteling works as follows:

- The employee calls ahead to book an office for a certain period of time.
- The employee is assigned an office or workstation depending on his or her level or function.
- Each office is outfitted with power and voice and data services.
- Calls are routed to the office by an automated digital switching system.
- A locker is assigned for personal items or storage.
- Each employee is permanently assigned portable pedestals and/or file cabinets, which can be rolled to the assigned office.

Several authors (e.g., Cook, 1993 and Eaton, 1994) use the pioneering work conducted at Arthur Anderson and Company consultants as a hoteling case study. After implementing the hoteling concept, the company was able to reduce its office space to 13 offices for 70 employees.

Using the above example, if each employee normally occupies a *gross* space of 250 square feet, with a fit-up cost of $30.00 and furniture costing $5k per workstation, a conservative estimate of savings for the first year alone would be:

Space savings 57 employees × 250 square feet × $30/square feet	$428K
Furniture savings	$283K
Operating costs	For benchmarking see Steelcase, 1991

For hoteling to work at its best, the facilities should be available to meet the demand for space and the office worker's requirements as much as possible (Harmon-Vaughan, 1995). The facilities manager should maintain:

- A profile of workers that lists individual needs
- Demand projections for hoteling facilities, so enough offices will be available when they are needed

In order to meet the above requirements, the hoteling model requires flexible offices.

Just-In-Time (JIT). The concept is much the same as hoteling and nonterritorial offices—build offices for only 20% of the employees. The difference with the JIT concept is that employees do not reserve space. Employees "drop-in" and occupy workstations on a first-come, first-served basis.

6.3.2.2   *The Office Outside of the Company Office*
The three major AWS strategies employed outside of the company office are:

- Telecommuting
- Satellite offices
- Virtual office

Telecommuting.   This is also termed "homework", and it permits the employee to work at home in his or her own office. The office is totally equipped for communication with clients and company personnel. It is provided with:

- Fax
- Copier
- Additional telephone lines
- Computer/modem/printer

Telecommuting is a major AWS that is growing at an increasing rate worldwide (Becker and Steele, 1995). Telecommuting is most popular among very large (greater than 1000 employees) and very small (less than 10 employees) companies.

Since 1991, the number of home offices in the United States has been increasing 29% annually. In 1993, 7.9 million workers were working from their homes. The person who telecommutes is equally likely to be male or female, married, and a white collar professional between the ages of 35 and 45 (Romei, 1992).

People elect telecommuting for a number of reasons including:

- More time to spend at home with families
- Less stress both getting to the office and working in it
- More flexibility in work schedules

Telecommuting is a natural fit with those whose work is normally on the road. Surprisingly, most people do not choose telecommuting to reduce childcare costs. Surveys show that most telecommuters use daycare.

Telecommuting is not for every worker in every company. Many workers are distracted by nonwork home chores. Some find the home socially isolating, and many just don't have the room for a home office. Thus while telecommuting may appear inviting, the relocation team needs to embrace the concept carefully.

Companies must also resolve issues that arise when their workers no longer work in the office (Harmon-Vaughan, 1995):

- Technology and furniture provided to the home is as expensive as that in the office.
- Security in the home is not as good as that in the office.
- Health standards for workers may apply in the home even though the company can't monitor or control them.
- Corporate liability, workers' compensation, and insurance are also factors for consideration.

Satellite Offices. Satellite offices are located outside of the company office in buildings that are located more conveniently to the worker's home. They can be single company sites or multioccupancy sites shared by several companies. They are equipped with the same technology as the home or office, but they might share a fax or copier.

The advantages of satellite offices over an office in a company building are:

- Reduction in the commuting distance and time
- Greater opportunity for privacy and concentration
- Alternative to telecommuting.

Satellite workers report that they have more flexibility in their schedules, permitting more time for family and social functions.

However, not all news is positive from satellite workers. The results from a survey conducted among satellite workers (Becker, 1993) indicated that:

- Technical support was not provided in a timely manner.
- Users were concerned about career opportunities (out of sight, out of mind).
- Managers found it difficult to schedule meetings and keep in contact with workers.

Virtual Offices. The virtual office is the concept that work can be performed anywhere, antyime. The virtual office is not tied to a home or a satellite building; its location is anywhere equipment is available to perform the work and communicate with colleagues. Today, with the availability of cellular communications, portable FAX machines, and portable computers, the virtual office can be located almost anywhere individuals are most productive—the home, the cottage, on a boat, or in the car (Aranoff and Kaplan, 1993).

6.3.2.3 Evaluating AWS for Your Relocation

On balance, AWS appear to be growing in popularity among workers and companies alike. Even so, case studies have indicated that there are situations where AWS has not worked well if at all.

So how does your relocation team determine whether the AWS is right for your move? Weiner (1994) provides a number of tips that are integrated into the following checklist.

Your team must ask of the company:

- What can be gained and lost by adopting AWS?
- Is the company willing to accept the major changes to their principles that will be required?
- How will the company know if AWS are working?

The team must ask similar questions of the workers:

- What do they gain and lose?
- Can they withstand the social isolation and the potential effects on their careers?
- Can their homes support telecommuting?

Weiner suggests piloting an AWS following a six-step plan:

1. Develop an action plan.
2. Determine candidates for the pilot study.
3. Evaluate the AWS options.
4. Implement the pilot plan.
5. Evaluate the results.
6. Decide on the next steps.

6.4   SPACE PLANNING CONCEPTS

Regardless of the workspace strategy that is selected to support the relocation—traditional or alternative—the company office space must still be planned. This section briefly addresses the techniques used to plan and the two major types of office design—open and closed plan. It also provides planning tips for the design team to consider, based on the experience of the author and others in the field. For more information, the reader should refer to Farren (1988) and Rayfield (1994).

6.4.1   Space Planning

The definitions of space planning are as numerous as space planners. Most professionals approach space planning as a process that begins with the collection of data on employees, adjacency requirements, and company standards and policies. Ideally the process ends with the optimal office layout for employee comfort and productivity.

It's a straightforward process that is only made complex by the desires of managers and employees to obtain the best offices for their group and themselves. Consequently, the process must be intentionally scheduled to accommodate design reviews at all levels of the organization. The space planning process consists of nine basic activities that are diagrammed in Figure 6.3 and explained below.

1. Identify the corporate principles that will affect the plan. For example, middle managers and above are to be located in closed offices. The team may have a substantial influence on these principles.

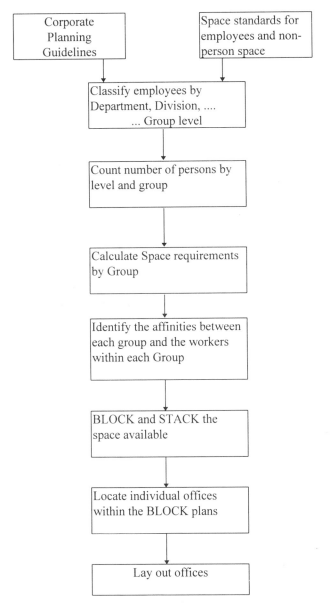

Figure 6.3. The space planning sequence.

2. Identify the space and design standards for each level of employee. These should be applied consistently across the organization to be fair to the employees who are not relocating.
3. Identify the nonperson space requirements for each group and those that are common across groups.
4. Classify the employees who are moving by level, department, division, group, and workteam. At some level these classifications will affect who moves where.
5. Determine the number of employees in each group.
6. Calculate the space requirements for each group.
7. Identify the affinities between groups and individuals within groups. In traditional plans, this information will determine who sits near whom.
8. Block out the areas required by each group on the floor plan.
9. Stack groups on adjacent floors of a multifloor building according to their adjacencies. If two groups have strong adjacencies, one may be located near the top of the stairs running between floors, the other at the bottom.
10. Locate individual offices within the block plan according to space standards, intergroup adjacencies, and circulation patterns.
11. Lay out the location of equipment in individual offices according to the occupants. This topic is explained in greater detail in Chapter 7.

6.4.2   Closed- and Open-Plan Offices

The design of the overall office is dependent on the concept of the individual office. Over the last 30 years, two office concepts—open and closed plan—have dominated space planning.

The open-plan office is configured with varying height partitions that are usually freestanding. The closed-plan office consists of floor-to-ceiling partitions that may be moveable or fixed.

A third type of office concept has no partitions between desks. This has been referred to as a "bullpen" configuration. It is mentioned in passing because it is still used in office buildings worldwide, however, it is not recommended.

Steelcase, in their 1991 office survey, published data on the prevalence of the three office concepts in three countries and the EEC. The data, which are graphed in Figure 6.4, illustrate large differences in the use of office concepts worldwide.

In Japan, for example, the open or "bullpen" configuration still dominated the office plan in 1991, while in the United States and Canada, partitioned (open-plan) and private (closed-plan) offices were more common. In Europe, open-plan offices were not as common as in North America. The majority of European offices were closed plan.

In the same survey, facilities managers predicted that over the next five years (by 1996) the most growth will be in open-plan offices. The data are illustrated in Figure 6.5.

Disregarding the bullpen concept, Table 6.2 lists the advantages of both open- and closed-plan offices.

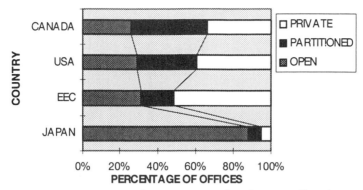

Figure 6.4. Percentage of open, partitioned, and private offices by country. Adapted from the Steelcase Worldwide Office Environment Index, 1991 Summer Series.

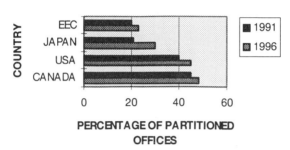

PERCENTAGE OF PARTITIONED OFFICES

Figure 6.5. Percentage of office workers occupying partitioned offices, by country: 1991 actual versus estimates from facilities managers. Adapted from the Steelcase Worldwide Office Environment Index, 1991 Summer Series.

Table 6.2. Advantages of Open- and Closed-Plan Offices

Open-plan	Closed-plan
• allows greater flexibility with furniture and personnel arrangements • allows for expansion and contraction of employees • provides more visual and physical interaction • provides exterior exposure • lowers equipment costs over life-cycle • conserves energy. Heat, ventilation and air-conditioning problems are reduced since there are no walls to obstruct airflow • facilitates wiring, and the cabling task is much easier through furniture units and panels • can be arranged to suit team requirements	• increases acoustic and visual privacy necessary for certain categories of work (the amount of visual and auditory privacy achieved depends on how it is designed and used) • increases security • makes it easier to individualize lighting • provides more environmental control • makes it easier to incorporate conventional furnishings • initial construction and furniture costs are typically lower than those using systems components • makes job status allocations straightforward

When open- and closed-plan offices are deliberately mixed together, they form an "integrated common plan." In this design, open offices surround closed offices, to increase privacy and acoustical isolation. In its purest form, the common plan uses closed offices for meetings, for administrative or personnel matters, or for noise-generating equipment or storage. Because open-plan spaces are separated from each other, they are isolated from noise generated by other open-plan spaces. Additional advantages of the common plan are that it:

- Meets multiple task and equipment requirements
- Uses both systems and traditional furniture
- Provides flexibility, expandability, and growth
- Provides security, privacy, and required separation

Experience has shown that the success of any office layout is dependent on how well the open-plan portion is designed. The following are some design recommendations for open-plan offices:

- Define functional groups located on an open-plan floor clearly by:
  —Signing (high-mounted)
  —Furnishings
  —Color
  —Lighting
- Do not use the open plan for jobs that require a quiet environment.
- Understand the nature of jobs before planning the space.
- Isolate workspaces from:
  —Sources of intermittent sounds
  —Areas of frequent conversations
  —Unnecessary traffic
- Ensure that the sound attenuation characteristics of free-standing partitions are appropriate to the task and environment.
- Put common destinations, such as restrooms, elevators, photocopying machines, and so on, close together, and make them accessible by direct routes.
- Position people who have many visitors close to the work area entrance.
- Place people close to those with whom they communicate frequently.
- Keep equipment close to the people who use it most often.
- Keep files and other reference material close to people who use them.
- Ensure that furniture satisfies the employees' need for personalization by:
  —Allowing some control over layout
  —Providing display space

Surveys show that most people do not like sitting with their backs to the entrance of their office, so many open-plan designs have freestanding desks that face outward, with panels to "protect" back and sides. Moreover, facing outward permits operators to look away from their tasks for visual relief.

Most office workers like to reduce eye contact, since eye contact invites conversation. Unless visual contact is a task requirement, the office should be designed to minimize eye contact by properly orienting furniture, or by using plants or panels.

6.4.3 Additional Planning Tips

As mentioned earlier, there are a number of texts that can provide detailed information on space planning. The purpose of this chapter is to consider the worker and relocation team issues in the topic. With this in mind, the following are tips that have been picked up from experience and from the literature that the relocation team may find helpful:

- Leave 5% of the space assigned to a "unit" empty to allow for expansion. Over the course of the relocation, the number of people assigned to groups will change, and this is one way of preparing for changes.
- Don't reduce the floor area assigned to an individual's office by any more than 25% in any one move.
- Provide common space for amenities for office workers, for example, large surfaces to wrap parcels.
- Corridors should be at least wide enough to permit two to three people abreast: 150–223 cm (60–84 inches).
- Brill (1989) recommends clear and hierarchical circulation patterns:
  —Boulevards—between departments
  —Main streets—between sections
  —Side streets—between groups
- Build offices to the building grid to simplify installation and maintenance. In one example a building was designed with a grid of 1500 mm (about 59 inches). The offices were designed to a 5 foot (60 inch) grid. Early in the construction the mismatches began to appear (e.g., walls creeping over light fixtures).
- Glass panels (sidelights) in offices transmit natural light to inside offices.
- The visual privacy of glass-walled offices, and conference rooms can be improved by etching figures into the glass at heights of between 160 and 180 cm (63 and 70 inches) above the floor.
- Visual privacy can be increased in open-plan offices by placing a half-width panel in the office entrance at an angle of 90 degrees to the corridor.
- Limit the number of office sizes to no more than three (preferably two).
- Pay close attention to the design of cabling systems used in your open-plan office. Most systems don't support flexible offices and high churn rates. Consider raised floor designs.

REFERENCES

Aranoff, S. and A. Kaplan (1995). Issues imparting today's offices. FM Journal, May/June, pp. 24–30.

Becker, F. (1993). Satellite offices. Premises and Facilities Management, April, p. 11.

Becker, F. and F. Steele (1995). Workplace by design: Mapping the high-performance workscape. San Francisco: Jossey-Bass.

Brill, M. (1989). Private offices or open offices: The politics and pragmatics of picking the right one. BOSTI, Publication No. 0189A.

Brill, M. (1991). The office as a tool. Teknion Report.

Cook, R. (1993). The virtual office space of the 1990s. FM Journal, May/June, p. 34.

Eaton, M. (1994). "Hoteling" maximizes space, enhances interaction. Building Design and Construction, May, p. 45.

Farren, C. E. (1988). Planning and managing interior projects. Kingston, MA: R. S. Means.

Harmon-Vaughan, B. (1995). New ways to work: Hoteling and homework. Haworth Office Journal, No. 12.

Rayfield, J. K. (1994). The office interior design guide: An introduction for facilities managers and designers. New York: Wiley.

Reinbach, A. (1994). At home in the virtual office. Buildings, March, p. 46.

Romei, L. K. (1992). Telecommuting: A workstyle revolution. Modern Office Technology, May.

Steelcase (1991). Worldwide office environment index summary report. Steelcase, Inc. Grand Rapids, MI.

Sullivan, C. C. (1994). The day after downsizing. Buildings, March, p. 32.

Weiner, B. M. (1994). Developing alternative workplace strategies as a competitive edge. FM Journal, September/October, p. 37.

ADDITIONAL READINGS

Becker, F. (1987). Managing an office relocation. Report prepared for the International Facility Management Association, November.

Becker, F. (1990), The total workplace: Facilities management and the elastic organization. New York: Van Nostrand Reinhold.

Harmon-Vaughan, B. and R. Fritz, (1994). The office of tomorrow. Proceedings, 15th Annual International Facility Management Conference and Exposition, November, p. 381.

Chapter Seven

Planning: Workspace Design

7.1 INTRODUCTION

During the course of the relocation, your project team will likely be faced with decisions on furniture, seating, and accessories when designing the individual workspaces of employees.

Discussion will inevitably include questions such as:

- Do we move with existing furniture or make a change?
- If we change furniture, do we buy new or use what we have?
- If we buy new, how do we decide which furniture and seating to purchase?

This chapter is about the design and layout of the physical workspace. It includes discussions about furniture, seating, and accessories that will affect the safety, health, and productivity of the employees. More specifically, this chapter is dedicated to four major objectives in workspace design:

1. Prevent acute injuries and illnesses, as well as those caused by repeated trauma that accumulates to eventually result in serious injury. This latter type of injury is referred to a cumulative trauma disorder (CTD).
2. Increase productivity of office workers by solving those problems that interfere with or slow down work.
3. Match the design of the workstation and layout of the office to work function.
4. Increase the comfort of each employee and his or her ability to access the tools needed to do the job.

This chapter does not cover those issues in the office that are beyond the scope of this book, such as computer systems and associated equipment (e.g., VDT, keyboard, mouse). These topics are well covered in other texts such as Joyce and Wallersteiner (1989). In addition, this chapter does not cover the design of software systems and their associated human–computer interfaces. For these topics, the reader is referred to texts by Booth (1991) and Galitz (1993).

The first objective above introduces the concept of cumulative trauma disorder. CTDs are a relatively recent consequence of the automated office that were not universally recognized until the late 1980's. Now, the potential for CTD injury has overshadowed other human factors topics that, at one time, influenced workstation design. This chapter, understandably, is influenced by worker health and safety.

In keeping with the theme of this book, this chapter concentrates on the development of tools that will help your relocation team address the workspace design problems that affect the relocation. These include:

- Avoiding injury and illness of office workers
- Determining user requirements through the use of checklists, analyses, and surveys
- Designing for the new generation of office equipment such as fax, laser printers, scanners, laptop computers, LANs, and modems
- Ensuring that design drives the availability and location of services, not the opposite
- Selecting the most appropriate furniture and seating for your requirements
- Fostering teams and teamwork
- Supporting alternative office strategies such as hoteling, satellite offices, and homework

7.2 WORKSTATION DESIGN

The design of the office workstation is influenced by four forces:

1. Science, in the form of design specifications
2. The goals of the company
3. The requirements of each individual job
4. The needs of each office worker.

The relocation team would do well to keep all four in mind when they reconfigure the new space.

A number of studies have demonstrated that properly designed furniture can increase productivity to the point where the cost of the furniture, seating, and office equipment can be paid back in about a year.

From the users' viewpoint, the furniture must provide comfort and functionality. Office workers want their workstations to meet the requirements of their jobs. They want enough storage and worksurface area to meet their needs, and they want the material they use to be convenient. Studies have shown that 1980's furniture, with few exceptions, was not designed to support the automated office. As a result, workers suffered discomfort, which affected both their well-being and their productivity. Attwood (1989) surveyed three groups of office workers to determine the effects of their jobs on their physical comfort. Using a discomfort rating survey, three groups of office workers—typists, traditional draftspersons, and computer-assisted design (CAD) operators—were asked to report their physical discomfort. The survey was completed for five consecutive workdays. Each day workers reported body discomfort in the morning before they began work and again in the evening before they left work. The results of the survey are shown in Figure 7.1.

The data showed a significant increase in reported discomfort between morning and evening. While the type and location of body discomfort varied from job to job, the discomfort report by VDT operators—typists and CAD operators—was similar, consisting of mid to upper body soreness and arm and wrist pain. The discomfort suffered by the traditional draftsperson was concentrated in the lower back. Further analysis demonstrated that each type of discomfort could be

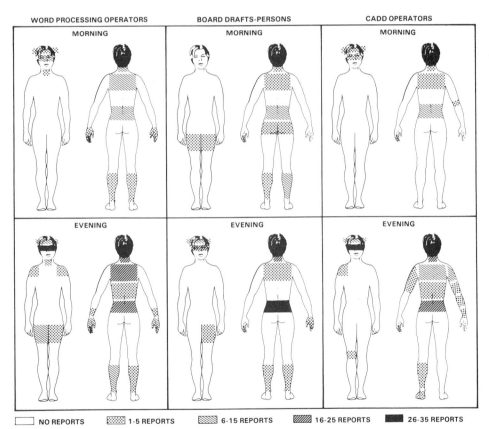

Figure 7.1. Summary of discomforts reported by each occupational group in the morning and evening. Reproduced with permission from Attwood (1989). Courtesy International Journal of Industrial Ergonomics.

traced to the design, or lack thereof, of the workstation. As this chapter unfolds, the origins of the data in Figure 7.1 become more evident.

The standards that are introduced in this chapter are focused on minimizing discomfort. The design goal is to achieve a neutral posture for office workers where the muscles that work to maintain body posture are as relaxed as possible. As an example, consider the posture of the head and neck as it affects the forward line of site. The muscles of the neck hold the head erect. When the head posture is properly balanced, the muscles are minimally stressed. As it turns out, the neutral head posture results in a normal line of site that is just below horizontal. This is shown in Figure 5.3. As a result, the objects that the operator looks at most often, the VDT for example, are best located within the visual field that is subtended by the angle between the horizontal and about 45 degrees downward from horizontal.

In practice, some operators prefer to work outside of this optimal visual angle. You will learn later in this chapter that user preference for the location of equipment and the adjustment of the workspace is frequently at odds with "what is good for them" scientifically.

7.2.1   Workstation Types

Figure 7.2*a* through *g* demonstrate some of the typical workstation configurations that are in use in offices today. Each has been developed to support a particular aspect of the user's job.

(a)

Figure 7.2. Range of typical office workstation designs. Reproduced with permission of SMED International, Calgary, AL.

(b)

(c)

Figure 7.2. *(Continued)* 115

(d)

(e)

Figure 7.2. (Continued)

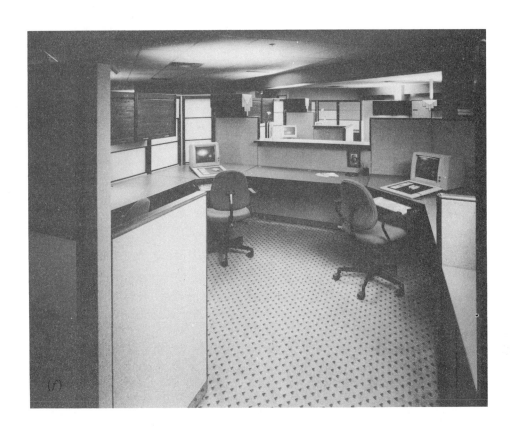

Figure 7.2. (Continued)

Workstations like those shown in Figure 7.2 can be divided into two major types, the second of which can be further divided into two classifications:

1. *Conventional furniture:* Comprised of individual components such as desks, credenzas, storage units, file cabinets, and tables.
2. *Systems furniture:* Also known as modular furniture, and comprised of interdependent components that can be assembled in many different configurations. There are two basic classifications of systems furniture:
   • Freestanding
   • Panel hung

7.2.2   Advantages and Disadvantages of Different Workstation Types

Each workstation classification has advantages and disadvantages that make it more useful in one application than in another. These are listed in Table 7.1.

The major advantage of systems furniture is its modularity and flexibility. However, many types of systems furniture cannot take the wear and tear of disassembly and reassembly in high churn conditions. On the other hand, conventional furniture is very robust if it can be moved as an integral unit. It also has the traditional good looks that appeal to middle and senior managers. However, as automation creeps steadily into all levels of the organization, good looks will inevitably be traded for function.

The efficiency of systems furniture is shown by its ability to provide the same functionality as conventional furniture but in less floor area.

Figures 7.3*a* and *b* illustrate two office configurations. One is composed of conventional furniture, the other of systems components.

Figure 7.3*a* illustrates a typical office setup for a senior manager that supports three different activities:

1. Desk work and VDT use
2. Small meetings at the desk location
3. Larger meetings around a table

This configuration typically requires 250–300 square feet (23.2–27.9 square meters). Figure 7.3*b* shows a much smaller office (220–225 square feet; 20.4–20.9 square meters) in which each of the activities above can be supported. The secret is the systems furniture configured with a "p-top" worksurface. All three functions can take place at the workstation. Similar space savings can be accomplished in smaller offices with the appropriate selection of systems components

7.2.3   The VDT Workstand

The freestanding portable VDT workstand is a valuable piece of add-on equipment. It is designed to support the computer and components, and, at the same time, provide some worksurface area and, with larger workstands, provide stor-

Table 7.1. Advantages and Disadvantages of Conventional and Systems Furniture

	Conventional Furniture	Systems Furniture	
		Free standing	Panel hung
Advantages	• Traditional formal good looks • Robust - can withstand multiple moves • Easy to move components for cleaning or to access services	• Traditional formal good looks • Modularity. Supports different configurations • Supports office automation • Provides same functionality in less space than conventional furniture	• Adjustable in height (usually 2.5 cm /1 in. increments) • Modularity. Supports different configurations • Best supports office automation • Provides the·same functionality as conventional furniture, but in less space
Dis-advantages	• Fixed height worksurfaces (minimal adjustment on the base) • Limited customization once built • Does not support office automation as well as systems furniture	• Fixed height worksufaces (minimal adjustment on the base) • Does not withstand the stress of office moves as well as conventional and panel hung • Difficult to move without disassembly	• When installed in private offices, panels encroach on floor space and can block access to services • Time and effort is required to dis- and re-assemble workstations • Not considered 'high-end' workstations • Does not withstand churn as well as conventional • Difficult to move without dis-assembly

age for books or binders. Figure 7.4*a* and *b* show two alternative designs for workstands, designs that can be compared for usability.

The workstand in Figure 7.4*a* is well designed to support the VDT task. It contains a pullout keyboard keeper beside a pullout worksurface that can support the mouse or open binders. All the storage is beneath the worksurface, as is the central processing unit (cpu) of the computer. For the user to access equipment or material stored under the worksurface, he or she must first store the pullouts to provide access to the bottom shelf.

The workstand shown in Figure 7.4*b* has no storage or obstructions under the worksurface. Instead it has been equipped with a free standing "hutch" that

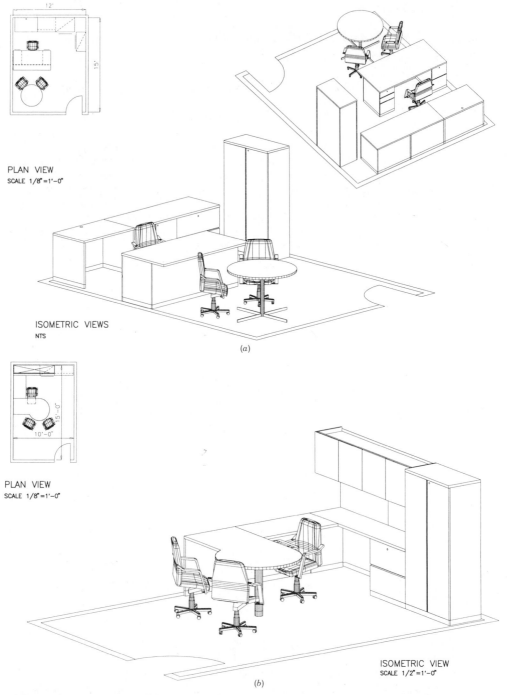

PLAN VIEW
SCALE 1/8"=1'-0"

ISOMETRIC VIEWS
NTS

(a)

PLAN VIEW
SCALE 1/8"=1'-0"

ISOMETRIC VIEW
SCALE 1/2"=1'-0"

(b)

Figure 7.3. Comparison of the space required for conventional and systems workstations that meet the same requirements. Published with permission of SMED International, Calgary, AL.

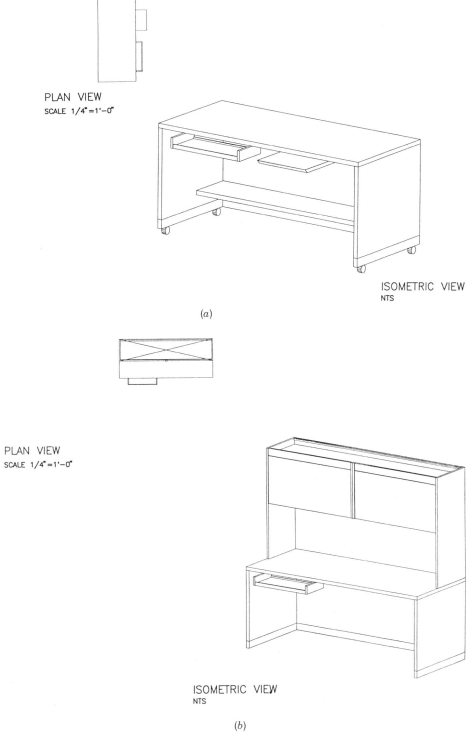

PLAN VIEW
SCALE 1/4″=1′-0″

ISOMETRIC VIEW
NTS

(a)

PLAN VIEW
SCALE 1/4″=1′-0″

ISOMETRIC VIEW
NTS

(b)

Figure 7.4. Alternative workstand concepts. Published with permission of SMED International, Calgary, AL.

stores binders, the cpu, or an optional printer above the worksurface within reach of the user. In today's office with the need to access a variety of equipment and material from the seated position, more use will be made of the vertical space available.

7.2.4   The Importance of Adjustability

The change in office workstyles in the 1990's and an appreciation of comfort and safety have put more focus on the need for worksurface adjustability.

Worker comfort and safety can be improved if the worksurface can be raised or lowered to accommodate the user. Panel hung worksurfaces can typically be adjusted in 1 inch increments through a wide range of heights. These adjustments must be made by removing the worksurace and reinstalling it at the new height. The operation is performed by staff who are trained in furniture assembly. The philosophy behind panel hung worksurfaces is that the height will stay the same as long as the same office worker is using the workstation.

With today's alternative work patterns, such as hoteling and satellite offices, many different workers may share the same workstation at different times, so the worksurface height should be quickly adjustable *by the user*. Table 7.2 recommends when to provide continuously adjustable furniture, versus furniture that requires tear-down and reassembly.

With the revolution in AWS, the next few years should see a high percentage of workstations being shared, thus raising the requirement for more continuously adjustable furniture.

Sit/stand workstations are becoming more popular as employees and facilities support staffs learn more about the positive effects on discomfort and fatigue of alternately sitting and standing to work. The concept of standing to work has been popular in some circles for many years. We're told that Winston Churchill, the British statesman, spent much of his time standing while performing office work.

The benefits of alternately sitting, then standing, while working include:

• Less total pressure on the intervertebral disks
• Improved blood circulation, which reduces feeling of fatigue

Table 7.2. When to Provide Continuously or Intermittently Adjustable Furniture

Continuously Adjustable	Intemittently adjustable
• Workstation is shared	• Job conditions don't change that often.
• Job functions vary from time to time requiring different worksurface heights.	• Only one user for the workstation at a time.
• Users want to sit or stand at their workstations	• No need or desire for the user to stand at the workstation.

- Movement of nutrients into the intervertebral disks
- Alternate use of different muscle groups

Sit/stand workstations can consist of two types:

1. A sit/stand fixed-height elevated worksurface, as shown in Figure 7.5
2. A variable-height worksurface that is adjusted manually or electrically, as shown in Figure 7.6*a* and *b*.

The disadvantage of the fixed-height elevated worksurface is that all other worksurfaces must be similarly elevated to be used effectively. The disadvantage of workstations with continuously adjustable worksurface heights is the difficulty of mounting storage cabinets over the worksurface. The cabinets would have to be raised with the worksurface.

7.2.5   Retrofit Versus New

New systems workstations typically cost in the range of $5k–$10k, depending on the material used to construct them, their size, and the amenities provided. Existing furniture can be upgraded to provide system-like configurations at a fraction of the original cost. Furniture upgrades can consist of the addition of accessories or of physical modification of existing furniture. Consider, for example, that a low budget way of developing a more functional workstation is to remove one pedestal from each of two identical double pedestal desks, then to join them to form an L-shape and fill the square formed in the center. The new workstation has more than twice the worksurface area of the original desks and no obstructions to movement below the worksurface between the two remaining pedestals.

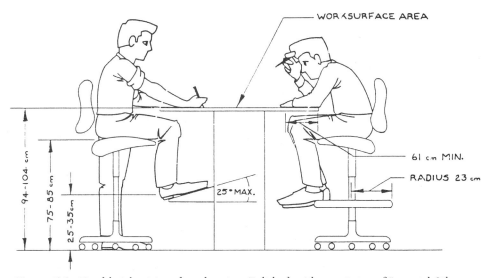

Figure 7.5. Fixed-height sit/stand workstation. Pulished with permission of Imperial Oil Limited, Toronto, ON.

(a)

(b)

Figure 7.6. Variable-height sit/stand workstation. (*a*) Adjusted to sitting height. (*b*) Adjusted to standing height. Photograph courtesy of Steelcase Inc., Grand Rapids, MI.

7.2.6   Functional Design

Office standards typically specify that the employees with higher rank are enti-tled to more office space and better quality furniture. While few might dis-agree that entitlements have their place, the provision of good quality furni-ture to senior staff should not be at the expense of the functional requirements of each office worker. Many workers at lower levels in the organization per-form tasks that require special consideration in the design of their furniture and services.

Consider, for example, three different tasks performed by three different workers who are at the same level in the organization. Each design can be implemented as a variation on a common workstation theme, as shown in the sketches in Figures 7.7 *a* through *c*. Each design begins with a basic "workwall," consisting of an overhead cabinet and a worksurface. Figure 7.7*a* illustrates a U-shaped modular configuration that could be developed for process engineers and geologists. The larger wing of the U consists of a 90 cm (36 inch) wide work-surface necessary to permit large drawings to be laid out. Figure 7.7*b* shows a bullet runoff that could be added to the workwall to create a table surface for meeting with clients. Figure 7.7*c* shows another U-shaped configuration. The secondary worksurface is 60 cm (24 inches) wide and is used for temporary stor-age of documents. The primary worksurface is a "P-top that can be used to meet with up to three other people.

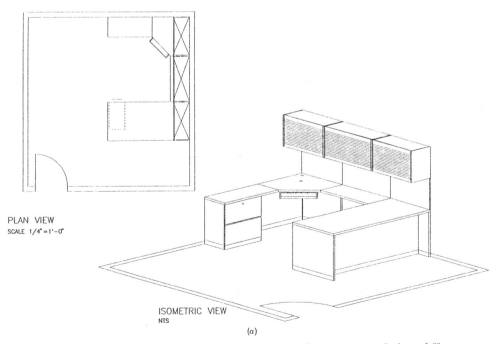

Figure 7.7. (*a*) through (*c*) Three variations of the same workstation to satisfy three different ways of working. Published with permission of SMED International, Calgary, AL.

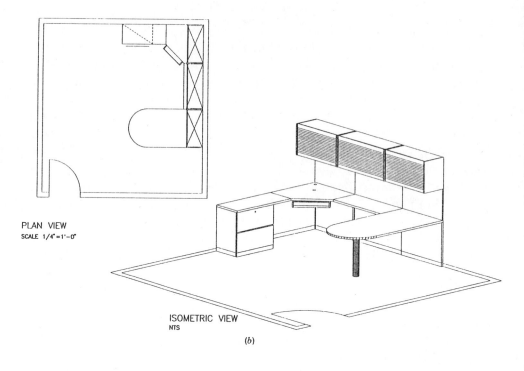

PLAN VIEW
SCALE 1/4"=1'-0"

ISOMETRIC VIEW
NTS

(b)

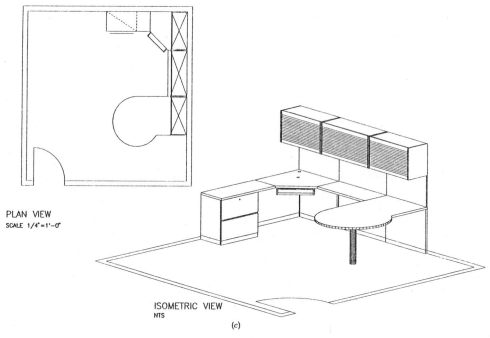

PLAN VIEW
SCALE 1/4"=1'-0"

ISOMETRIC VIEW
NTS

(c)

Figure 7.7. (Continued)

The above example illustrates the use of modular components integrated to a common furniture section—the workwall. The number of design variations needed may be determined after ergonomics professionals have thoroughly analyzed the tasks performed in the organization. A task analysis of each position is essential in order to identify the proper furniture configuration for each worker.

Table 7.3 illustrates the results of a task analysis that was performed by the author in one organization. The row headings outline the types of tasks that may be performed in an electronic office. They range from computer use to filing. The column headings illustrate the degree to which each task is performed. Column A indicates light or occasional use; column C indicates heavy use. The cells identify the job of the office worker who might perform each task at the level indicated. For example, the cell at the top left-hand corner represents a senior manager who uses the computer less then two hours per day, does no filing or faxing, and so on. Row 5 of Table 7.3 represents the other extreme. It describes a task that combines the elements in the row above it. So, the cell in the bottom right-hand corner of the table represents a job that consists of multiple tasks at the highest level of effort.

Table 7.3. Job Types Corresponding to Office Activities

Activity	A. Light Use	B. Moderate Use	C. Heavy Use
1. VDT use	Executive Manager	Professional (e.g. engineer) Technician Secretary	Customer Service Representative Journalist Writer Data Entry Typist CAD Operator Tele-marketer
2. Telephone Use	Manager Executive Professional	Purchaser Secretary	Receptionist Telephone Switchboard Operator Tele-marketer
3. Access to files and binders	Manager Professional	Engineer Architect Sales manager	Sales staff Purchasing agent
4. Worksurface requirements - Meetings - Paperwork	 Manager Manager	 Professional Sales staff	 Supervisor Design architect Engineer Geologist Admin Assistant
5. Combined use of: - Computer - Telephone - Files/storage - Worksurface	Manager	Technical sales person	Sales staff Purchasing agent Customer service representative

Table 7.4 has the same headings as Table 7.3. The difference is that the cells specify the furniture that might be required to satisfy the characteristics of the tasks in Table 7.3. The senior manager would be well served with a double-pedestal desk and a table for meetings. The customer service representative (CSR), on the other hand, requires a workstation to accommodate the systems and filing requirements of the job. In addition, he or she also requires a good layout (perhaps in the shape of a "U") that would permit easy access to the equipment, files, phones, and so on.

The above example illustrates a technique for specifying furniture and equipment requirements. It begins by identifying the tasks performed in each job

Table 7.4. Furniture that Would Support Selected Office Activities

Activity	A. Light Use	B. Moderate Use	C. Heavy Use
1. VDT use	(3-hours per day) Conventional desk and credenza modified with a keyboard keeper, articulating arm to hold the computer and a floor support for the computer, or Modified credenza	(3-5 hours per day) Conventional desk and credenza with a workstand	(> 5-hours per day) Workstation designed to support computer equipment. Adjustable workstation height may be required depending on other requirements
2. Telephone Use	Conventional telephone	Speaker phone upgrade	Headset with plug-in
3. Access to files and binders	Conventional desk with pedestals and credenza. Storage units within 2-3 m (6-9 ft) of seated position	Independent free-standing files in work area. 1-2 m (3-6 feet) from seated position.	Files and binder storage become integral part of workstation (U- or L-shaped) with overhead storage.
4. Worksurface requirements - Meetings	Guest chairs in front of conventional desk, or Meeting table and chairs	Meeting table and chairs	Bullet or P- runoff in an L- or U-shaped workstation
- Paperwork	Conventional desk	Upgrade with a rectangular table behind desk or a credenza modified to work at.	Rectangular, bullet or P-runoff as part of a U-shaped workstation. (Worksurface area is determined by activities)
5. Combined use of: - Computer - Telephone - Files/storage - Worksurface	Conventional desk (1A.) Credenza or free-standing files or storage units within 2-3 m (6-9 ft) of seated position. Phone on desk	Conventional furniture in U-workstation consisting of: - Desk on one side - Computer table in center - Credenza or files at the other side Phone located between files and computer table.	Full U-shaped workstation with rectangular runoffs fitted with 2-HI files or pedestals Phone located between files and the VDT

classification, then analyzes each task to determine the furniture, equipment, and layouts necessary to support that task.

7.2.7   Support for New Office Equipment

For those readers who have facility experience, the issue of location of services should have special meaning. Power, voice, and data outlets have traditionally interfered with the layout of office furniture. In some cases, they are located on walls against which a systems panel has to be positioned. In other cases, they are monuments in the floor that force the furniture to be positioned away from the wall, wasting valuable floor space. Wall mounted services require furniture manufacturers to create access panels in the wall gables to accommodate the services. This preamble leads to a very important principle in office design:

Do not let the location of services drive the design of the office!

With the advent of new office equipment provision of services takes on a new meaning.

Few would argue that the design of office equipment, is changing much more rapidly than that of the furniture designed to support it. For example, the original personal computer (PC) was wider and not as deep as its counterpart today. So, while a 60 cm (24 inch) deep worksurface would support a 286 model cpu, the same surface is too narrow to house more recent machines, which are longer.

One trend that appears to be increasing in the 1990's is the use of portable equipment in the office. The laptop computer is a good example. Sometimes the laptop "docks" with office equipment that is designed to provide power and is equipped with a remote monitor, keyboard, and printer. Other times, however, the laptop is used as a standalone device that connects to:

- Power
- Printer
- Telephone (modem) lines
- System networks (e.g., LANs)

from connections that are terminated at receptacles in the office. In the past, the receptacles were located in the wall behind the furniture. It is important today to make these connections more convenient for the portable user. In other words, they need to be more accessible in the form of power strips or pop-up service models at the desk surface. Figure 7.8*a* and *b* illustrate an example of one style of pop-up receptacle that can be installed into the worksurface.

It's been my experience, however, that with the many different types of connections on the market, some equipment won't easily mate with the service connection. For example, the integral plug and power adapter for one computer, as shown in Figure 7.9, might be difficult to use with some of the receptacles designed for use in the surface power strips.

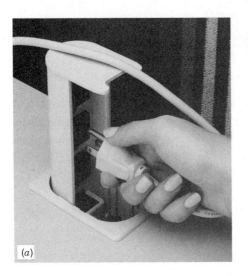

Figure 7.8. (a) and (b) A pop-up receptacle for use by equipment on the worksurface. Reproduced with the permission of Byrne Electrical Specialists, Rockford, MI.

Figure 7.9. Surface receptacles must be designed to accommodate a wide range of equipment.

130

7.2.8　Workstation Specifications

Since 1985, when the first legislative standard for VDT workstations was issued in West Germany, a number of guidelines have been developed for use worldwide.

In North America two standards for voluntary use have been issued, one in the United States (ANSI/HFS, 1988) and the other in Canada (CSA, 1989).

Each of the standards is prescriptive rather performance-based. Prescriptive standards specify design details such as recommended heights of worksurfaces above the floor. Performance based standards merely prescribe what the workstation is to accomplish, for example, design for worker comfort, rather than how to make it happen.

The above standards and several excellent texts are available that provide recommended dimensions for workstations. While the value of specific dimensions in each standard may differ slightly, the dimensions are similar, since they are based on the same anthropometric data. Figure 7.10 summarizes the recommended dimensions from the CSA standards, while Figure 7.11 illustrates the minimum workstation width and depth recommended by the ANSI/HFS standards.

Standards are consensus documents that often require years to produce. Consequently by the time they are issued, they are often out of date. This was the case with both the ANSI and CSA documents. In 1988/89 when these standards were issued, computer pointing devices such as mouses and trackballs were already in wide use. The potential for cumulative injury when using point-

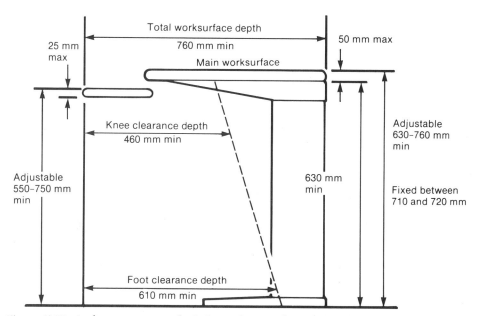

Figure 7.10. Anthropometric standards for workstation design. With the permission of the Canadian Standards Association, and copyrighted by CSA, 178 Rexdale, Blvd., Rexdale, ON, M9W 1R3.

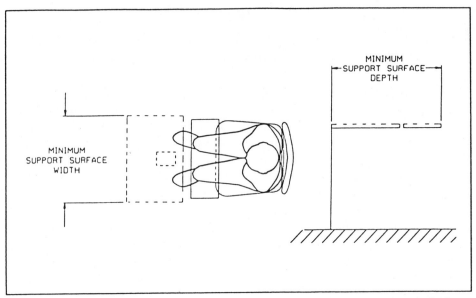

Figure 7.11. Minimum width and depth recommended by the ANSI/HFS VDT Standards.
Reprinted with permission from *American National Standard for Human Factors Engineering of
Visual Display Terminal Workstations* (ANSI/HFS 100-1988), 1988. Copyright 1988 by the
Human Factors and Ergonomics Society. All rights reserved.

ing devices is high, yet neither the ANSI or CSA documents address them. Nor
does either document address the standing workstation in terms of workstation
height, manual versus automatic positioning, the need for memory, the design
and location of controls, or the need for a foot-rail to reduce back discomfort.
De Chiara et al. (1991) provide the following recommendations for standing
worksurface height and for the use of sit/stand workstations:

- Both the worksurface (keyboard surface) and the display monitor must
  move through 31.7 cm (12.5 inches) of travel from 72.4 cm (28.5 inches) to
  104.1 cm (41 inches)—see Figures 7.6*a* and *b*.
- Adjustment controls, designed for hand operation, must be located within
  the operator's extended reach envelope.

Another issue about standards that is often debated is whether they reflect real-
world practice. Standards are often a compromise between what should be done,
from a scientific viewpoint, and what is practically and economically possible.
Dimensional ranges such as the range of worksurface heights of a seated workstation are based on the requirements of the 5th percentile female and the 95th percentile male. To extend these requirements to the 99th percentiles would increase
the adjustment range substantially and would be prohibitively expensive.

Designs based on anthropometric dimensions may not take into account the
way office workers prefer to use their furniture. Grandjean (1988), for example,

conducted a study to determine the settings of VDT workstation dimensions preferred by VDT operators. The data are shown in Table 7.5; also shown for comparison are the recommended dimensions from the CSA standards.

Clearly, users and designers differ in opinion about the adjustment range. In addition to being designed for computer use, workstations must also be designed to accommodate other requirements, such as horizontal reach on the worksurface, vertical reach to overhead storage, and reach to the sides for access to printers and faxes. The limits of forward reach for a small (5th percentile) seated operator are given in Figure 7.12. The reach envelopes for the 5th percentile standing operator are reproduced in Figure 7.13. Figure 7.14 provides guidelines on the range for the side reach for avarage male and female operators.

Figure 7.15 provides recommendations for the primary work areas of seated operators. The areas are defined as:

- Close work area is defined out to a radius of 300 mm.
- Primary work area is defined by the area of the worksurface that is swept by arm motions pivoting at the elbow.
- A large area for occasional reaches is defined by the full extension of the arm and twisting of the upper body.

7.2.9   Analyzing Workstation Requirements

You will recall that a major objective of the workstation is to support the work function, hence the wide variation in workstation designs that are available to accommodate the wide range of tasks that office workers perform. What you need to determine, therefore, is which configuration is right for your office workers. It's tempting to believe furniture manufacturers who claim that a particular configuration will satisfy the requirements of a specific "job," but does it really? Each furniture configuration has been designed to *directionally* satisfy the demands of a particular job, but the only way to know how well the configuration fits the job is to determine what the worker's job is. In other words, analyze the job to determine the range of activities that define it.

 Table 7.5. Preferred Settings for a VDT Workstation Versus Recommended Settings

Dimension	Preferred Settings (Grandjean, 1988)	Recommended Settings (CSA, 1989)
1. Keyboard height	700-850 mm (27.6 - 33.5 inches)	630-790 mm (24.8 - 31. inches)
2. Distance between front edge of table and back wall	600 mm to 800 mm (at foot level) (23.6 - 31.5 inches)	460 mm to 610 mm (at foot level) (18.1 - 24. inches)

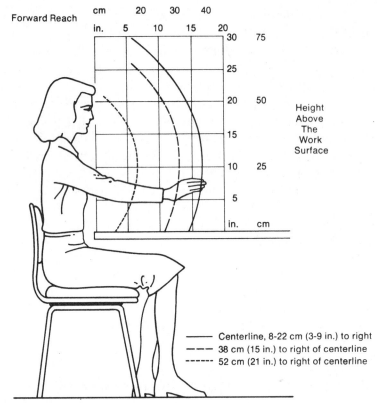

Figure 7.12. Reach envelopes for the seated operator. Reproduced with permission of Institute of Industrial Engineers, 25 Technology Park/Atlanta, Norcross, GA 30092, (707) 449–0461. Copyright © 1995.

Task analysis is a process that breaks a job into its component activities so that each activity can be analyzed for its human factors/ergonomic requirements. The process is at the heart of human factors design. In its most general application, one could say that task analysis is responsible for the design of every workspace configuration that has ever been produced. Even if a "secretarial" workstation has been configured to satisfy the general activities performed by most secretaries, however, your question still should be: "What is the configuration that will satisfy *our* secretaries?"

Task analysis does not have to be a complex exercise that takes months to conduct and results in a different configuration for every worker. In fact, the tasks of your office workers can likely be supported by analyzing only a few design factors, for example, worksurface area requirements, and by then determining the values that suit the way your office workers work. In addition, the number of basic configurations that will suit your operation can likely be limited to about five. However, within each configuration, the modules required will vary by individual needs, for example a two-high lateral file instead of two pedestals. You will also find that the "handedness" of the configuration will be driven by the room orientation, by the preferences of the worker, or by the flow of work

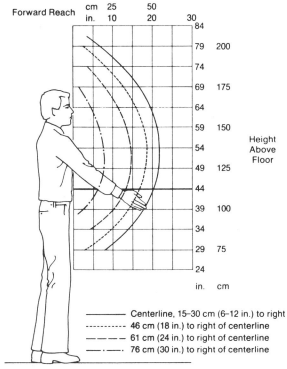

Figure 7.13. Reach envelopes for the standing operator. Reprinted, with permission, from Eastman Kodak Company (1983).

Figure 7.14. Guidelines for side reach of seated operators. Published with permission of Imperial Oil Limited, Toronto, ON.

135

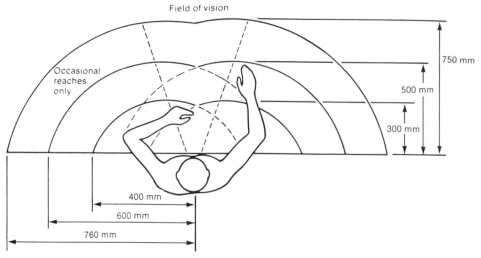

Figure 7.15. Recommended horizontal reach envelopes of seated workers. With the permission of the Canadian Standards Association, and copyrighted by CSA, 178 Rexdale, Blvd., Rexdale, ON, M9W 1R3.

 Table 7.6 presents a workstation needs assessment tool that can be used to conduct a simple analysis of the tasks that your office workers perform. It can be used to assess the tasks performed by every worker or, if there is a large number of workers who perform similar tasks, used to assess a sample workers who perform the same task. The tool examines the following major design factors:

- *The worker:* In terms of body size, visual corrections, handedness, and any physical limitations. It also establishes whether the workstation is shared with others. If so, the adjustability requirements can be determined.
- *Activities:* Seven activities cover over 95% of what workers do in their offices. The percentage of time spent performing each task will help determine configuration requirements.
- *Worksurface area:* These requirements are based on the support materials used, the type of office equipment used, and the nature of the job.
- *Storage and filing:* These requirements must be determined both for personal and work use. Within the work requirements, the worker estimates the percentage that is important and is given an opportunity to declare whether some of the storage and filing space is unnecessary.
- *Equipment requirements:* Computer requirements are particularly important. We know that computer style and the amount of support equipment can affect worksurface area and configuration.

It should be noted that the paper and book sizes in Table 7.6 are based on United States standards and will have to be modified for use elsewhere.

Table 7.6. Workstation Needs Assessment

Employee Name: _____ **Room No:** _____ **Date:** _____

Height in shoes(cm/in): _____Right- or left-handed? (R/L) _____

Corrective lenses? (Y/N): _____ If YES, are they bi- or trifocals? (Y/N): _____

Any physical limitations? (Please explain) _____

Do you share your workspace? (Y/N) _____ If YES, with whom? _____

   If YES, how many days per week do you use it? _____

A. Principal Office Activities:

Please choose from the following list the principal office activities that you perform and the percentage of time that you will spend on each over the next year. Then answer the questions in each section that correspond to the activities you perform.

Principal Activity	% Time	Go To Section
1. Computer use	_____	B
2. Desk work (reading, writing, etc.)	_____	C
3. Filing/storage	_____	D
4. Telephone use	_____	E
5. Collating	_____	F
6. Fax/copy use	_____	G
7. Meetings in own office	_____	H
8. Meetings outside of office	_____	
9. Other activities (please explain)	_____	

B. Computer Use

1. What type of computer do you use in your office?
   (a) Desk top model _____
   (b) "Tower" (floor) model _____
   (c) Laptop _____
   (d) Other (explain)_____

2. If you answered "laptop", go to question 2(a); Otherwise go to question 3.
   (a) Do you use an external monitor, keyboard and pointing
       device with your laptop for desk work? (Y/N)   _____
   (b) Do you use it as a stand alone computer? (Y/N)   _____

Table 7.6. *(Continued)*

3. What tasks do you perform on your computer and for what percentage of time?

          Task   **% Time?**

    (a) Data/text input?   _____

    (b) Graphic design?   _____

    (c) CAD design?   _____

    (d) Software development?   _____

    (e) Other (explain)   _____

4. What type of support materials do you use while operating your computer?

          Material   **% Time**

    (a) Documents (letter size)   _____

    (b) Books (28 × 43 cm; 11 × 17 in.)   _____

    (c) Binders (28 × 43 cm; 11 × 17 in.)   _____

    (d) Printed output (55 × 35 cm; 22 × 14 in.)   _____

    (e) Large drawings (60 × 90 cm; 24 × 36 in.)   _____

5. In addition to a VDT, keyboard, and mouse, do you use any other specialized computer devices? (Y/N)

    (a) Pointing devices (specify)   _____

    (b) External disk drives   _____

    (c) Printer/plotters   _____

    (d) Other devices (specify) _____

C. Desk Work

1. What type of support materials do you use?

          Material   **Yes/No**

    (a) Reports (letter size)

    (b) Binders (opening to 28 × 43 cm; 11 × 17 in.)   _____

    (c) Computer printer output (opening to 55 xx 35 cm; 24 × 14 in.)   _____

    (d) Drawings (up to 90 cm; 36 in. square)   _____

    (e) Other (specify) _____

2. What other equipment or material is routinely on your worksurface while you are performing desk work?

Table 7.6. *(Continued)*

Equipment/Material	Yes/No
(a) Telephone	_____
(b) Calculator	_____
(c) Stacks of paper in temporary storage	_____
If yes, how many stacks?	_____
(d) Other items of material (specify)	_____

3. How many projects could you be working on at any one time? _____

D. Filing and Storage

	cm	in
1. Hanging files can be measured in cm (in.):		
(a) How many cm (in.) of hanging files do you have?	_____	_____
(b) How many cm (in.) of those do you have to access:		
i. Frequently	_____	_____
ii. Occasionally	_____	_____
iii. Infrequently	_____	_____
(c) How many cm (in.) of hanging files could you discard or put into records retention?	_____	_____
2. Books and binder storage can be measured in cm (in.):		
(a) How many cm (in.) of storage do you have?	_____	_____
(b) How many cm (in.) of those do you access		
i. Frequently	_____	_____
ii. Occasionally	_____	_____
iii. Infrequently	_____	_____
(c) How many cm (in.) of storage could you discard or put into records retention?	_____	_____

3. Personal storage can be measured by drawers (10 cm/4 in. high) or by cm (in.) of shelf space.
   (a) How many drawers full of personal storage do you have? _____
   (b) How many cm (in.) of shelf space to you have? _____ cm? or in.?
   (c) How How much could you reduce your personal storage by?
       i. Drawers? _____
       ii. Shelf space? _____ cm? or in.?

4. How many piles of paper might you have on your desk/credenza _____ at any one time?

Table 7.6. (Continued)

5. Special requirements for the storage of office supplies? (Y/N). If YES, please explain.

_____.

_____

E. Telephone Use

1. Which activities would you perform while you use the telephone?
   (a) Writing? (Y/N)   _____
   (b) Accessing the computer? (Y/N)   _____
   (c) Accessing files/drawers? (Y/N)   _____
   (d) Other (explain) _____

F. Collating

1. What do you collate in your office? Please answer Yes or No to the following:
   (a) Letters/envelopes for a distribution list?   _____
   (b) Reports?   _____
   (c) Presentations?   _____
   (d) Other items? (Please explain) _____

2. Collating space can be measured by the number of pieces of paper in a letter or a report that must be laid out on your worksurface at the same time.
   (a) What is the typical number of pages that you would normally   _____
       lay on your desk at the same time?

G. FAX/Copy Use

1. Do you have a fax machine on any part of your workstation? (Y/N)   _____

2. Do you have a copy machine on any part of your workstation? (Y/N)   _____

3. Are you required to add paper or change ribbons or cartridges? (Y/N)   _____

H. Office Meetings

1. How many meetings to you typically hold in your office in a week?   _____

2. How many people typically attend your meetings?   _____

3. What types of materials would you and your attendees bring to the your meetings?
   (a) Reports?   _____
   (b) Open reports (23 × 43 cm; 11 × 17 in.)   _____
   (c) Other materials? (Please explain) _____

The output from the needs survey provides a range of values, for example, length of hanging files, from which the range across all office workers can be determined. Figure 7.16 for example, illustrates a design configuration that was based on the needs of a class of office workers. Overhead storage, in this example, was set at 260 cm (108 inches), which satisfied 95% of the users.

7.2.10   What to Look for in Office Furniture

Table 7.7 provides a checklist of criteria that can be used to evaluate and compare furniture systems, furniture manufacturers, and furniture dealers. While the aim of Table 7.7 is to provide a list of those ergonomic characteristics that support the office worker, other recommendations to examine the quality of the

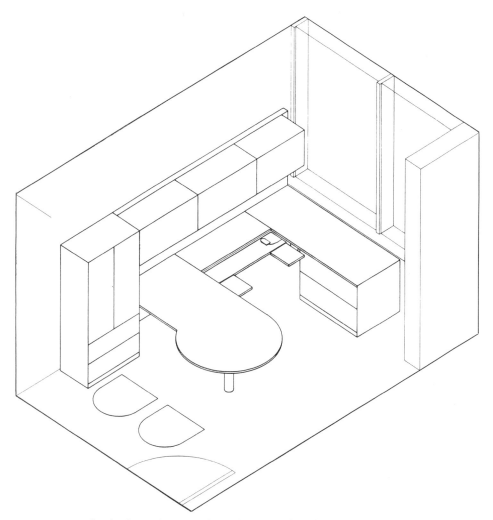

Figure 7.16. Sketch of a workstation whose design was based on a needs assessment of operators. Published with permission of Imperial Oil Limited, Toronto, ON.

Table 7.7. Selection Criteria for Furniture Systems

Checklist Item	Rating (1= poor; 5= excellent)	Importance (1= unimportant 5= important)	TOTAL SCORE [Col. (2)x(3)]
Product Design Criteria 1. Safety • Sharp edges • Pinched fingers • Obstructions (e.g. head, knees)			
2. Up-to-date • Designs that are able to satisfy contemporary issues in office ergonomics - Communications - Printers - Alternate keyboard designs - Pointing devices - Storage, filing - Oversized VDTs - Task lighting - Sit/stand requirements			
3. Modularity • Able to be reconfigured to meet functional requirements ⇒ From the basic building blocks ⇒ In minimal time • Number of basic modules available			
4. Compatibility • Between successive new product lines			
5. Height adjustability • Continuously adjustable, or • Manually adjustable (worksurfaces may have to be detached)			
6. Lighting • Minimal reflected glare from the worksurface • Adjustable intensity			

142

Table 7.7. (Continued)

Checklist Item	Rating (1= poor; 5= excellent)	Importance (1= unimportant 5= important)	TOTAL SCORE [Col. (2)x(3)]
7. Flexibility/Configuration • Minimum number of parts • Ease of reconfiguration (time to disassemble and re-assemble) • Ease of adjustment (leveling) • Availability of design guides, templates, etc. to support office layouts			
8. Aesthetics • Color options • Finishes available • Appearance • Ability to match original surface colors and textures in replacement furniture			
9. Meets design specifications for dimensions and operation			
10. Wire management • Convenience • Accessibility • Supports worksurface access to services (e.g. power, voice and data)			
11. Mockups: Willing to set up full-scale office mockups for employees to view and grade			
12. Durability • Able to meet BIFMA requirements. • Able to withstand repeated dis- and re-assembly • Edges of worksurface, drawers and doors will not detach			
13. Warranty			

Table 7.7. (Continued)

Checklist Item	Rating (1= poor; 5= excellent)	Importance (1= unimportant 5= important)	TOTAL SCORE [Col. (2)x(3)]
14. Full line of products available • Chairs, filing cabinets, desks, systems furniture • Different levels of furniture grades available (administrative to executive)			
15. Labeling - supports purchasers inventory/labeling systems (if any)			
16. Geographic delivery location limitations (if any)			
17. Packaging • Minimal waste to landfill, reuses material • Ability to protect product during delivery			
Service Criteria 1. Designers available in-house • Pre-installation advice			
2. CAD capabilities of dealers or manufacturers			
3. Post installation audit • Small projects (less than 'X' workstations) • Large projects			
4. Post installation deficiency corrections • Time to identify • Time to fix after identification			
5. Ordering procedures • Directly from CAD? • Easy to understand catalogue and process			

Table 7.7. (Continued)

Checklist Item	Rating (1= poor; 5= excellent)	Importance (1= unimportant 5= important)	TOTAL SCORE [Col. (2)x(3)]
6. Delivery lead time / Geographic order location • Guaranteed earliest delivery • Quick ship program? • Rapid ship program? • Method of delivery			
7. Reports (usage, service calls, etc.)			
8. Ongoing product support • Repairs (time to respond and availability of parts) • Warranties			
9. Servicing account • Sales rep availability and response time • Response time on problem resolution • Handling damaged items on delivery			
10. Method of invoicing			
11. Electronic data invoicing capabilities			
Price criteria 1. Unit pricing/discounting structure			
2. Dollar/volume discounts			
3. Future products			
4. Payment terms			
5. Shipping costs, if any			
6. Taxes, duty or brokerage charges, if any			

Table 7.7. (Continued)

Checklist Item		Rating (1= poor; 5= excellent)	Importance (1= unimportant 5= important)	TOTAL SCORE [Col. (2)x(3)]
7.	Restocking charges			
8.	F.O.B. point			
9.	Returns/cancellation charges, if any			
10.	Installation charges			
11.	Design charges			
12.	Other service charges			
13.	Repair costs			
14.	Reconfiguration charges			
Supplier Criteria 1.	Member BIFMA			
2.	Financial stability			
3.	Proven service record (should supply references)			
4.	Proven product quality			
5.	Demonstrated quality control program in place			
6.	Demonstrated safety program in place (WC fees are not excessive)			
7.	Type of organization: public, private			
8.	Organization: Dealer network, or direct from the manufacturer			

NOTE: If any of the above product or service items are graded low, there may be a cost associated with the item which would then be included in the financial analysis.

furniture and the performance of furniture manufacturers and dealers are also provided. The table also provides a method of evaluating the selection criteria across furniture manufacturers. In column 2, manufacturers are rated on their ability to meet each criterion. Column 3 is the teams' rating of the relative importance of each *criterion*, so that importance remains the same for each supplier. Column 4 provides the total score on each criterion for each manufacturer. The total score is the product of the "rating" in column 2 times the "importance" in column 3. This table is provided as a separate file in the computer disk provided with this book, so it can be modified as necessary.

7.3   OFFICE SEATING

The office chair may be the most important piece of personal furniture in the office. Certainly, it's the piece of furniture that the worker has most contact with. In many companies, the office chair is the only piece of furniture that relocates with the employee.

When we change from a standing to a seated position, the curvature of our spine changes and we put more pressure on the intervertebral disks (Grandjean, 1988). The upright seated posture is difficult to maintain for long periods of time. Hence we slump forward, sometimes leaning on our elbows to make notes and read. This posture relaxes our back muscles but increases the pressure on our intervertebral disks.

The more we can increase the angle between our body and legs, the less pressure we put on our disks. If we recline to increase the angle, the more body weight is taken by the chair, thus reducing muscle stress. Studies have also shown that a proper lumbar support can also reduce disk pressure and muscle stress. Hence a reclined seated position that allows an angle of 110 to 120 degrees between trunk and legs reduces pressure on our disks and stress on our back muscles.

Unfortunately, with contemporary office furniture, we can't work in a reclined position. To do so, the worksurface would have to be angled. Under special circumstances, when for medical reasons workers must sit in a reclined position, we have provided them with an angled worksurface. We found that writing is unaffected up to a worksurface angle of about 20 degrees. We also found that work materials such as papers can be managed with the use of bean bags or magnets, and that pens and pencils can be controlled with a lip at the front of the worksurface.

Under normal circumstances, the office worker will continue to work at a horizontal worksurface and will vary his or her posture between reclined, erect, and slumped forward, thus shifting the stress between different muscle groups. Hence the job of the office chair is to support the way the office worker works.

A recent innovation in office seating is the forward-tilting seat pan that can form an angle of about 100 degrees between trunk and leg without the necessity of redefining the seat back. However, the forward tilt must be limited to about 10 degrees to prevent the occupant from sliding forward.

7.3.1   Office Seating Guidelines

Figure 7.17 illustrates a number of desirable features of a well-designed office chair. As a minimum, the chair requires:

- Five casters for stability
- A "gas-lift" height adjustment
- A seat pan that is firm, yet well cushioned, covered with nonsticking fabric and designed with a rounded front that will not put pressure on the underside on the thighs
- Good lumbar support in the backrest
- Ability to recline the backrest
- Choice of armrests or no armrests.

In addition, the better chairs will optionally provide:

- An adjustable seat pan angle that has a forward tilt
- High backrests to provide head support for employees to lean back from time to time to relax the back muscles
- Arm rests that are adjustable in height, width (distance from each other), and can rotate to provide support for the arm when using a pointing device

Guidelines that recommend the dimensions and adjustment ranges of each of the above are provided later in this section.

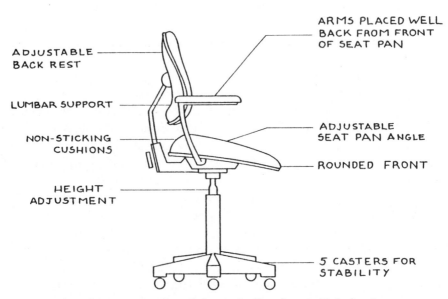

Figure 7.17. Characteristics of a well-designed office chair. Published with permission of Imperial Oil Limited, Toronto, ON.

Office chairs support several types of tasks, each emphasizing different design features:

- Task chairs, used at VDT workstations, must be the most adjustable of all chairs and take advantage of each of the above features.
- Desk chairs require good back support, a recline feature and, therefore, high backrests.
- Meeting chairs are shared by many people. They must be equipped with the widest range of height adjustment. They should also recline, but do not need high backs since they are not used for long periods of time.

All reclinable chairs should be designed so that:

- The seat pan does not tilt upward when the backrest reclines.
- The lumbar support follows the lumbar area of the spine when the occupant leans back.

Table 7.8, with the help of Figure 7.18a through c, lists the dimensions and adjustment ranges recommended by the ANSI/HFS-100 (1988) and the CSA(1989) guidelines. Sources for dimensions that are not covered by the above guidelines are referenced .

As a general comment, the recommendations from the CSA guidelines agree with those of the ANSI/HFS guidelines. They vary only in lumbar support height and angle of seat pan adjustment. The lumbar height recommended by Grandjean seems most appropriate. Note 3 in Table 7.8 appears to be the driving force for backrest angle adjustment.

The quality of seating varies widely from one manufacturer to the other. It is recommended that office seating meet the quality standards of the Business and Institutional Furniture Manufacturers Association (BIFMA).

7.3.1.1   Evaluation of Office Seating

The recommendations for dimensions and adjustability of office chairs, which are listed in Table 7.8, are only as good as the test methods used to measure them. The ANSI/HFS standards (1988) provide methods for measuring:

- Compressed seat height
- Seat reference point
- Seat angles
- Back height
- Seat depth

Table 7.9 provides recommended methods for measuring:

- Seat pan width
- Seat arm height

Table 7.8. Recommended Dimensions and Adjustment Ranges, in cm (inches), for Office Chairs (Refer to Figure 7.18 for Dimension Definitions)

Dimension Name	Tag	ANSI (1988)	CSA (1989)	Other
Seat Pan Height from floor[1] (Weighted seat pan)	H	40.6 to 52.0 (16.0 to 20.5)	38 to 52 (15. to 20.5)	
Depth	D	38 to 43 (15 to 17)	38 to 43 (15 to 17)	
Breadth[2]	B	45 (17.7)	45 (17.7)	
Seat pan angle (degrees)[3]	A	0 to +10	-3 to +4	
Upholstery compression (max)[4]	--	--	--	3.8 (1.5)
Seatback Height of lumbar support above the seat pan	L	15.2 to 22.9 (6 to 9)	20 to 25 (7.9 to 9.8)	10 to 20[5] (4 to 8)
Width at the lumbar support (min)	X	30.5 (12)	35 (13.8)	
Top of backrest above seat pan	T	--	38 to 53 (15 to 21)	--
Backrest angle (degrees)[3]	V	--	+5 to +15	+15 to -10
Armrests Inside width (min)[2]		--	45 (17.7)	--
Forward of seatback (max)	G	--	30 (11.8)	--
Width (min)	--	--	5 (2)	--
Covering[4]		--	--	fabric
Height above seat pan	C	--	20 to 25 (7.9 to 9.8)	18 to 23[4] (7 to 9)

Footnotes

[1] Compressed seat height

[2] Chairs with seat pans wider than 45 cm should ensure that the inside width of the armrests is adjustable

[3] Angle between the torso and thigh depends on both the seat pan and backrest angles. The torso/thigh angle should be allowed to range between 90 and 110 degrees

[4] Imperial Oil Guidelines (1984)

[5] Grandjean (1988)

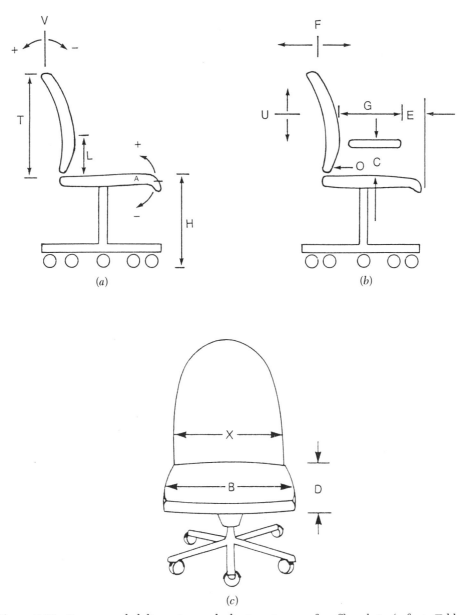

Figure 7.18. Recommended dimensions and adjustment ranges for office chairs (refer to Table 7.8 for dimension definitions). Published with permission of Imperial Oil Limited, Toronto, ON.

Table 7.9. Office Chair Evaluation Procedures

A. Seat Pan Width

1. Measure the seat pan width by placing a straightedge in the line that has been drawn 125 mm from the end of the 90F[1] nearest the seat back.
   [*Note:* Where chair arms interfere with the placement of long straightedge, calipers or a telescoping rule should be used.]

B. Seat Arm Height

1. For seat arm height, place the straightedge across the seat arms at approximately the location of the 125 mm line across the 90F.
2. Measure the distance from the base of the 90F to the bottom of the straightedge and add 1.6 cm (the width of the plywood that the 90F is made from). Record result.

C. Armrest Distance From the Back of the Seat

1. Place the straightedge across the front surface of the armrests.
2. Measure the distance from the back of the 90F to the straightedge and add 1.6 cm. Record result.

D. Seat Back Width

1. Estimate the point on the seat back where the lumbar support protrudes the most.
2. Place a straightedge across the seat back at that point.
3. Measure the distance between the outermost edges of the seat back (even though the fabric may not go to the outer edge). The distance would include any molding that is on the outer edge.

E. Backrest Angle

1. Loosen seat back tension as much as possible.
2. Push the 90F back as much as possible so it approaches the seat reference point.
3. Set the joined ruler to 90 degrees and place it against the seat pan and seat back beside the 90F.
4. Tilt the seat back to its maximum rearward position. Remove the 90F.
5. Adjust the angle of the jointed ruler so it once more contacts the seat back. (Be sure that the ruler does not move from the seat reference point.
6. Place the protractor on the upright portion of the ruler, and read the angle.
7. Allow the seat back to tilt to its fully forward position.
8. Repeat (4.) and (5.). Record the result.

---

[1] The 90F is a right angled form (see sketch below) that resembles a seat pan and seat back set at right angles. Each face is about 30 cm wide and 50 cm long. It is made from plywood, 1.6 cm thick. A slot is cut into the seat pan face to allow a ruler to pass through vertically and touch the floor. The ruler can be positioned anywhere in the slot.

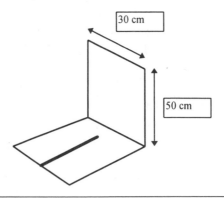

30 cm

50 cm

- Distance between front of armrest and seat back
- Seat back width
- Backrest angle

7.3.1.2   Seat Preference

It has been my experience that office workers will prefer one office chair over another, even though both meet design specifications and each has the same fabric finish. Hence the final decision about which chair to purchase, all other things like cost, delivery, and quality being equal, should be made by the employees.

A few years ago, the author in cooperation with Ms. Jean Dalton of the Dominion Foundry and Steel Company (DOFASCO) developed the Office Chair Evaluation Form shown in Table 7.10. The form is completed by office workers after they have evaluated the chair for two days. The result of each evaluation is a score between 25 and 125.

A study procedure, presented in Appendix 1, provides design techniques, test conditions, and sampling methods based on a paired-comparison technique. The result provides a prioritized list of chairs, which will help the relocation team with the selection.

7.3.2 Implementing an Office Seating Program

Office workers are not generally familiar with the operation of new chairs or the correct way of adjusting them. In many companies, chairs just appear in the office and the worker is left to his or her own abilities to learn how to use them and how to adjust them correctly. In most cases the results are poor.

A seating program must have two components.

1. Good chairs that arrive with good instructions. Good instructions do not necessarily mean a complex manual that employees won't read or keep (Figure 7.19, for example, provides simple, easy to understand instructions on a sticker attached to the new chair).
2. Employee training on seat operation and adjustment.

7.4   FILING AND STORAGE

The design and location of files and storage systems can have three major consequences for an office worker; they can affect:

1. Worker safety
2. Worker efficiency
3. The usability of the system

Table 7.10. Office Chair Evaluation Form

Chair Make:	Chair Model:
Evaluated by:	Date:

Circle the number (1 to 5) that best describes your opinion of each design element. Check the appropriate boxes (❑) when you feel that a problem exists.

PLEASE ANSWER EVERY QUESTION. If a question is 'not applicable' to the chair that you are evaluating, mark N/A in the COMMENTS column.

Design Element	Rating Scale poor best	Problem?	Comments
1. Seat pan adjustment - ease of adjustment - range of adjustment	 1 2 3 4 5 1 2 3 4 5	 Not high enough ❑ Not low enough ❑	
2. Seat pan angle adjustment - ease of adjustment - range of adjustment	 1 2 3 4 5 1 2 3 4 5		
3. Seat pan comfort - depth - width - padding	 1 2 3 4 5 1 2 3 4 5 1 2 3 4 5	 Too long ❑ Too Short ❑ Too narrow ❑ Too wide ❑ Too Soft ❑ Too hard ❑	
4. Backrest Comfort - curve at lower back - width - interference with movement - height	 1 2 3 4 5 1 2 3 4 5 1 2 3 4 5 1 2 3 4 5	 Too flat ❑ Too far out ❑ Too high ❑ Too low ❑	
5. Backrest Height Adjustment - ease of adjustment - range of adjustment	 1 2 3 4 5 1 2 3 4 5		
6. Backrest angle adjustment - ease of adjustment - range of adjustment	 1 2 3 4 5 1 2 3 4 5		
7. Arm rests - width between arm rests - size - comfort - interferes with task - safety (pinching) - adjustment	 1 2 3 4 5 1 2 3 4 5 1 2 3 4 5 1 2 3 4 5 1 2 3 4 5 1 2 3 4 5	 Too wide ❑ Too narrow ❑ Too wide ❑ Too narrow ❑ Too hard ❑ Too soft ❑ Not adjustable ❑	
7. Chair movement	1 2 3 4 5	Moves too easily ❑ Not easily enough ❑	
8. Stability (tip resistance)	1 2 3 4 5		
10. Lack of sharp or protruding objects	1 2 3 4 5		
11. Overall rating	1 2 3 4 5		

Source: Reproduced with the permission of Dominion Foundry and Steel Company (DOFAS-CO), Ltd, Hamilton, ON, and Imperial Oil Limited, Toronto, ON.

154

Figure 7.19. Example of easy-to-understand chair operation instructions that are convenient for the user. Published with permission of Simo Dow.

Typical office filing and storage systems can include:

- File cabinets
- High storage on shelves
- Overhead storage for workstations
- Under surface (desk) files and storage

This section examines each type of filing and storage system in terms of each of the consequence headings. Much of this section is in list form, so it can be easily made into a table or checklist.

7.4.1 Filing Cabinets

Three major types of filing cabinets include:

1. Vertical files
2. Lateral files
3. Fixed shelf lateral files

The advantages of the fixed shelf lateral file over vertical and lateral files with roll-out shelves are:

- Fixed shelf unit has fewer push-pull operations (only the front panel to the shelf requires opening).

- Fixed shelf file does not easily tip, since the weight distribution never changes.
- Cost of fixed shelf cabinets and associated file supplies are competitive with those of roll-out units.
- Fixed shelf equipment maximizes use of office floor space. For example, a fixed shelf unit that requires (0.42 square meter (4.5 square feet) of floor space would replace a lateral rollout that requires 0.767 square meter (8.25 square feet) of space (see Figure 7.20).

The following guidelines touch on the efficiency of use of any paper files:

- They should be located within the user's reach from a standing position.
- Reach to a file should not exceed about 1.25 times the person's height (Grandjean, 1988). For a small female office worker, the maximum height should be less than about 190 cm (75 inches).
- File systems should be designed and implemented to minimize the time required to store and retrieve files. Filing efficiency may be improved by:

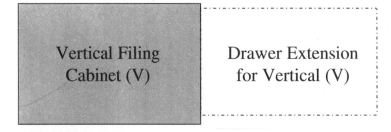

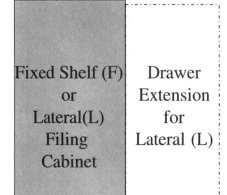

Dimension	V	L	F
File Space (cm)	254	325	345
Floor Area (m²)	0.63	0.77	0.42

Figure 7.20. Comparison of the floor space required by vertical, horizontal, and fixed shelf horizontal filing cabinets. Published with permission of Imperial Oil Limited, Toronto, ON.

> —Locating the most frequently used files in the most accessible location (e.g., standing or seated waist height)
> —Visually coding files to make them easier to identify (coding may be by color, symbols, or short legends)
> —Using manually driven or mechanized units whenever retrieval volume is high
- Using modular file systems

The safety of filing systems can be improved with these ideas:

- Pullout files should be tip resistant:
- They can be bolted to the wall.
- They should be fitted with an interlock to ensure that two drawers cannot be pulled out at the same time.
- File cabinets should not have pinch points or sharp edges.

7.4.2   High storage

High storage on shelves is meant to house infrequently accessed materials that may be beyond normal reach. To access materials on high shelves:

- Stairs or stair ladders must be provided instead of rung ladders. Stairs and stair ladders should be inclined at 50 to 70 degrees to make climbing easier.
- Provide stairs for items that require two hands to grasp .
- For bulky items or items weighing more than 13 kg (28 lb.), provide ramps or elevating platforms.

7.4.3   Overhead Storage

For a seated operator, overheads should be located low enough so a small female can access items from storage units in front of her. This limits the maximum height to about 74 cm (30 inches) above the *seat pan* of the operator, that is, about 20 inches above the worksurface. Figure 7.13 illustrates the forward and upward reach of a user in a seated position; overhead storage units should be situated within this range.

Frequent reaching to grasp, remove, and lay heavy binders on desks can lead to cumulative injury of the waist, arm, and shoulder. Thus in jobs requiring frequent handling of binders, the binders should be stored at worksurface height. Figure 7.21 illustrates a workstation in which the overhead storage unit has been mounted on the desk to assist retrieving and replacing binders.

7.4.4   Desk Files

Files are typically stored in pedestals or two-high filing cabinets beneath the worksurface. Safety issues associated with desk files include:

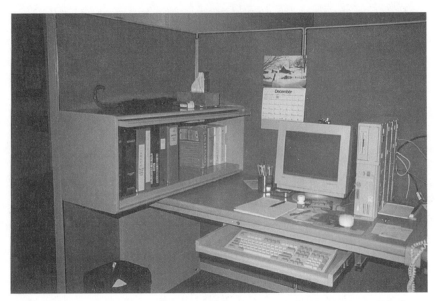

Figure 7.21. Rearrangement of an overhead cabinet to make it more accessible for frequent use of heavy binders. Published with permission of Exxon Chemical Company, Houston, TX.

- Pinch points
- Potential tripping hazard if drawers are left open
- Back injuries if files require twisting to use them

7.4.5   Storage Checklist

 The relocation team may want to offer suggestions to the employees in the form of a brochure or awareness session that discusses the items in Table 7.11. This may be used in connection with the needs survey in Table 7.6.

7.5   WORKSTATION AND SEATING ACCESSORIES

Accessories discussed in this section are those that are intended to reduce the potential of soft tissue injuries (CTDs) or to increase efficiency. They do not consist of items such as letter trays, pencil holders, or wastebaskets, but, rather of items that are fitted to workstations or chairs and may be retrofitted to existing furniture to make them safer.

7.5.1   Keyboard and Mouse Support

Carpal tunnel syndrome (CTS) is one of the most frequently occurring classes of CTD. It develops over time when office workers are exposed to a combination of risk factors including:

Table 7.11. Storage Checklist for Office Workers

To develop an effective storage system for your workspace:

- MAKE a written list of the material used in your job such as:
  —Paper
  —Rolled drawings
  —Books
  —Addresses
  —Supplies (e.g., staples, paper clips)
  —Hand equipment (e.g., stapler, three-hole punch)
  —Files
  —Computer printouts

  - INDICATE for each item the typical size, shape, and weight (e.g., one- versus two-hand lift)
  - DECIDE how much of each item must be stored
  - CLASSIFY each item according to the frequency with which it would be used
  - LOCATE the "active" items close to you, the "dead" items in remote files
  - IDENTIFY the storage system that is best for the items used frequently
  - DECIDE on its location (e.g., heavier items requiring a two-handed lift should be centrally located)

- Large forearm-wrist angles
- High frequency movements
- High force in the fingers
- Lack of proper recovery periods

Large angles between the wrist and forearm can be caused by the poor placement of the keyboard relative to the worker and worksurface, or by misuse by the office worker. Figure 7.22 illustrates poor wrist posture that could be due to bad work habits or the misalignment of the keyboard.

Two types of accessories have been developed to reduce the potential for injury due to wrist angle. Figure 7.23 shows one version of a keyboard keeper that is used to adjust the keyboard to the proper height. Figure 7.24 illustrates a wrist rest that provides support for the wrists while typing. As well as providing support, the wrist rest also forces the wrists up and reduces the angle between wrist and hand. Table 7.12 provides design recommendations for keyboard keepers and wrist rests that should be considered when purchasing them.

The problems typically caused by the overuse of a mouse or trackball are in the arm and shoulder of the user, owing to the lack of proper arm support. Most combination keyboard keeper and armrest accessories are not designed to support the arm. Wrist rests located at the mouse position can place the entire weight of the arm on the wrist and can aggravate an existing CTD condition. Support should be provided for the forearm and can be in the form of armrests on an office chair or of armrests that are built into the workstation. Figure 7.25

Figure 7.22. Poor hand posture while using a computer keyboard.
Published with permission of Imperial Oil Limited, Toronto, ON.

Figure 7.23. Adjustable height keyboard keeper.
Photograph courtesy of Steelcase Inc., Grand Rapids, MI.

illustrates a prototype pullout armrest that was designed by the SMED
Manufacturing Company. The armrest can be attached to the underside of any
surface. It extends outward up to 30 cm (12 inches) and is fitted with a pad
whose thickness can be varied to match the thickness of the worksuface, that so
the arm remains parallel to the mouse.

7.5.2   Document Holders

The optimal visual field for the VDT was defined in Section 5.13 as +/- 45
degrees either side of the line of site. To minimize head and eye movements, the
support documents from which data are entered into the computer should be
located as close as possible to and at the same height as the VDT (Figure 7.26);

Figure 7.24. A commercially available wristrest. Reproduced with the permission of Ergonomic Design, Inc.

*Table 7.12. **Design Recommendations for Keyboard Keepers and Wrist Rests***

Keyboard Keepers
- Adjust vertically through a minimum range of 15 cm (6 inches)
- Equipped with a supporting surface large enough to support keyboard and pointing device. If the pointing device is a mouse, the area required to support it is normally 15 cm (6 inches) square.
- Should not have any sharp corners or edges or obstructions on the underside that would injure the user or catch clothing
- Angle of the support surface cannot vary unless the angle of the surface that supports the pointing device can vary independently of the main surface

Wrist Rest
- Made of firm pliable material like sponge rubber
- Covered with material that will not promote sweating and will absorb sweat
- Top of the wrist rest should be at about the same height as the space bar of the keyboard

Figure 7.25. Retrofit armrest developed to support the forearm while using a pointing device. Reproduced with the permission of SMED International, Calgary, AL.

Figure 7.26. Commercially availabe document holder. © 1996 by Fellows Manufacturing Co. Reproduced with the permission of Fellows, 1789 Norwood Avenue, Itasca, IL, 60143-1095.

Figure 7.27. Commercially available footrest. Reproduced with the permission of WorkRite, Ergonomic Accessories, Inc., Norvato, CA, 94945.

a document holder is designed to hold the materials used in such a position. A well-designed document holder has the following characteristics:

- Can position the documents in the optimal visual field close to and at the same height as the VDT
- Consists of a support surface that is large enough to hold the required documents
- May be equipped with a task light that illuminates the documents independent of the level of ambient lighting

7.5.3   Footrests

When office chairs are raised to their extreme height, the seat pan is often too high for shorter workers to rest their feet comfortably on the floor. Footrests are used to support the feet so shorter workers can sit back comfortably in their chairs and take the pressure off of the underside of their thighs (Figure 7.27). Well-designed footrests have the following characteristics:

- Height is adjustable up to at least 10 cm (4 inches).
- The angle of the footrest is adjustable.
- The footrest is designed not to slip on floors or carpets.
- Width is at least 40 cm (16 inches).
- Depth is at least 30 cm (12 inches).

REFERENCES

ANSI/HFS 100-1988 (1988). American national standard for human factors engineering of visual display terminal workstations. Santa Monica, CA: Human Factors Society.

Attwood, D. A. (1989). Comparison of discomfort experienced at CADD, word processing and traditional drafting workstations. International Journal of Industrial Ergonomics, 4, pp. 39–50.

Booth, P. A. (1991). An introduction to human-computer interaction. Hillsdale: Lawrence Erlbaum Associates,.

CSA (1989). Office ergonomics: A national standard of Canada, CAN/CSA-412-M89. Rexdale, ON: Canadian Standards Association.

DeChiara, J., J. Panero, and M. Zelnik (1991). Time-saver standards for interior design and space planning. New York: McGraw-Hill.

Eastman Kodak Company (1983). Ergonomic design for people at work, Volume I. New York: Van Nostrand Reinhold.

Faulkner, T. W. and R. A. Day (1970). The maximal functional reach of the female operator. AIIE Transactions 2: pp. 126–131.

Galitz, W. O. (1993). User interface screen design. Boston: QED Publishing.

Grandjean, E. (1988). Fitting the task to the man, 4th edition. New York: Taylor and Francis.

IOL (1984). Guidelines for office ergonomics. Toronto, ON: Imperial Oil Limited.

Joyce, M. and U. Wallersteiner (1989). Ergonomics: Humanizing the automated office. Cincinnati, OH: South-Western Publishing.

ADDITIONAL READINGS

McCormick, E. J. and M. S. Sanders (1982). Human factors in engineering and design; 5th edition. New York: McGraw-Hill.

Sanders, M. S. and E. J. McCormick (1993). Human factors in engineering and design, 7th edition. New York: McGraw-Hill.

Chapter Eight

Planning: Human Factors Considerations in the Design of Special Areas and Services

8.1 WAYFINDING

8.1.1 Introduction

The performance of a facility is determined, in part, by how well people can be directed from one part of the building to another to meet their individual objectives. Wayfinding is the system that determines how easily a visitor can arrive at his or her destination. The purpose of this section is to:

- Familiarize your relocation project team with the issues in wayfinding
- Provide a simple method for evaluating the wayfinding system in a facility
- Recommend techniques for designing an appropriate wayfinding system

Wayfinding is a specialized field that covers more detailed information than can be addressed in this section. This section is intended to provide enough information to allow you and your team members to interact with the wayfinding specialist, not to make any of you experts in wayfinding.

In a multitenant building the characteristics of the wayfinding system may be specified by the building owner. In this case the project team may have no other option than to evaluate the facility and place the indoor signage in the most appropriate locations. In a single tenant or owned building, the design of the wayfinding system will likely be controlled by the building manager and can be influenced by the requirements of the relocation, in which case the relocation project team will be able to use more of the recommendations given herein. In either event, this section should provide the team with the tools necessary to improve a very important part of the facility that affects office workers.

The individual components of a wayfinding system consist of:

- Architectural elements and space within the building. Elements include landmarks such as elevator banks, escalators, and stairwells, or large structures such as fountains or sculptures. Space might include the shape of the basic structure of the building—whether U-, L- or H-shaped—or whether it has a central atrium.
- Signage; which for the purposes of this section will include all forms of visual assists such as word signs, directional signs, directories, and maps.
- Nonvisual wayfinding information, such as voice signs and directories, tactile signs, or textured walkways.

Clearly then, a wayfinding system is not just visual signing. In fact, if the other wayfinding components are properly designed, there is less need for visual signs. However, signage will continue to play a major role in wayfinding, so the majority of this section will deal with signs as a way to meet the users' information needs.

A poor wayfinding system can cause visitors to get lost and when a person is lost he or she:

- Can become disoriented (which can evoke further reactions)
- Can become anxious and stressed
- Can become angry

Lost visitors can also affect others. For example:

- The building management may spend on unnecessarily great deal of their time directing visitors.
- Angry visitors may vandalize the facility—another cost.
- Staff time is wasted when the visitor is late.
- An angry visitor may not have a good interaction with the tenant.

All visitors use a combination of techniques to find their way to their destination. Most will try to obtain a cognitive map of the facility by studying the architectural components of the building. The predominant behavior is a sequential process of

- Gathering information
- Making a decision
- Executing the decision

The wayfinding system should support this process by providing the visitor with:

- The right amount of information at each decision point
- In the right form so he or she can make the correct decision.

Many existing wayfinding systems are not designed to provide the visitor with proper information systems because of:

- Message ambiguity
- Information overload
- Sign systems that are illegible due to poor design or poor lighting
- Sign systems that are poorly located, and thus not seen by the visitor
- Lack of information; including gaps that leave the visitor stranded

Well-designed wayfinding systems have special meaning for the physically, perceptually, and mentally disabled. The next section provides methods for evaluating how well your wayfinding system works for both the able bodied and disabled visitor.

8.1.2 Evaluating Your Wayfinding System

Several methods have been developed to evaluate signage systems. The two methods described below employ either

- visitors to the building, who can offer information, or
- checklists, which can be used by the facilities team to make an evaluation.

Wayfinding systems for new space are designed based on extensive criteria that have been developed and recorded in various guidelines and texts that are referenced in this chapter. Depending on the situation, you may want to skip evaluation techniques and proceed to Section 8.1.3, which discusses design issues

8.1.2.1 Visitor Evaluations

The most efficient way to determine whether the current wayfinding system is doing its job is to listen to and observe visitors. Visitor complaints and opinions can be collected by building occupants who have *the most contact* with the public.

Receptionists are often the targets of lost and confused visitors. Therefore the team needs to interview receptionists (and security guards). Ask them to keep a log of problems and complaints. Find out:

- What the most asked questions are
- How many people show up at reception because they are lost

Another way of learning from visitors is to follow and observe them as they make their way to their destinations. Visitors should be easy to identify in front of the lobby directory.

Finally, the best way to learn from users is by conducting a usability test on the wayfinding system. Usability testing is a technique that is used to evaluate the human–system interface. It is commonly used to evaluate software systems (to ensure they are "user-friendly") and to evaluate the usability (ease of use) of equipment such as remote controllers.

The principle behind usability testing is to follow and observe the users as they test the system. Observation is typically done visually or with a video recorder for later analysis. Each user is encouraged to provide a running commentary on his or her experiences. When the user comes to a complete impasse, he or she is advised how to continue once the reason for the impasse is recorded.

The subjects for usability testing can be selected to represent any part of the user population, including disabled visitors. The test administrators can even subject the user to mild stress through the use of incentives and instructions. For example, the user may be under instruction to arrive at his or her destination within a limited time period.

8.1.2.2   Checklist Evaluations

Table 8.1 provides a basic checklist that can be used to evaluate the interior signage and wayfinding system. It has been shortened and adapted from the extensive evaluations reported in Arthur and Passini (1990). The checklist evaluates aspects of system components that are designed for disabled visitors as well as those used for able bodied visitors with normal perceptual and mental abilities.

Table 8.1. Checklist Evaluation of the Interior Wayfinding System

Building: _____   **Location/City:** _____

Date: _____   **Evaluated by:** _____

Remarks
- You should approach this evaluation as a visitor to the building.
- The visitor may be disabled physically, perceptually, or mentally, so try to evaluate each situation from the point of view of a disabled visitor.
- The checklist is organized to follow a route that the visitor may use to get to a particular destination.
- The visitor is assumed to be starting from the lobby. Hence this checklist does not address any of the wayfinding issues associated with finding the building, parking, or accessing the lobby.

A. General Questions
    1. Identify systems that are in poor repair or don't operate. _____
    2. Identify makeshift signs (e.g., handwritten). _____
    3. Identify signs that are obsolete._____

B. Main Lobby

B1: Inside the Main Entrance

1. Unobstructed view of the information desk or building directory? (Y/N) _____

2. Phone to reception or message phone at the entrance for use by the visually impaired? (Y/N) _____

3. Signs directing visitors to the building directory or reception if they are not immediately visible? (Y/N) _____

B2: Information Desk

4. Located in the lobby (Y/N) _____

5. Identified by letters at least 10 cm (4 inches) high as a reception or information desk? (Y/N) _____

B3: Building Directory

6. Identified by letters at least 10 cm (4 inches) high as a building directory? (Y/N) _____

7. No line in the directory is higher than 160 cm (63 inches) above the floor? (Y/N) _____

8. Information grouped into bundles of five-lines separated by spaces?(Y/N) _____

9. Destination, or destination zones (e.g., medical services) are in letters at least 2.2 cm (0.9 inch) high? (Y/N) _____

10. Location of destinations are by floor, or if a one floor building, by office number? (Y/N) _____

11. Building map showing floor plan with architectural highlights is nearby? (Y/N) _____

12. Light level (lux)? _____

C. Elevators and Stairs

C1: Elevator Lobby

1. Signage or messaging system directs you to the proper elevator? (Y/N) _____

2. Call buttons are easily found and easy to use? (Y/N) _____

3. Arrival of the elevator and direction of travel is announced visually and auditorally? (Y/N) _____

4. Low intensity sound directs visually impaired visitors to the proper cab? (Y/N) _____

5 Map of floor and "You are here" are located on lobby walls of the each elevator bank or at each lobby exit? (Y/N) _____

6. Alternate "map" system is available for visually impaired visitors? (Y/N) _____

7. Directions to stairs are provided? (Y/N) _____

8. Floor number printed and raised for touch on each side of each elevator entrance? (Y/N) _____

Table 8.1. *(Continued)*

C2: Elevator Cars, Interiors

9. Car controls located no more than 140 cm (55 inches) or less than 90 cm (35 inches) from the floor? (Y/N) _____

10. Visual floor indicators at least 2.2 cm (0.9 inch) high? (Y/N) _____

11. Auditory signal (tone and voice) that identifies floor and car direction? (Y/N) _____

12. Braille (tactile) markings for each control and emergency system? (Y/N) _____

C3 Stairwell Doors, Corridor Side

13. Sign identifing stairwell is located 130 to 160 cm (51 to 63 inches) above floor? (Y/N) _____

14. Bottom of window in stairwell door (to see users on the other side) is located at most 130 cm (51 inches) above the floor? (Y/N) _____

15. Lighted overhead Exit signs above door? (Y/N) _____

C4: Stairwell Doors, Stairwell Side

16. Floor number at least 10 cm (4 inches) high located on the wall beside the door, between 130 and 160 cm (51 and 63 inches) above the floor? (Y/N) _____

C5: Stairs

17. Nosings of treads are a different color from the rest of the tread? (Y/N) _____

18. Light provided to see stairs under normal and power out conditions? (Y/N) _____

D. Corridors and Intersections

D1: Corridors

1. Are directions to destinations repeated on long corridors? (Y/N) _____

2. Emergency alarms are equipped with visual and auditory signals? (Y/N) _____

3. Corridor wall projections, projecting more than 10 cm (4 inches) and mounted less than 160 cm (63 inches) above the floor, are extended to at most, 65 cm (26 inches) above the floor? (Y/N) _____

4. Alternative auditory or tactile information for visually impaired visitors? (Y/N) _____

D2: Intersections

5. As many directional signs as corners at the intersection? (Y/N) _____

6. Signs mounted between 130 and 160 cm (51 and 63 inches) above floor? (Y/N) _____

7. Sign characters are at least 4 cm (1.6 inches) high? (Y/N) _____

Table 8.1. (Continued)

8. Ceiling mounted signs (as well as wall mounted) at busy   _____
   intersections? (Y/N)

9. Alternative auditory or tactile directional information available _____
   for visually impaired visitors? (Y/N)

E. Department Offices and Reception Areas

E1: Entrances

1. Destination signs using same plain language as directory   _____
   located beside doors or entranceways? (Y/N)

2. Signs use letters at least 2.2 cm (0.9 inch) high? (Y/N)   _____

3. Signs are located between 130 and 160 cm (51 and 63 inches) _____
   above the floor? (Y/N)

4. Alternative auditory or tactile destination information   _____
   available for visually impaired visitors? (Y/N)

E2: Reception Area

5. Reception area identified by sign with letters at least 10 cm _____
   (4 inches) high? (Y/N)

6. If no receptionist, is it immediately apparent where to go for _____
   information? (Y/N)

E3: Open-Plan Offices

7. Destination zones, destinations marked by overhead signs with _____
   letters at least 10 cm (4 inches) high? (Y/N)

8. Offices identified with wall (partition) mounted signs? (Y/N) _____

9. Map on entrance to office area showing layout and individual _____
   destinations? (Y/N)

10. Alternate auditory and tactile map information available for _____
    visually impaired visitors? (Y/N)

11. Tactile office numbers on visual signs? (Y/N)   _____

Source: Adapted from Arthur and Passini (1990), with permission of Public Services Canada.

8.1.3 Wayfinding System Design Technologies

In order to design a proper wayfinding system, you need to know the information that visitors require to make their way to destinations in your facility. In general the following information is required:

- General information about the building, which can be given by:
  —Building directories
  —Building layouts that show the features of each floor such as elevators, stairwells, escalators, business zones, foyers, washrooms

—Reception areas
—Self-help kiosks and telephones
• Directional information to a particular destination, which can be provided by:
—Elevator directories
—Directional signs perhaps with braille features
—Map displays
—Self-help telephones
—Talking signs for the visually impaired
• Destination identification:
—Visual signs with braille features
—Talking signs

8.1.3.1   Helping Visitors to Process Wayfinding Information

Not all visitors require the same information or have the ability to process the information to the same extent, so as a design principle, the wayfinding system should be designed for the most disadvantaged, as long as that does not, in turn, disadvantage other visitors.

Under conditions of stress, due to time pressure for example, the visitor may act impatiently, not taking the time to assimilate the information provided. Whenever possible, these people should be accommodated.

Under normal conditions, the human does not store and process information as well as the simplest computer. Humans read signs quickly, assimilate the information into short-term memory, then set off to their destination. Short-term human memory has limited capacity and loses information easily and quickly. Hence it's important not to provide too much information at one time. The amount of information that can be processed can be increased if we can chunk it into something more meaningful. For example, the telephone number 1-800-VISIT-NYC is much easier to remember than its numeric equivalent 1-800- 847-4869(2).

8.1.3.2   Deciding What Information to Provide

Visitors generally proceed in a sequential manner moving from one decision point to another until they reach their destination. The wayfinding designer must solve two problems:

1. Where are the decision points
2. What information does the visitor need at each decision point

The previous section described methods to determine answers to these questions by using visitors. For new facilities where visitors' comments are not available, the wayfinding designer can use a "walk-through" technique to simulate different destination scenarios. The walk-through is conducted with naive users using plan drawings and mockups of the wayfinding system.

8.1.3.3   Deciding How to Provide the Wayfinding Information Required
The type of information required at each decision point will suggest the
wayfinding component required to provide it (e.g., directional sign or map).
However, the design of the particular component can determine whether the
information is assimilated by the visitor. Table 8.2 recommends major design
considerations for each component.

Table 8.2. Design Considerations for Different Wayfinding Components

A. Multimodal Signs
1. All information and direction signs should be designed to provide visual/auditory
    and/or tactile information.

B. Lobby Directories
1. Directory should be located within sight of the lobby entrance, or visitors who can-
    not see it directly should be directed to it with signs.
2. Directory should be identified with letters at least 10 cm (4 inches) high.
3. Destination information should:
    • Not be positioned higher than 160 cm (63 inches) from the floor
    • Be provided with characters at least 2.5 cm (1 inch) high
    • Be limited to destination or destination zone and floor or office number.
    • Be grouped into bundles of five lines separated by a space
    • Be visible under current lighting conditions

C. Elevator Lobby Directories
1. Same names on elevator lobby directory as on the main lobby directory
2. As many directories provided as banks of elevators.
3. Should provide more detailed destination information than lobby directories.
4. Consist of map displays with "You are here" indications that direct visitors toward
    destination. Map displays should contain architectural components to act as land-
    marks for the visitor and clear expressions of the circulation system.

D. Directory Signs
D1. General Design and Mounting Recommendations
1. Mount between 130 and 160 cm (51 and 63 inches) above the floor. If intersection
    is heavily traveled, install overhead signs as well as wall-mounted.
2. Characters should be at least 2.5 cm (1 inch) high.
3. As many directional signs at corridor intersections as there are corners at the inter-
    section.

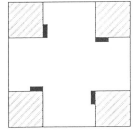

Location of direction signs at a corridor
intersection. Reproduced from Arthur
(1988) with the permission of Public
Services Canada.

4. No more than two directional arrows per sign. If another arrow is required, use another sign.

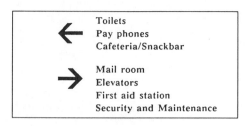

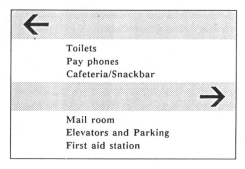

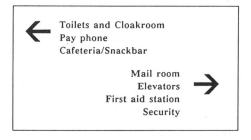

Methods of displaying or laying out directional information. Reproduced from Arthur (1988) with the permission of Public Services Canada.

D2. Message Considerations
5. Use as few words as possible to get message across
6. Message is consistent with other signs and directories
7. Use unambiguous words

D3. Readability Features
8. Use san serif characters, e.g., Helvetica. For a given character size, they can be read at about a 25% further distance than serif characters.
9. Visual angle: under ideal conditions of contrast and lighting a 2.5 cm (1 inch) high character can be identified at 12.2 m (40 feet)
10. Copy position: include a large enough border around the text to ensure that the message is separated from the environment.
11. Contrast: black characters on a white background provide the best contrast for reading. If colored letters on a colored background are necessary, suitable and unsuitable color combinations are given in Table 5.3.

E. Destination Signs
1. Should indicate room number and room use, for example, name of occupant, printer room, copier, or electrical closet

174

Table 8.2. (Continued)

2. Should be mounted between 130 and 160 cm (51 and 63 inches) above floor
3. Characters should be at least 2.5 cm (1 inch) high.

F. Consistency
1 Consistency of design, sizes, message, and mounting locations maintains visitors' expectations and improves usability.

8.2   CONSIDERING THE DISABLED WORKER

8.2.1   Introduction

A disability can be defined as a reduction in the efficiency of one or more of our body systems, making it difficult to carry out major activities such as moving, walking, seeing, hearing, speaking, breathing, learning, or understanding.

Each of us has likely suffered from a temporary disability at one time or another. We have broken a limb or pulled a muscle, making it difficult to work and to get around. We have lost our voice, making it difficult to communicate, or we have had a temporary loss of stamina, making it difficult to climb stairs or do repetitive work. About 20% of the population of most industrialized countries suffers a permanent deficiency of one or more of the body systems.

The relocation project team needs to consider the accommodation of the disabled worker in the new location. Even if there are no permanently disabled workers in the current workforce at the time of the project, there will be at some time in the future. Hiring practices are changing in most countries, making it unlawful to discriminate against workers with disabilities. Also, there is a very good chance that at any one moment, a significant percentage of your able bodied workers will be temporarily disabled.

Not only does legislation make it unlawful to discriminate in hiring practices, it also demands employers to provide "reasonable" physical accommodation for disabled workers or disabled visitors to the worksite.

While a disability is a reduction of efficiency in any body system, there are some disabilities that are more common than others. Kearney (1992) provides estimates of the percentages of major disabilities in the United States; the findings are summarized in Table 8.3.

The following subsections describe the most common complaints that are received from disabled workers.

8.2.2   Parking and Building Access

For the mobility impaired and wheelchair-bound worker, a major challenge is accessing the building from the handicapped parking area. While many buildings have installed ramps for wheelchair use, they have not always considered other obstacles in the path to the building, for example, small bumps or joints

Table 8.3. Percentage of the US Population Suffering from Various disabilities

Category of Disability	% of US Population
• Mobility (ambulatory/wheelchair)	10
• Visual	5
• Hearing	3
• Other	2
Total	**20**

Source: Adapted from Kearney (1992).

can halt a wheelchair or affect its control. In fact, any interface that requires people to pass over a gap or step over a threshold or obstacle can be a problem for the mobility impaired worker. Foyer and hallway space may be too restricted to maneuver wheelchairs properly, and doors may be difficult to use.

8.2.3   Elevators

Proper design of elevators is especially important for the mobility and visually impaired worker.

The minimum interior dimensions of the elevator cab to permit a wheelchair to turn around are 137×173 cm (58×68 inches). The elevator floor-to-cab threshold should be at the same height and the gap between them as narrow as possible. Elevator buttons should be lowered so they can be reached by a wheelchair-bound worker. Unfortunately, most guidelines call for buttons to be mounted so low that they are difficult for standing passengers to operate. If legislation permits, a panel of buttons at wheelchair height can be installed on one side of the door and another panel for use by standing passengers can be installed on the other side. Elevator doors should remain open as long as required for the mobility impaired user.

The visually impaired worker requires special consideration in the design of information systems. Call buttons should be installed in the center of each wall of each bank of elevators. Cars going up should emit a single tone when they arrive at the elevator lobby. Cars going down should emit a double tone.

The doors of the cab should stay open long enough for the worker to find the threshold and enter the car. A steadily emitting low-frequency tone should remain on as long as the doors are open to guide the user to the elevator threshold. The illumination level at the threshold should be at least 50 lux (5 ft.-c).

Inside the cab, buttons for each elevator function and floor indicator should be in braille or raised numbers. The locations of each function should be standardized, and each should light when selected and extinguish when the car leaves the floor. A tone should advise the occupants as the cab passes each floor and the arrival at a floor should be announced verbally.

8.2.4 Restrooms

Restrooms should be designed to assist the mobility, visually, and hearing impaired workers. The entrance to the restroom should not be obstructed by small lobbies with doors on each side. The inner door should be eliminated. One or more stalls should be large enough for the wheelchair user to maneuver (173 × 173 cm minimum: 68 × 68 inches). Urinals in men's rooms should have a maximum rim height of 43 cm (17 inches). A minimum clearance of 76 × 122 cm (30 × 48 inches) should be provided in front of the urinal.

The top surface of one or more washbasins should be no higher than 86 cm (34 inches). Knee clearance should be a minimum of 69 cm (27 inches), and should extend back below the basin 48 cm (19 inches). A clear floor space 76 × 122 cm (30 × 48 inches) should be provided in front of the washcounter. One or more washbasins should be provided with levers on the taps.

The location and layout of restrooms should be the same in all parts of the building to assist visually impaired users. In addition, signs should be designed with maximum contrast. Male and female door symbols should be standardized and installed with raised figures.

Emergency signals should be audible within the restroom for hearing-impaired workers. For the deaf worker, a flashing light will warn him or her of an emergency.

8.2.5 Water Fountains

Water fountains should be designed for wheelchair access as discussed for washbasins. Controls should be placed on the front of the fountain.

8.2.6 Signage

Special signs are required for visually impaired users. Letters should be designed for persons with 20/60 vision (i.e., at 20 feet, a visually impaired person can identify the same size letters as a normally sighted person can identify at 60 feet). Maps need to have larger symbols and letters and for the blind, raised characters and symbols.

Talking signs are currently available to provide directional information to blind users. The signs provide location and direction information when activated by a small transmitter; the transmitter would normally be available from reception or security.

8.2.7 Other Design Issues

The disabled have mentioned many other facilities design issues that should be addressed, even though they are less important. In the interests of brevity you are refered to this chapter's references for further information.

8.2.8   Planning to Accommodate the Disabled Worker

The relocation team should address the needs of the disabled in the new office space. If the building is for multitenant use, the team must ensure that the owner complies with all applicable regulations in base building design. Responsibility for disabled design often rests as much with the tenant as with the landlord.

Designing for use by the disabled can be made more efficient by following the program steps outlined in Table 8.4.

8.3   MEETING AND CONFERENCE ROOMS

In every business people have to get together from time to time for a common purpose. The reasons for meeting together are varied and include:

- Training
- Team work
- Issue resolution
- Information dissemination
- Focus group interaction
- Audio conferencing
- Teleconferencing

Each of the above meeting types places different space, services, and equipment requirements on the meeting/conference room. The purpose of this section is to provide you with guidelines on the design and location of meeting and conference rooms and the services that each requires. When possible, the guidelines are formatted as tables and figures to make them more understandable and usable.

8.3.1   Design Considerations

In addition to the specific guidelines that follow, there are a number of general issues around the design and location of meeting and conference rooms that should be noted.

- *Room sizes:* Meeting and conference rooms are usually designed to accommodate different sized groups. For the purposes of this section, meeting rooms are divided into:
  —Small   (5–8 occupants)
  —Medium   (8–15 occupants)
  —Large   (16–24 occupants)
  Meetings smaller than five persons can generally be held in an individual's office. Meetings with more than 24 attendees require exceptionally large rooms that many companies do not normally set aside space for. They are generally held off-site or in the cafeteria.

- *Number of meeting rooms:* The number of meeting rooms of a particular size that your company requires depends on how your company operates. For team-based, open-plan environments, one small meeting room may be require for every 12–16 office workers. Marketing departments may required one small meeting room for every 5–8 workers.

Table 8.4. Eight-Point Plan to Ensure a Barrier-Free Facility After Relocation

1. Form the accommodation team:
   - Team should be composed of people who have worked on disability issues in the past. They need not belong to the project team.

2. Foster awareness:
   - Familiarize the team members with applicable laws governing barrier-free accommodation. Major legislation for disabled workers has been in effect in most jurisdictions for 10 to 15 years. [A description of the major pieces of legislation in North America can be found in Snell (1988), Kearney (1992) and Bosco (1994).]
   - Visit other facilities to observe how their teams handled their design issues.
   - Visit with members of organizations for the disabled to learn how experts view accessibility issues.

3. Hire a consultant who is knowledgeable about barrier-free access:
   - Many designers, architects, and general contractors are not familiar with governing legislation or have little or no experience with practical implementation.

4. Survey the facility that you are moving into:
   - Design of the survey should be determined by the standards in existence at the time (e.g., Americans with Disabilities Act Accessibility Guidelines, ADAAG)
   - The Building Owners and Managers Association (BOMA) has published an 80-page checklist that you can use to survey your facilities.
   - Use disabled consultants to help evaluate the facility. Ensure that they conduct a "walk-through" of the building.

5. Review drawings of proposed tenant fit-out to determine where access problems may be created, for example, by design and location of wayfinding.

6. Analyze data to:
   - Determine the cost of each potential accommodation. Cost estimation guidelines for retrofitting existing buildings are available from many organizations, for example, Public Works Canada (1994). Typically, the cost of disabled accommodation is less than 1% of the construction cost of new buildings.
   - Prioritize potential accommodations into those that are "readily achievable."
   - Determine the extent to which discretionary accommodations can be supported with relocation funds.
   - Plan those accommodations that will be paid for out of other budgets or implemented after the relocation is complete.

7. Design accommodation solutions that best use existing structure, layouts, and equipment.

8. Implement accommodations.

There are two ways to estimate your meeting room requirements. The first is a survey of past use of existing meeting rooms. The second is a survey of the group managers to determine their future needs. The latter survey should be combined with the space needs analysis that was discussed in Chapter 6. Open-plan offices are not designed for meetings. They do not provide speech privacy and are not always large enough to accommodate more than two persons. Hence as a general design principle, the higher the percentage of open plan offices in the total office space, the more meeting rooms are required.

- *Location*: Meeting rooms generally produce more traffic in and out than normal offices. Attendees may come from outside the building as well as inside. For these reasons, the relocation team should consider locating meeting rooms:
  — As close as possible to floor entrances to reduce traffic and the noise and disruption to other workers
  — Near restrooms
  — Near food delivery services and visual aids providers
- *Space:* The area required for meeting/conference rooms depends on how the room is used. Table 8.5 provides guidance on the area required per attendee for three major uses.

Table 8.5. Space Recommendations for Meeting/Conference rooms by function

Function	Area (per person)	
	Square Meters	**Square feet**
1. Auditorium style	1.4	15
2. Regular meetings	1.9	20
3. Classroom style	3.7	40.

- *Noise considerations:* Meeting rooms should be sound insulated to prevent workers in adjacent offices being disturbed by the sound of spontaneous laughter and chatter, or by the sound from video tapes or audio- or tele-conferencing.
- *Support areas:* Breakout rooms are often required adjacent to large meeting rooms to support team or training activities. Often large meeting rooms can be divided by portable partitions to create breakout space or space to set up buffet meals.

8.3.2   Furniture

Meeting room furniture should be designed to support meeting activities. Table 8.6 provides some general advice on meeting room furniture.

Table 8.6. Guidance in the Selection of Meeting Room Furniture

Furniture	Guidance
Chairs	• Equipped with gas lift height adjustment. • Reclining backrests • Seat pan does not tilt upward when backrest reclines.
Tables	• Rectangular tables are generally more space efficient than round or square tables • Should be able to be reconfigured in large meeting rooms. • Rule of thumb for small areas is that the length of the table, in feet, is about the same as the number of people that can comfortably sit at it. More detailed requirements are given in a later paragraph.
Counter space or credenza	• Provide for collating or for coffee/food services • Minimum size for small rooms is 60 cm X 150 cm (24 inches X 60 inches)
Storage cabinet or credenza	• Provide to store meeting supplies and equipment.

8.3.3   Services

Meeting rooms in the 1990's must provide more services for the attendees than those of the past. Visual aids are much more sophisticated than they were in the past. Video and audio conferencing are common, and the equipment is becoming portable enough to go into any meeting area. In addition, it is common today for meeting attendees to bring laptop computers to meetings to refer to data or for notetaking. With these changes in mind, services recommendations for meeting rooms are listed in Table 8.7.

Table 8.7. Recommendations for the Provision of Services in Meeting Rooms

Service	Recommendation
Power	• At table in a center-mounted surface distribution strips or under the table. • On walls around the meeting room
Data	• Located at the 'presentation' end of the room.
Voice	• Under the table for audio conferencing • At the presentation end of the room • On the credenza or counter
Cable TV	• At the presentation end of the room
FAX, Copier	• In office services areas located adjacent to (or nearby) meeting rooms • In the meeting room itself

8.3.4   Wall Coverings

The surfaces of the meeting room walls should support the way that groups operate in meetings. Table 8.8 provides minimum recommendations for meeting room wall surfaces.

8.3.5   Personal Space Requirements

Figures 8.1*a* and *b*, reproduced from de Chiara et al. (1991), provide the dimensions required to comfortably seat attendees in two meeting rooms configurations, one with a rectangular table, the other with a round table. The values of each of the dimensions are listed in Figure 8.1*c*.

8.3.6   Lighting

Meeting rooms located on the outside of a building have access to two types of illumination—natural and artificial. Recommendations for the use of each are provided in the following subsections.

8.3.6.1   Natural Light
- In the northern hemisphere, meeting rooms should be located on north facing walls to reduce glare and the solar heat load.
- Black drapes or opaque vertical or horizontal blinds should be available to darken the room when visual aids are used.

Table 8.8. Recommendations for Wall Surfaces in Meeting/Conference Rooms

Design Feature	Comment
Tackable surfaces	Tackable surfaces should be provided on the three walls surrounding the wall at the 'presentation' end of the room. The surfaces can consist of: • Full tackable surfaces between 91 and 198 cm (36 and 78 inches) above the floor. • Tackable strip, running parallel to the ceiling at 198 cm (78 inches) above the floor.
Mounting rails	• Run parallel to the floor at about 91 cm (36 inches) above the floor. • Grooved to prevent presentation boards from sliding off the rail as they lean against the wall.
Projection Screen	• Retractable ceiling-mounted screen at the presentation end of the room.
Marker boards	• On wall at the presentation end of the room

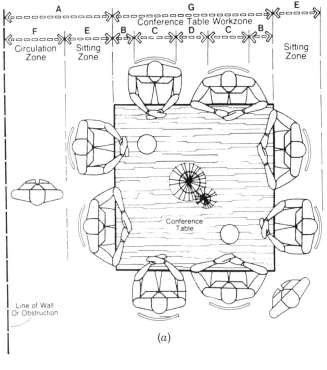

(a)

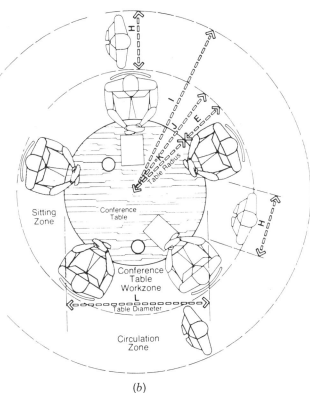

(b)

	in	cm
A	48–60	121.9–152.4
B	4–6	10.2–15.2
C	20–24	50.8–61.0
D	6–10	15.2–25.4
E	18–24	45.7–61.0
F	30–36	76.2–91.4
G	54–60	137.2–152.4
H	30	76.2
I	72–81	182.9–205.7
J	42–51	106.7–129.5
K	24–27	61.0–68.6
L	48–54	121.9–137.2

(c)

Figure 8.1. Space required to comfortably sit meeting attendees. (*a*) At a rectangular table. (*b*) At a round table. (*c*) Values of the dimensions. From J. de Chiara et al., *Time-Saver Standards for Interior Design and Space Planning* (1991). McGraw-Hill. Reproduced with the permission of The McGraw-Hill Companies.

8.3.6.2   Artificial Lighting
- Three independently controllable lighting systems should be installed in each meeting room as follows:
  —*System 1:* Ambient lighting above the meeting table to provide general illumination for meetings
  —*System 2:* Recessed incandescent or fluorescent wall washers to illuminate the three nonpresentation walls
  —*System 3:* Recessed incandescent or fluorescent wall washers to illuminate the presentation wall
- Separate sets of lighting controls should be located on the wall inside *each* entrance door and at the presentation end of the room (on the wall or on a separate console).
- Each of the three lighting systems should be dimmable from off to maximum intensity. The intensities should be infinitely adjustable or adjustable in four equally spaced levels (e.g., off, $\frac{1}{3}$ maximum, $\frac{2}{3}$ maximum, and maximum).
- For teleconferencing, in addition to the above lighting systems, a separate set of flood lights should be mounted above and behind the camera and directed at the attendees as they face the camera. In addition, "white" boards and camera units for hard-copy transmission should be equipped with separate lighting systems.

8.4   RESTROOM DESIGN

Restroom facilities should be designed to meet the following objectives:
- Ensure user comfort
- Ensure that all equipment is convenient to use
- Ensure user privacy
- Support sanitation requirements
- Ensure ease of use by disabled users

The purpose of this section is to provide the relocation project team with the human factors principles that are the underpinnings for the design of restroom systems. This section will not deal with the detailed design of the systems installed in restrooms. For design information, you should consult your architects or mechanical designers.

The remainder of this section will be in the form of a checklist that the team can use in design meetings with design specialists or to evaluate the completed facilities.

The facilities and supplies required in a restroom include:

- Toilets
- Urinals
- Washbasins
- Shelves for packages/briefcases
- Coat hooks in stalls and on restroom walls
- Proper lighting

- Faucets
- Hand soap
- Hand towels
- Waste bins
- Drinking water
- Temperate wash water

- Emergency lighting
- Signs and labels
- Toilet paper dispensers
- Sanitary napkin dispensers
- Sanitary napkin disposal
- Nonslip floors

 Principles for the design and installation of each of the above are contained in Table 8.9.

 Table 8.9. Checklist of Human Factors Principles in the Design of Restrooms

Design Area	Human Factors Principles
Location	❏ Between the entrance to the floor (e.g., elevator lobby) and the employees' workstations ❏ Near meeting and conference rooms
Washbasins	❏ Designed to be as self-cleaning as possible - contoured shape - waterstream directed away from drain
Faucets	❏ Single stream of tempered water (43 °C, 110 °F) ❏ Faucet stream should not splash on the user ❏ Require minimal hand contact by users (e.g. push to start, automated stop) ❏ Easy to operate (e.g. automatic on/off) ❏ Signs should be posted near faucets that have a novel operation to advise users how to use them ❏ Convenient for mobility-impaired users
Hand Soap	❏ Soap is dispensed ❏ Location convenient to the washbasin ❏ Location is convenient for mobility-impaired users ❏ Easy to use ❏ Can be operated with minimum user contact
Hand towels	❏ Paper towels are preferred over roll towels or blow dryers ❏ Towel dispensers located near the washbasin ❏ Convenient for mobility-impaired users
Waste bins	❏ Convenient for mobility-impaired users ❏ Located near the washbasin
Drinking water	❏ Available in disposable cups or ❏ From a fountain ❏ Convenient for mobility-impaired users

Table 8.9. (Continued)

Shelves	❑ Located inside the restroom entrance for large parcels and briefcases ❑ Located at each washbasin for small items that must remain dry such as purses, office papers, watches, rings and glasses
Hooks	❑ One on the wall of each restroom stall ❑ Several provided inside the restroom entrance for coats and umbrellas
Lighting	❑ Ambient (100 to 200 lux; 10-20 ft-c) ❑ Parabolic or directed light over washbasins ❑ Emergency lighting
Signage	❑ Directional signs to restroom located on the building walls ❑ Male/female designations on the restroom doors ❑ Informational, such as instructions to operate restroom equipment ❑ Designed for use by the visually-impaired user
Toiler paper/Sanitary napkin dispensers	❑ Located as conveniently as possible for the user ❑ Designed for ease of use.
Non-slip floors	❑ Floor should be made of material that does not become slippery when wet
Privacy	❑ Urinals separated by a modesty panel ❑ Toilet stalls provided with locks
Ventilation	❑ Outdoor ventilation rates of 25 litres per second (50 cubic feet per minute) for <u>each</u> toilet and urinal (ASHRAE, 1989)
Number of toilets and urinals	❑ Meets local building codes ❑ In the absence of local codes, meets the following minimum requirements:

Number of male or Female office workers	Number of Facilities	
	Toilets	Washbasins
1-9	1	1
10-24	2	1
25-49	3	2
50-74	4	2
75-100	5	3

NOTES:
- Additional facilities are installed when walking distance is excessive.
- For male restrooms, up to 1/2 the toilets may be replaced with urinals
- At least one disabled facility is recommended per building
- Consider both meeting and cafeteria capacity when determining the number of facilities to install.

REFERENCES

Arthur, P. (1988). Orientation and wayfinding in public buildings. Public Works Canada, Architectural and Engineering Services, Ottawa, ON, October.

Arthur, P. and R. Passini (1990). 1-2-3 Evaluation and design guide to wayfinding: Helping visitors find their way around public buildings. Public Works Canada, Architectural and Engineering Services, Ottawa, ON, Report Control No. AES/SAG 1-4: 86-15, March.

ASHRAE (1985). Ventilation for acceptable indoor air quality. American Society of Heating, Refrigerating and Air-Conditioning Engineers, Inc., Standard 62–1989.

Bosco, P. (1994). The ADA: Today, and tomorrow and tomorrow? Buildings, April, p. 62.

DeChiara, J., J.Panero and M. Zelnik (1991). Time-saver standards for interior design and space planning. New York: McGraw-Hill.

Ebrecht, M. (1989). Planning for change. Meeting the needs of the disabled and the elderly. Canadian Facility Management, Winter, p. 34.

Kearney, D. S. (1992). Meeting the needs of ADA Part 1: Reasonable physical accommodation and Part 2: Reasonable psychological accommodation. FM Journal, May/June, p. 35.

Public Works Canada (1994). Barrier-free design cost guidelines. Public Works and Government Services Canada, Catalogue No. P35-76/1994.

Snell, H. (1988). Barrier-free design—Planning and designing a facility for everyone. Proceedings, Canadian Facility Management Conference, Toronto, ON, May, p. 19.

ADDITIONAL READINGS

Arthur, P. (1994).Wayfinding is good business management. International Facilities Management Association, Toronto chapter Fall '94 Education Day, October.

Leibrock, C. (1994). Dignified options to ADA compliance. Facilities Design and Management, June, p. 56.

McWilliams, J. E. and K. N. Jensen (1995). Effective signage reduces confusion, costs. FM Journal, May/June, pp. 45–46.

Mumford, S. (1993). The ADA: Striving to comply. Buildings, April, p. 47.

Mumford, S. (1994). The ADA: How much is enough? Buildings, November, p. 31.

Owens, D. D. (1993). Facilities planning and relocation. Kingston, MA: R.S. Means Company.

Passini, R. and G. Shiels (1987). Wayfinding in public buildings. Public Works Canada, Architectural and Engineering Services, Catalogue No. AR 56B, July.

Petrino, M. A. D. (1994). Understanding the lessons of ADA. Building Operations Management, October, p. 24.

Rambo, R. L. (1994). ADA compliance update. Building Operating Management, May, p. 30.

Steelcase (1994). Design for disability. Workwell, Edition No.1, p. 28.

Terry, J. L. and G. A. Austin (1995). A problem-prevention strategy for facility managers. Building Operating Management, January, p. 38.

Chapter Nine

Implementation of the Relocation

════════════

9.1 INTRODUCTION

Up to this point in the book, we have been dealing with the myriad details in preparing for the move. This chapter begins a new phase in the relocation process—the move itself. The sections in the chapter cover all phases of the physical relocation and deal with minute details that could not be adequately covered in earlier chapters.

Each phase of the actual move is a logistical maze in which the relocation team can quickly get lost unless potential issues are identified and dealt with upfront. Once the moving trucks arrive, it's too late to plan.

The physical relocation is the most disruptive element in the project. If it is not done properly the fallout can be crippling to the credibility of the relocation team. Inadequate planning for the relocation and poor execution and follow-up to the physical move can:

- Increase moving costs
- Affect the productivity of workers, which in turn, angers supervisors and management
- Disrupt and anger employees
- Lower employee morale

To help the relocation team navigate the maze, advice for the relocation process is contained in the following sections:

- *Information gathering:* Addresses the people, the furniture, and the equipment

189

- *Planning the move:* Looks at the details of the move
- *Scheduling and tracking the move*
- *Working with the mover:* Examines moving, storing, and tracking the furniture and equipment
- *Preparing employees for the move:* Discusses how to provide them with the information they need to fulfill their responsibilities for the relocation
- *Supervising the move.:* Shows how to ensure that the physical move is successful
- *Postmove follow-up*

Many of the topics presented in this chapter have been introduced elsewhere in the book. However, this chapter deals in depth with each aspect of the physical move.

Many of the headings for this chapter are discussed in other texts and articles, but in an effort to maintain the human-centered orientation of this book, only those issues that affect the team and its clients will be highlighted.

9.2   INFORMATION GATHERING

The objectives of this section are to:

- Illustrate the importance of gathering complete information
- Provide advice on how to gather the data

9.2.1   People Information

Clearly, in order to relocate people, the relocation team must know how many people will move, what groups they belong to, and where they will be moved to. Each of these issues was addressed in Chapter 6 on office planning.

However, keeping track of the number of people who will move in each group may be one of the most formidable tasks the team will face. Unfortunately for the team, business goes on after the relocation is announced. Groups hire and fire and reorganize as the team plans and executes the move. The more time that is taken to complete the project, the more the organization will change from start to finish. In one relocation, for example, the employee numbers reportedly changed 13 times, and some people who were relocated at the beginning of the project were moved again at the end.

In Chapter 2, the need for a team representative from Personnel Coordination (PCoor), sometimes referred to as Human Resources was identified. In many organizations, plans for employee transfers, promotions, and staff reorganizations are treated as privileged information and are not voluntarily passed on to the relocation team. A PCoor representative on the team can maintain current employee counts without necessarily identifying people, thereby violating employee confidences.

9.2.2 Asset Management

Keeping an accurate track of equipment and furniture in an organization is an expensive and time-consuming chore. The tracker is often in the unenviable position of being out of the information loop when furniture and equipment is purchased, moved, replaced, or sent for repair. Often employees trade equipment or commandeer a chair or table after hours.

9.2.2.1 Justifying the Asset Management System

For high churn organizations or those contemplating a major relocation, a computer-based asset management system that provides an inventory database and tracking system is essential. It is used to:

- Assist in planning the power and data/voice requirements of new or refurbished offices.
- Determine the "size" of the move in terms of the number of pieces of equipment and the number of boxes required. (Note that employee books, binders, and personal items need to be inventoried separately prior to the move.)
- Ensure that the mover and the relocation team have the same count.
- Schedule the moves.
- Track furniture and office equipment into and out of storage.
- Determine the disposition of furniture, that is, whether to move it, discard it, replace it, or refurbish it.
- Identify furniture, by inventory tag, or by the room plan of each new office, so the employee knows if his or her furniture has arrived.
- Help develop a preliminary budget for the relocation.
- Identify valuable items such as antique or expensive furniture, art, or memorabilia for archives.
- Specify the manpower required to move large or cumbersome pieces or to disassemble workstations, some of which may be oddities that require special skills to reassemble.
- Identify those pieces of furniture and equipment that will require special handling (e.g., that will not fit in the elevator of the new building).
- Prepare budgets and taxes. Capital assets can generally be "written off" for tax purposes. Hence a program of continual updating can be budgeted.
- Determine compliance with standards.

9.2.2.2 Completing an Inventory

Many companies provide asset management services. They may specialize in such services or may be divisions of furniture or equipment suppliers. Many of the asset management providers have developed specialized computer databases. The relocation team should be aware that if they change suppliers, the database may no longer be supported.

To complete an inventory, the team needs to consider three things:

- The makeup of the inventory team

- The design of the asset management system
- The information that is obtained for each piece of equipment

Inventory Team. The team should be comprised of knowledgeable people. Resist the temptation of employing students or other contract workers or even the employees of the asset management company unless they have been properly trained to collect the data. Some furniture may require disassembly, other equipment may need to be discarded, and only those with proper training can make those judgments.

Asset Management System Design. The asset management system that is selected should have the following characteristics:

- It should use a commercially available database.
- Application programs (i.e., reports and search routines) should meet the relocation team's needs and be easy to use.
- It should provide a way of scanning furniture in the field and identifying it without having to access a computer at another location. Many portable scanners are equipped with computers and enough memory to identify the equipment owner or room location.

Information Obtained. Enough information should be available for each piece of equipment or furniture so the organization can relocate it and can identify it for financial purposes. Table 9.1 is an example of an inventory form that could be used in the asset system and that would satisfy relocation needs.

In some cases, computer tracking requires information about the capabilities of the machine (e.g., hard disk capacity, memory, fax/modem). These characteristics could be added to Table 9.1, or a separate database and inventory form could be created for them.

We have found that the initial inventory is much faster to complete if the inventory team is provided with a book that contains *photos* of each piece of equipment and a *bar code* that describes the equipment. The team member can scan the bar code corresponding to the photo of the equipment to enter it automatically into the database.

Each bar code label should be placed in a standard location defined for each type of equipment. That way, all team members know where to look when they need to identify a piece of equipment. The bar coded tag should also be placed in an easily accessible location.

An initial inventory of the furniture and equipment in a 50,000 square foot area can take as much as 175 person-hours to complete (Stern and Gordon, 1989).

9.3 PLANNING THE MOVE

Project planning is the umbrella activity that determines how each phase of the relocation will be performed and by whom. Move planning is a subactivity of the

Table 9.1. Data Fields Recommended for the Asset Management System

Asset No.	Location	Type of Asset	Make	Model	Size (LxWxH) m	Color	Condition P= poor F= fair G= good	Special Needs for Relocation	Market Value

project that identifies each of the minute details of the move, assigns them to the move team, and specifies the order in which they will occur. Move planning is typically the responsibility of the move coordinator.

Move planning and coordination can be contracted to outside services. Architects and moving companies often offer move planning services in addition to their primary services. Experience shows planning and coordination are given less attention by those who do not specialize in the field. As you might realize by now, however, this activity cannot be handled as an afterthought.

Move planning and coordination consultants can provide excellent service and should be considered if the move involves more than 100 people or if the needed experience is not available in-house. Consultant services range in price from $(US) 50 to $(US) 140 (in 1996 dollars) per person moved.

Regardless of whom you use—architects, furniture dealers, moving companies, or specialists—check their experience and references. If they are not successful, the damage they can cause to the credibility of the relocation team or the reputation of the company will far exceed the cost of a good consultant.

This section is divided into four subsections, each representing a phase of the move.

1. Preparing for the move
2. Preparing for move-out from the old building
3. Loading and transporting furniture, equipment, and personal belongings
4. Preparing for the move-in to the new building

Every effort is made to provide the information in forms that can be used directly by the relocation team (e.g., checklists and tables).

9.3.1 Preparing for the Move

The move team should be comprised of those people who have experience with the relocation to date and those whose expertise will be invaluable if and when issues crop up during the move. It should minimally consist of the following personnel, either on-site or on-call:

- *Project team*
  —Move coordinator
  —Move coordination assistants
  —Scheduler
- *Department representatives:* Involved in their own departments' moves:
  —Department coordinators
- *Building services:* At each end of the move:
  —Security
  —Locksmiths
  —Building managers
  —Loading dock/elevator supervisors
  —Electricians and mechanics

- *Moving company*
  —Coordinator assigned to the team
  —Furniture assembly personnel
  —Movers
  —Warehouse staff
- *Information management*
  —Voice/data technicians

Move issues that must be considered prior to the move include:

- Schedules
- Move-out, move-in checklists for employees, supervisors, and the move team
- Staging the move at each end
- Booking special equipment required for the move
- Booking elevators and loading docks at each end
- Notifying service providers such as insurance companies
- Preparing the old and new buildings
- Planning the transportation activity
- Establishing command and control functions
- Understanding by-laws for noise, traffic access, and parking
- Arranging for permits and licenses.

The following sections address each of these issues

9.3.2   Preparing for Move-Out from the Old Building

In addition to furniture inventories and tagging, which are addressed elsewhere in this section, other activities are required immediately before the move. These include:

- *Disconnections:* Voice, data, and electrical services must be disconnected from all furniture and equipment.
- *Disassembling and wrapping:* All workstations and oversize pieces of furniture will need to be disassembled and wrapped. Items of special value will also need wrapping.
- *Protection:* Carpets, floors, ceilings, walls, doorways, and handrails must be protected against damage.
- *Preparation of elevators:* All elevators used to transport furniture and equipment will need to be prepared. Passenger elevators should be equipped with padding, and ceilings my need to be removed to accommodate large pieces of equipment. The elevators should be under full control of the move team. Often, oversize pieces of furniture and equipment are loaded onto the roof of the elevator cab.
- *Provision of moving materials:* These should be provided to team members and employees according to the move schedules.

- *Cleaning up:* The old building will need cleaning after the move-out.
- *Deactivation of security alarms:* This must be arranged for.
- *Security:* Arrangements must be made for security and, if necessary, with the police for traffic control.
- *Loading docks and access:* These must be arranged for.
- *Coordinating dates:* Dates must be coordinated with building services or the landlord.

9.3.3   Loading and Transporting Furniture, Equipment, and Personal Belongings

If loading and transportation are not performed as efficiently as possible, back-ups can occur at the "from" location, and people will be idle at the other end. Moreover, the schedule may relax, resulting in the loss of loading dock and elevator privileges.

The route that the moving vans will use should be checked for restrictions such as:

- Construction detours
- Traffic obstructions (e.g., low clearance)
- Weight restrictions
- Turn restrictions by time of day
- Events that may produce traffic delays

Many companies count the number of pieces moving out of one building and into the other. This is especially important for secured files, valuable furniture, art, and other valuables.

9.3.4   Preparing for the Move-In to the New Building

The new building is typically the unknown factor in the move. Location of services and service panels, size and operation of elevators, and access through indoor hallways and doors require special attention prior to the move. More specifically, the move-in issues include:

- *Wayfinding:* This is important for both the movers and the move team. Until the open space is defined by systems furniture, the team needs guidance with the use of ceiling hung and wall-mounted signs.
- *Parking:* This should be arranged for move team members.
- *Layout plans:* These should be posted on individual offices; floor plans should be posted on elevators and strategic walls. The move coordinator should be provided with a complete set of plans.
- *Regulations:* The move team needs to know about any regulations governing access to the buildings, such as:
  —Loading dock restrictions

—Elevator availability
—Protection of floors, walls, ceilings, handrails, elevators

A walk-through with the building manager can pinpoint areas to protect and can identify existing damage.

- *Arrangements:* These will include
  —On-site security
  —Traffic control, if required
  —Deactivating security alarms
  —Cleanup after move-in
- *Preparation of elevators:* This was discussed in Section 9.3.2.
- *Furniture and equipment holding area:* A spot must be established to act like a buffer between incoming items and those that are transported to the appropriate floor.
- *Elevator service:* Arrangements should be made in advance for the movement of critical or perishable material.
- *Evaluation of access:* Both access to the building and the capacity of elevators must be determined.
- *Interface:* The interface between loading docks and moving vans should be evaluated.
- *Connections:* Voice, data, and electrical services will need to be connected.
- *Assembling:* Workstations and furniture will need assembly.
- *Coordination of dates and schedules:* Building services or the new landlord must be consulted.

9.4   SCHEDULING AND TRACKING THE MOVE

The relocation schedule is comprised of a number of subschedules that detail specific phases of the project. The move schedule is the most detailed subschedule since it must account for each activity, however minute, during the move.

This section does not address routine topics that are part of every schedule. Instead this section deals with the origin of schedule activities and provides the move team with a computerized aid to help make a very intricate and complex issue a little easier to manage.

9.4.1   The Weekly Move Coordination Schedule

Most phased moves operate on a weekly schedule that determines exactly who will move when, from where, and to where. The week prior to the move, the team has a good idea who is moving and where they are moving from and to, but the move has not been locked in yet. There are many factors that can upset move plans, including reassignments, unplanned team activities, or moves delayed from previous weeks because people were not ready or construction was not complete.

While move plans can change up to minutes before the move begins, the schedule typically firms up a week in advance.

Table 9.2 illustrates a typical detailed move schedule that looks forward approximately six weeks into the future. The columns identify the date of the move, the move number (if more than one on the same day), the group and department coordinators involved, the number of people who will be moved, and the from–to buildings and floors. Not shown in this schedule are the names and exact locations of the people moved.

This table underscores the nature of the detail available at any given time. Note that for December 5th, seven moves are scheduled in detail. But, for the period January 15th through February 7th, the data are still sketchy, depending on the completion of other activities such as exact employee numbers or the completion of construction. At the next weekly meeting, the plans for future moves will firm up.

9.4.2   The Evergreen Move Schedule

The number of pieces of data involved with the move are substantial. Each employee needs to know:

- From–to assignments
- Move dates and times
- Furniture and equipment assignments
- Departmental coordinator
- New telephone numbers

The data required by the departmental move coordinator includes:

- Names and locations of employees assigned to him or her
- Dates of moves
- From–to locations
- Equipment and furniture assignments

The telecommunications coordinator requires information such as:

- Employee names
- From–to assignments
- Move dates and times and input information such as:
  —Telephone numbers at each location
  —Data ports at each location

The move coordinator assigns employees:

Table 9.2. Typical Move Schedule for a Phased Relocation Among Several Buildings

Date: December 4, 1995

Chairperson: E.H. Wallper, 555-8338

Date (YY/MM/DD)	Move No.	Group Contact	# to be moved	FROM (Bldg/floor)	TO (Bldg/floor)
95/12/05	01	Fisher/Troffer/Tannenbaum	3	925/1	1310/7
	02	Fisher/Credit (Dept 5.5)	9	925/3	1310/7
	03	Nelson/Jones (Travel)	1	925/2	1310/5084
	04	Nelson/Kristoff/Farn/Mortz	3	101/3	1310/5
	05	Weer/Simmons	1	65/4113	1310/5080
	06	Aikins/Wismer/Chin/Leups	3	80/3	1310/8
	07	Moore/LeClerc/Woo	2	101/345N&S	1310/8
95/12/07	01	Helsome/Nyle- HR	2	925/3	65/3
95/12/08	01	Maintenance-/Denver	8	1310/6	1310/6
96/01/15	01	Marketing-/Joddim	70	1300/3	80/1
96/01/24	01	IM-/Martin	100	1300/2	YT
96/02/07	01	Business Information-/Reingold	4	101/7	YT
TBN		Credit-/Rath	9	80/3	80/1 (80/2)

Next Meeting: December 12th, NOON to 2:00pm, Room101-1711C

- "To" locations
- Move dates

The mover needs to know

- Employees who are moving
- From–to information
- Times and dates of moves

In short, each person involved with the move provides and/or receives data about the move, and these data are constantly changing. Under normal circumstances the horrendous task of tracking and updating the data falls on the shoulder of the move coordinator.

In addition to having the data associated with the move managed, employees, supervisors, and departmental coordinators expect to be told what they have to do to prepare for the move and when they have to do it. The next section provides checklists that are developed for each participant. Each is keyed to move dates and times.

The coordination and communication of these data can be managed by a database management system (DBMS). The DBMS lets you:

- Collect, organize, find, display and print information about the move
- Restrict access based on who is authorized to change the data and who can only read it
- Link the data to checklists that are sent to employees in hard copy or by electronic mail

The key to the DBMS is the linkage between the individual groups of data that are provided by each person assigned. For example, the information table used by the telecommunications coordinator might resemble Table 9.3. The telecommunications coordinator would be able to enter or modify only those data in the columns to which he or she has access.

At the same time, the space planner needs to be able to assign new offices to employees, and may need to access an information table such as the one located in Table 9.4. The space planner would be able to enter or modify data only in those columns to which he or she has access.

The departmental move coordinator is the beneficiary of the data entered in the preceding tables. He or she is able to enter or modify the data in the columns in Table 9.5.

The key to the ease of accessing this information is the relationship between the tables. Note that a common piece of information in each table is the employee name. Each piece of data about a unique employee is maintained in a master table to which some team members contribute information, while others just read it. The reports illustrated in the tables above can be accessed on a local area network (LAN) or can be sent to the participants in hard copy. If a number of

Table 9.3. Information Required or Entered by the Telecommunications Coordinator

Employee Name	FROM Location			TO Location		
	Building/Office	Telephone No.	Data Port No.	Building/Office	Telephone No.	Data Port No.

Table 9.4. Office Assignments by the Space Planner

Employee Name	FROM Location	TO Location

different people are entering information, LAN access is the most convenient, timely, and efficient way to manage the DBMS.

Appendix 3 presents the Evergreen Move Schedule, a DBMS that has been designed to accommodate the various people associated with a typical move. These include:

- Employee
- Manager of a business group
- Move coordinator for the business group
- Telecommunications coordinator (voice/data)
- Space planner
- Mover
- Move coordination assistants
- Building managers and staff

In addition, the Evergreen application file is provided on a disk that is included with this book. The file was developed using Microsoft® Access® and will require the user to have Access installed on his or her computer to use the application.

9.5   Working With The Mover

A number of excellent papers have been written about writing the specifications for a move (Farren, 1989) and choosing the moving company.

In summary, the bid specification should include the information that can affect your contract with the moving company:

- Number of employees to move (include those who may be scheduled to move more than once)
- Number of square meters (square feet) of space that the employees occupy
- Move dates and times
- Special equipment, such as computers or invoice readers, that require special handling
- The from and to locations
- Special moving problems such as elevator restrictions, loading dock restrictions, or traffic restrictions

Table 9.5. Data Provided to the Move Coordinator

Employee Name	Move Group	Move Date	Move Time	FROM -- Building/Office		TO -- Building/Office	
				Location	Telephone	Location	Telephone

The specification also outlines your particular requirements with regard to:

- Protection of buildings, equipment, and furnishings
- Provision of boxes and moving materials
- Move scheduling and sequencing
- Number of movers for each move task (e.g., assemblers, movers, truck loaders, elevator loaders)
- Special moving equipment to be provided
- Employee supervision

Finally, the specification outlines the financial conditions which both you and the mover will agree.

For simple moves, the provision of information to the mover, your special requirements, and the financial terms can be straightforward. For complex moves, which may take place in phases over weeks or months and may involve the temporary storage of equipment and furniture, it's much more difficult to specify employee numbers, move dates and times. In these cases the contract with the mover may involve agreement to general concepts, such as cost per employee moved, rather than agreement to detailed items such as checking time sheets or inventorying moving boxes. In many ways your contract will be written like a partnership that is renegotiated routinely as issues come and go. Many readers will not believe that such a deal can be struck in the age of suits and litigation, but you may have no other choice. A rigid contract based on checks and balances may not work well over the long term.

Stern and Gordon (1989) estimate the cost of a commercial move at $(US) 0.75 to $(US) 2.00 per square foot. Personal experience is about $(US) 1.40 per square foot (1996 dollars) for all costs associated with a large relocation involving multiple moves, furniture storage, and disposal.

Selecting the mover obviously involves checking several things:

- Ask to see references for moves of size and complexity similar to yours.
- Investigate the financial stability of the moving firm. The last surprise you need is for the mover to declare bankruptcy with his warehouse filled with your furniture.
- Check on the mover's insurance coverage and performance bonds.

Other issues that affect the lives of office workers and the relocation team also need to be discussed and agreed to as part of the contract negotiations. Furthermore, if your company is as conscientious about reducing injuries and illnesses as many others, you will want to monitor the moving company to ensure that their safety performance during your relocation is exemplary. Table 9.6 addresses safety issues that your company may want to consider during the phase of contracting with the mover.

The mover can agree to be part of the employee orientation and educate employees about moving issues. For example, the mover can advise employees how to help reduce moving costs by unpacking and returning boxes quickly.

Table 9.6. Guidelines for Reducing the Risk of Injury During the Move

A. Employee issues
1.   Provide moving cartons that employees can handle: a) Normal sized plastic moving boxes, filled with books, papers and other personal belongings can weigh 25-30 Kg (55-66 pounds) and are so wide that they are awkward to lift and maneuver. They were designed to move large quantities quickly, not for the safety of the office workers who have to fill them. The weight of cartons should not exceed 15 Kg (33 lb.) and the distance between handholds should not exceed about 60 cm (24 inches).   b) Plastic moving cartons are generally more stable than collapsible cardboard cartons   c) Ensure that moving cartons are equipped with good handholds
2.   Supply moving materials that are "user friendly":   They need to be easy to apply and remove and safe for skin and clothes
3.   Load and lift moving cartons at waist height not from the floor. Employees should be instructed to place empty cartons on a credenza, desktop or other stable surface when they are empty.
4.   Educate employees on how to load and carry moving cartons: a) Keep cartons close to the body while carrying them   b) Do not twist while picking up cartons or carrying them. Look ahead to ensure that the walkway is clear of obstructions.   c) Pack cartons so the center of gravity is centered and is as low as possible.   d) Unpack file cabinets and shelves from the top down, and reload them from the bottom up.
5.   Read the carton labels: Don't stack more together than is recommended.
6.   Don't try to lift more, or more often than you can. If you are sore or tired, rest.
7.   Use a stool or ladder to reach items on upper shelves. Don't stand on a chair or other unstable surface.
B. Mover Issues
1.   Use equipment that is provided to help lift or carry.
2.   If an object is heavy or bulky: a) Get help to lift it, or   b) Break it down into lighter or more manageable pieces before lifting it.
3.   Push carts, whenever possible, don't pull them. Pulling puts more strain on the joints of the body. While pushing, make sure to look ahead for obstructions or slippery surfaces.

As a partner in the move, the moving company can be encouraged to use their experience to find ways of making the move more efficient.

Movers can also provide services that are often required for large moves covering a long time period.

- Temporary storage is often required, especially if temporary office (swing) space is required.
- Furniture and equipment donations can often be brokered by the mover because of their connections in the industry.
- It may be possible for the mover to arrange for the sale of executive furniture.
- The mover may also be able to arrange the sale of furniture to employees. The sale can be conducted in the mover's warehouse on a weekend. The company may want to make the sale an event by providing food and drink for the employees and by donating the profits from the sale to charity.

In summary, your relationship with the mover cannot be adversarial. It cannot be based solely on contractual clauses and close monitoring. For long, complex, and potentially expensive moves, your relationship with the mover and his or her employees can vary the final cost by thousands of dollars. This is not to imply that contracts are unnecessary and monitoring is not required. On the contrary, one person from your team dedicated solely to monitoring the mover, and auditing invoices for materials, boxes, and time can easily save your company twice the salary of that team member.

9.6   PREPARING EMPLOYEES FOR THE MOVE

At no time during the relocation is it more obvious that this is a "people-project" than when the team is interacting with the workers who will be relocated. The team has four major responsibilities to the workers in preparing for and implementing the actual move:

1. Communication
2. Education
3. Easing the burden
4. Providing support at all times

This section provides the relocation team with advice and materials to help them meet their responsibilities. The guidelines and checklists that are introduced in this section are also on the computer disk provided with this book.

9.6.1   Orientation

The purpose of the orientation meetings with employees is to communicate and educate. The meetings should support the written material that employees receive about the move by reviewing and discussing it. At the same time, the orientation meetings provide information that cannot be addressed as effectively in written materials. Orientation meetings need to be held both before the move takes place (premove meetings) and after the move has been completed (postmove meetings).

The premove meetings are used to accomplish the following goals:

- Educate:
    —Train employees how to prepare their offices for the move by addressing:
    Timing
    Support materials provided
    Labeling of furniture, equipment, and moving boxes
    How to pack
    —Inform employees of records management policies and guidelines for purging old files and equipment.
    —Teach employees how to read office floor plans.
- Review:
    —Openly discuss the reasons for the relocation.
    —Review how the relocation will be accomplished, who is in charge, and when it will take place.
    —Review the support mechanisms developed for the office workers.
    —Review the workers' roles and responsibilities.
    —Respond to questions from employees on any topic associated with relocation.
- Inform:
    —Install mockups of the new office layouts or have photographs of mockups available for the workers to examine.
    —Demonstrate any new equipment such as chairs or office equipment.
    —Describe principles developed to move contents, furniture, and equipment, depending on the type of move that's taking place. An example of a meeting handout explaining such policies is given in Table 9.7.

To accomplish each of the above goals requires the presence of management and technical staff, which may include:

- Departmental coordinators
- Move coordinator
- Records management representatives
- Representative from the moving company
- Building managers from the buildings represented at the meeting

9.6.2   Purging Contents

Over the years, each of us accummulates files, books, brochures, manuals, equipment, and trinkets that are no longer useful. The packing and moving exer-

Table 9.7. General Policies on the Relocation of Contents, Furniture, and Equipment

---

1. WHAT MOVES FROM YOUR PRESENT OFFICE TO THE NEXT?

The following policies generally apply depending on whether the move is to an interim or a final location or whether you are staying in your current building or moving to another . Separate policies exist for asterisked (*) items depending on the building you are moving **TO.**

If you have a question, please contact [TBI][1] , your Departmental Coordinator, at EXT. [TBI].

Within Building Move

	Items that move to new office	Items that don't move to new office
Interim Location	- personal items - telephones - computer systems - desk chairs - guest chairs	- corporate art - furniture - white boards - plants - appliances
Final Location	- personal items - telephones - computer systems - furniture - all chairs - white-boards - corporate art	- appliances

Between Building Move

	Items that move to new office	Items that don't move to new office
Interim Location	- personal items - computer systems - desk chairs - guest chairs	- corporate art* - furniture - white boards - telephones - plants - appliances
Final Location	- personal items - telephones - computer systems - furniture - all chairs - white-boards - corporate art	- corporate art* - furniture - white boards - telephones - plants - appliances

[1] TBI = To Be Inserted by the relocation database

2. QUALIFICATIONS

Interim Moves
Every effort will be made to ensure that each employee makes no more than one interim move.

Furniture
Furniture will not generally be moved between buildings to an interim location. Exceptions include:
- Desk chairs
- Personal computer terminal stands
- Furniture that must move with the job (e.g. CAD workstations)

Table 9.7. (Continued)

Equipment
- Computer equipment and workstations move with the position/department, not the employee.
- Photocopiers do not move.
- FAX equipment moves with the Department

Corporate Art
- Corporate art is to be moved only by the Art Coordinator. It does not move between buildings
- Personal art should be packed in your moving boxes. If it requires special handling, contact your Departmental Coordinator.

Telephones
- Do not pack telephones. They will be provided at you new location.

---

cise presents an excellent opportunity to purge the materials that are no longer required. Both the worker and the company can benefit from throwing away unneeded material. Reducing the amount of office material means less packing/unpacking for the office worker and lower moving expenses for the company. Reductions of 40–60% of files and printed material are common during the premove purge sessions. The following information is intended to provide the relocation team with guidance and ideas about the purging exercise:

- Coordinate all purge programs with the company's records management group.
- Describe what to throw away and what to do with it. Do you keep binders and toss the contents? Do you gather old equipment for tax donations?
- Develop guidelines for the employees to follow.
- Keep the program light, make an event out of it:
  —Casual dress on purge day
  —Competition for the highest percent reduction, or the most weight discarded
- Advertise the event: What to throw out, where to put it, and why (recycling, dollars saved).

9.6.3 Move-Out Checklists and Materials

Orientation meetings, relocation newsletters, and office visits are extremely valuable ways to educate and inform the office worker about the impending move. These do not, however, provide the detailed instructions that the worker needs to successfully complete the move. Detail is provided by checklists. They advise the office worker not only what to do but when and how to do it.

The move-out checklist provided in Table 9.8 is an example of the information the workers need before the move. The checklist is part of a "moving on kit" that contains the materials required for the employee to pack and find his or her way to the new location. The kit could include:

Table 9.8. Move-Out Checklist

EMPLOYEE'S MOVE CHECKLIST

[This is one of four different checklists that will be generated by the relocation database depending on whether the employee is involved in an interim or final move or is moving within his/her current building or is relocating to another building]

Employee Name: ___[TBI]¹ _____   **Present Location:**
____[TBI]_____

Date/Time of Move-out: __[TBI]_____   **New Location:**
_____[TBI]____

The checklist that follows helps you prepare for the upcoming move. By now, you should have received moving boxes and a package entitled "Moving On -- Moving Kit". It provides you with the stick-on labels and pens that you will need to mark your furniture and boxes. Please follow the checklist and pack and label as you have been advised. If you have a problem, call your Group Coordinator _____ at EXT. _____, or the Move coordinator at EXT. _____.

STEP 1: CHECK MATERIALS
❏ Count moving boxes

STEP 2: LABELING

Be sure to label moving boxes before they get full (and very heavy). Do not do any heavy lifting. GET HELP.

All items you move must be labeled with:

    a. Your name [should be completed before the employee receives form]
    b. Your New Bldg/office No. [should be completed before the employee receives form]
    c. Number of the Box, e.g. "Box 1 of 7"

STEP 3: LARGE ACCESSORIES
❏ Separately label desk pads, glass tops and other items too big to fit into moving boxes.
❏ Separately label white boards, cork boards, and other wall accessories.

STEP 4: PACK BOXES
❏ Small items (paper clips, pens etc.) into envelopes
❏ Breakables: Wrap carefully in newsprint provided

STEP 5: ART, PHOTOGRAPHS
❏ Wrap small items in the newsprint provided
❏ Have larger pieces crated. Call EXT: _[TBI] and leave message -- name, location, items to be crated, new office location, when move will take place. (Please try to contact craters 24-hours before the move).

Table 9.8. (Continued)

STEP 6: COMPUTER EQUIPMENT

- ❏ Label all pieces of electronic equipment (e.g. VDTs, CPUs, keyboards, mouses, printers, FAX machines and copiers)
- ❏ All computer equipment - VDT's, CPU's, Printers, etc.) will be serviced and packed by IM staff or their contractors.

STEP 7: PREPARE FURNITURE

If you have CONVENTIONAL FURNITURE (e.g. desk, credenza), GO TO ITEM A. If you have SYSTEMS FURNITURE, GO TO ITEM B.

A. CONVENTIONAL FURNITURE

Desks
- ❏ Empty Desk
- ❏ Leave all drawers unlocked

File Cabinets - Lateral
- ❏ Empty completely
- ❏ Lock all drawers

File Cabinets - Vertical
- ❏ Does not need to be emptied
- ❏ Lock all drawers

Storage Cabinets
- ❏ Empty completely
- ❏ Lock doors

Credenza, Book Cases
- ❏ Empty completely
- ❏ Lock all drawers and sliding doors

Wall shelves
- ❏ Pack all items on wall shelves

- **If furniture is moving with you, the keys are your responsibility.**
- **If funiture is moving to storage or to another location, tape the keys as follows:**

Desks:	Inside upper right hand drawer
File Cabinets:	Outside front, top section
Credenza:	Outside front
Bookcase:	Outside, top front
Storage Cabinets:	Outside, top of door

Table 9.8. (Continued)

B.   SYSTEMS FURNITURE

All components of the furniture <u>must be emptied</u> including:
- desks,
- drawers,
- credenzas,
- bookcases and
- file/storage cabinets

- **If furniture is moving with you, the keys are your responsibility.**
- **If furniture is moving to storage or to another location, tape the keys as follows:**

Pedestal:	Inside the top drawer
Overhead Cabinet:	Outside front, beside lock
Lateral Cabinets:	Outside top, front

C.   MISCELLANEOUS FURNITURE
- Chairs: Label
- Coat Racks: Label

STEP 8: PREPARE PLANTS
- Label company plants on the pots. They will be moved by the movers.
- Take all personal plants with you. Movers will not be responsible for them.

STEP 9: KEYS
- Leave office keys in the door when you leave for the last time.
- Place special items belonging to the old office or building (e.g. washroom keys, special passes) in the cloth bag that came in your move kit. It was made to hang on your doorway.

[1] TBI = To be inserted by the relocation database.

- Packing instructions to reinforce the packing workshops that each employee attended
- Packing labels, tape, and pens
- A bag for keys, badges, and so on, that has been designed to hang on the office doorway
- A pocket card or brochure that provides each employee with the information that they will need to find and access their new offices, and to contact coordinators if they have a problem

The departmental move coordinator could also be provided with a package that includes:

- A list of their employees moving, the times and dates of their moves, and the from/to locations

- A move checklist that is developed to follow up with their employees. An example of such a checklist is presented in Table 9.9
- Giveaways, for example, a T-shirt or hat that identifies them during the move

In one relocation (Devlin et al., 1992) move coordinators were given a two-headed screwdriver (with logo) to disconnect computer cables.

It's important to note that Tables 9.8 and 9.9 could each be generated from the database supporting the Evergreen schedule that was introduced in Section

Table 9.9. Moving Your Group

CHECKLIST FOR DEPARTMENTAL MOVE COORDINATORS

The checklist that follows will help you prepare and assist your work colleagues for the "move-out" and "move-in". If you encounter any problems please contact one of the following:

FUNCTION	NAME	TELEPHONE
Move Coordinator	[TBI]	[TBI]
'FROM' Building Coordinator	[TBI]	[TBI]
'TO' Building Coordinator	[TBI]	[TBI]
Telecom Coordinator	[TBI]	[TBI]
IM Coordinator	[TBI]	[TBI]

Attached is a list of the office workers you are responsible for, their 'FROM' and 'TO' locations and the times and dates of their moves.

STEP 1: COORDINATE MOVE-OUT
Contact each worker, the day before their move-out, to ensure that each:
- ❏ has received their 'move-out' kits
- ❏ will be able to complete packing on time
- ❏ has received their moving boxes

❏   Ensure that floor plans have been completed for the new offices of each office worker.

STEP 2: COORDINATE MOVE-IN
Contact each worker the morning of the move-in to ensure that:
- ❏ Each has received all boxes, furniture and equipment
- ❏ Furniture and equipment has been located according to the floor plan
- ❏ All equipment is operating properly

❏   Meet with colleagues in Room [TBI] at [TBI] am/pm to discuss problems encountered and to answer questions associated with the new location.

TBI = To be inserted by the relocation database.

9.4.2. The database contains all of the names, dates, times, and locations that are required by the checklists. The materials are merely database reports that can be printed for distribution by the departmental move coordinator or by a member of the project team.

9.7   SUPERVISING THE MOVE

By now, the planning for the move is complete, offices are packed, and the movers are on the way. As a supervisor of the move, your job is to get everything out of the old location and into the new, on-time and without incurring additional expense. You have seven major responsibilities.

1. To complete a premove audit of both the existing and new buildings (or new floors of your current building) to note existing damage to floors, walls, ceilings, and elevators. Without this information and a sign-off by the building managers, your company may get charged to repair existing damage.
2. To ensure that floors are protected with plywood or masonite, and that the walls and wood trim are covered with cardboard and the elevators with pads.
3. To audit the movers
   - To ensure that crew sizes are as specified
   - To monitor hours of work

   Your report to the relocation team will be used to check invoices.
4. To ensure that the correct items move out of the existing location in the correct order and that they go to the correct location in the new building. Typically, the objective is to complete one floor at a time in the new location no matter where the furniture and equipment come from. You will likely have developed a color-coding scheme to sequence the move.
5. To supervise the disassembly and reassembly of furniture and the disconnection and reconnection of electronic equipment.
6. To ensure that all equipment is working properly, for example:
   - Workstations have power.
   - Telephones are connected.
   - Computers are powered and connected to their LANs.
7. To ensure that all spaces are cleaned when the move is completed.

To accomplish your objectives, you need the support of the relocation team and some basic rules to follow:

- The move should be supervised at each end. Supervision at the sending end could be provided by the departmental move coordinators who coordinated the tagging and packing of furniture and equipment.

- You should have been provided with the people necessary to make the move a success:
  —Security at each end
  —Someone who knows how all furniture and equipment comes apart and goes together
- All move supervisors should be in constant communication by radios or cellular phones.
- No deviations should be permitted from the approved layouts. The exception is if the furniture and/or equipment does not fit the space available.
- No one should be on the move site except those involved in the move. And those involved in the move should wear distinctive clothing or headgear so they will be easy to spot.
- No special requests should be made of the movers.

9.8   POSTMOVE FOLLOW-UP

The postmove follow-up has four major objectives:

1. Welcome employees to their new home.
2. Orient employees to new building, new equipment, and new procedures.
3. Ensure that employees unpack and check the operation of their equipment.
4. Identify and correct deficiencies.

This section is limited to the activities performed within the first hours or days of the move. Chapter 10, Postoccupancy Evaluation, is dedicated to debriefing all individuals involved in the move to learn how to improve the next relocation.

9.8.1   Welcoming Employees

Remember your first day in your new job? You met new colleagues, learned new ways of working, and you familiarized yourself with new surroundings. It was not likely a pleasant experience. Keep this in mind when your workers come into their new space for the first time. Here are some ideas to make them feel more comfortable when they arrive.

- Chocolates, flowers, and/or a small momento of the move on each employee's desk
- A card signed by the CEO
- Coffee and doughnuts with their new group

9.8.2   Orienting Employees

Employee orientations can be accomplished in at least two ways:

1. Orientation packages:
   - For each employee, providing information about the building, work policies, and the neighborhood. This was discussed in detail in Chapter 4. An example of an orientation package is given in Table 9.10.

Table 9.10. Summary of Topics to Consider when Preparing the Package to Orient Employees to Their New Building

Welcome to your new home

General information
- ❏ Mailing Address
- ❏ Main Building contacts/Telephone Numbers
    - Include a stick-on label with the major numbers that the employee can remove from the booklet and place on his or her telephone.
- ❏ Maps and floor plans:
    - plans of each floor that point out the location of the most used, or most important areas of the new building including:
      - Emergency exits and evacuation routes
      - Elevators: Passenger and shipping
      - Cross-over floors
      - Medical centers/ first aid stations
      - Health and fitness centers
      - Room Numbering conventions
      - Meeting Rooms
      - Cafeterias/ vending areas/ coffee locations
      - Tuck shops
      - Shipping/ receiving
      - Mail room
      - Library
      - Graphics and reproduction
      - Restricted areas such as computer rooms, finance
      - Parking

- ❏ Main switchboard Telephone/FAX
    - Hours of operation

Building services
- ❏ Building Services - HELP lines
- ❏ Computer HELP line
- ❏ Safety and security
- ❏ Meeting and events coordination
- ❏ Archives
- ❏ Copying
- ❏ Office Equipment HELP line
- ❏ Mail/Courier Delivery
- ❏ Health center
- ❏ Audio-visual resources
- ❏ Records control

Building Policies
- ❏ Mail delivery and pick up
- ❏ Meeting and function reservations
    - How to reserve   - Lead time required
    - Charge numbers   - On and off premises
- ❏ Building Access:
    - regular hours
    - After business hours
    - Parking

Table 9.10. (Continued)

___

❏ Courier	- visitors
- who to call, latest times for pickup	❏ FAX: Outgoing/Incoming
- Incoming packages	❏ Records control
❏ Safety and security	❏ Parking policies
❏ Smoking	❏ Fire/emergency procedures and drills
❏ Home numbers and addresses of employees	❏ Taxis for business
❏ Hours of work	❏ Mandatory and floating holidays

Transportation

❏ By car:	❏ By public transport
- maps to and from major roadways	- bus/subway stops
- show one-way and restrictions by time of day	- cost information

Outside services

Packaged as a pocket booklet that employees can carry with them. Should contain maps to services in the immediate area showing the location of the following:

❏ Restaurants	❏ Coffee shops
❏ Banks/ ATMs	❏ Directions to nearest shopping centers
❏ Dry cleaners	❏ Convenience stores

Local merchants may be willing to develop a coupon book with discounts to introduce employees to their services.

Move related, short term issues

Prepare a note that asks employees for their understanding and patience with a few last-minute difficulties that were encountered during the move.

❏ Services that might not yet be working, e.g. air conditioning, switchboard
❏ Last minute construction, carpet installations
❏ Furniture adjustments

___

- For supervisors, advising them how to welcome employees. Table 9.11 provides a checklist that supervisors may want to use to welcome new employees and get them acquainted with their new location and work-mates.
2. An orientation meeting. One variation on the orientation meeting that was reported by Devlin et al. (1992) was a scavenger hunt. Workers were required to find an item in each department, thus making them find each department. Those who completed the hunt received a wristwatch emblazoned with the company logo.

9.8.3   Unpacking and Checking Equipment

When the office workers arrive at their new workplace for the first time, they require some direction in addition to their welcome. Table 9.12 is an example of a move-in checklist that will guide employees on the completion of their move.

Table 9.11. Moving-In Checklist for Supervisors

The following checklist is designed to help supervisors welcome employees to the new building, orient them and explain any policies and problems that are specific to their new building or their new jobs

STEP 1: WELCOMING EMPLOYEES

❑ Greet the employees at the door or at the elevator when they arrive.

❑ Make individual appointments with each employee or advise them that a group meeting has been arranged. Tell them when and where the meeting will take place.

❑ Provide employees with a floor layout ("You are here") and show them how to find their office.

STEP 2: GETTING ACQUAINTED

❑ If meeting with employees individually:
 • Show them around the office
 • Familiarize them with the facilities and general procedures. Use the list in Table 9.12 as a guide.
 • Take them to lunch

❑ If meeting in a group:
 • Demonstrate the facilities and review general rules and procedures. Use slides or go through the orientation booklet. Use the list in Table 9.12 as a guide.
 • Explain any jargon used in the new building
 • Make employees aware of social groups active in the building

❑ Take your employees to lunch.

STEP 3: POINTS TO COVER DURING EMPLOYEE ORIENTATION

Locations

❑	Building/facilities	❑	Cafeteria location and hours
❑	Security office	❑	Where to get employee ID cards
❑	Parking	❑	Office supplies
❑	Medical clinic	❑	Mail rooms
❑	Coffee stations	❑	Lost and found
❑	Travel office		

Policies

❑	Security	❑	Charge codes/cost centers
❑	Recycling	❑	Safety
❑	Harassment	❑	Travel
❑	Smoking	❑	Business ethics
❑	Furniture/seating	❑	Dress Codes
❑	After hours/weekends	❑	Ergonomics
❑	Benefits	❑	Support for the disabled

Table 9.11. (Continued)

Schedules/Procedures

❑	Travel expenses	❑	Parking policies
❑	Fire and emergency	❑	Lunch and break schedules
❑	Canteen, coffee wagon schedules	❑	Mail and courier policies
❑	Computer passwords and logon access	❑	Staff meetings

The informal organization

- ❑ What is the culture and preferred working style of the group?
- ❑ What does the supervisor really expect?
- ❑ What is considered the best way to get things done?
- ❑ What are the roles and responsibilities of each group member?
- ❑ How do people usually communicate?
- ❑ Who do I call in the event of an illness or other absence?
- ❑ How does the performance review system work?
- ❑ When do people normally come to work and go home?

Support Systems - who to call, where to go?

❑	Computer	❑	Fax
❑	Telephone	❑	Relocation services
❑	Facilities	❑	Industrial Hygienist
❑	Child Care	❑	Safety Specialist
❑	Health Care	❑	Ergonomics Advisor
❑	Graphics and reproduction	❑	Copying
❑	'HELP' Desk	❑	Travel advances
❑	Meetings and events	❑	Travel reservations
❑	Library	❑	Visual aids
❑	Mail services	❑	Business cards

9.8.4 Identifying and Correcting Deficiencies

As the employees unpack and check out their equipment, they should be completing a checklist of any deficiencies that they encounter. An example of a deficiency checklist is given in Table 9.12.

The deficiencies identified by each employee can be quickly consolidated into a "punchlist" of problems that can be corrected quickly. It's important that a team of technicians remains on-site for two or three days after move-in to respond to the punchlist. The team should consist of:

- Movers and installers to adjust/repair furniture and equipment and collect boxes
- Building technicians to adjust air flow and repair lighting and electrical problems
- IM and telecommunications technicians to repair system and telecommunications deficiencies

Table 9.12. Moving-In Checklist for Employees

EMPLOYEES CHECKLIST FOR GETTING SETTLED INTO YOUR NEW BUILDING

EMPLOYEE NAME: ___[TBI] ____   **NEW LOCATION:** ____ [TBI] __

Welcome to [TBI]. The checklist that follows will help you get settled into your new office. Please follow the checklist and check off items as you complete them. If you have a problem please contact [TBI], your Departmental Coordinator, at EXT [TBI].

STEP 1: CHECK OFFICE
- ❏ Count moving boxes delivered to ensure that they were all received
- ❏ Check the location of your furniture and equipment against the floor plan that is attached to your office door.
  If furniture and/or equipment is not located properly, note on the 'deficiency checklist' provided and contact your move coordinator. **DO NOT UNPACK UNTIL YOUR FURNITURE AND EQUIPMENT IS IN THE CORRECT LOCATION IN YOUR OFFICE.**
- ❏ Turn on all equipment and check its operation. If the equipment is not operating properly, call your Departmental Coordinator and list problems on the deficiency checklist.

STEP 2: UNPACKING
- ❏ Unpack boxes as soon as possible
- ❏ Itemize any damage on the deficiency checklist
- ❏ Call EXT [TBI] for box pickup
- ❏ Remove/discard tags, tape, paper etc. in the garbage bags that are provided in this package.

STEP 3: WALL MOUNTING
- ❏ Mark the wall locations for wall mounting items. Use the sticky pads included in your move package.
  They will be installed overnight by building technicians. **DO NOT ATTEMPT TO HANG THEM YOURSELF.**

STEP 4: SECURITY
- ❏ Test all keys and passes included in your package. Call EXT: [TBI] if you have a problem.

STEP 5: GROUP MEETING
- ❏ Please meet with your old and new work colleagues for coffee and snacks at [TBI] am/pm in Room [TBI].
  Bring your questions with you.

Table 9.12. (Continued)

Deficiency Checklist

To be used on completion of the move to identify:
- Damage to personal or company property
- Items or equipment or facilities that are not working properly
- Items or equipment that are missing

Please complete the following checklist and submit the completed form to your
Departmental Move Coordinator: _____ Room: _____
Extension: _____

| Name: _____ Room No.: _____ Extension: _____ | | |
| Date of submission: _____ | | |
Description of Deficiency	Deficiency type - Damage (D) - Not working (NW) - Missing (M) or describe in your own words	If personal item, what is the replacement cost?

Please submit completed form to your Departmental Move Coordinator

TBI = To be inserted by the relocation database.

Finally, the move supervisor needs to check any damage that might have been done to the building. Be sure to compare any damage found against the original damage audit.

REFERENCES

Devlin, H. J., L. Howell, and D. H. Morton (1992). A moving experience. Proceedings, 13th Annual International Facility Management Conference and Exposition, New Orleans, LA, October 4–7.

Farren, C. E. (1989). Streamlined project management. Tutorial T:1, International Facilities Management Association '89 Conference, Seattle, WA, November 1.

Stern, R. M. and B. Gordon (1989). Making a move that won't mean your job. IFMA Journal, February, pp. 20–31.

ADDITIONAL READINGS

Becker, F. (1987). Managing an office relocation. Report prepared for the International Facility Management Association, November.

Cheikin, L. (1991). Moving the facility—What's it all about? Proceedings, 12th International Facilities Management Conference and Exposition, San Diego, CA, November 10-13.

Dennis, H. and D. A. Brown (1992). Merging and moving at Comerica Bank: Putting people first in a complex relocation plan. FM Journal, May/June, p. 42–44.

Engel, P. (1987). Corporate moves: Managing the confusion. Facilities Design and Management, April, pp. 64-67.

Himes, P. E. (1991). Effectively managing complex renovation projects within occupied conditions. Proceedings, Annual Meeting of the Canadian Association of Facilities Management, Toronto, ON, April.

Kamp, D.D., C. Neumann, and D. Woodward (1994). More than a move … A corporate relocation case history. Proceedings, 15th Annual International Facility Management Conference and Exposition, St. Louis, MO, November 6–9.

McDonald, J. H. and T. Huckfeldt (1988). Staff relocation: Reducing the hidden costs. Bank Administration, November.

Mortimer, B. R. (1994). Do you know where your assets are? Canadian Facility Management, June, p. 22.

Tuttens, N. (1990). Coordinating office relocations. CFMA Conference, Toronto, ON, April.

Whitson, B. A. (1991). The physical moves checklist. Expansion Management, Atlas/Guide, p. 55.

Chapter Ten

Postproject Evaluations

═══════════════

10.1   INTRODUCTION

In Chapter 9, the postmove follow-up was described as a period of time after the move was complete during which deficiencies were corrected. The follow-up is conducted after each individual move, whether of one person or a hundred, and could take one day or several weeks to complete. The follow-up activities were generated from deficiency lists that were developed as soon as the move was complete.

The postproject evaluation is different from the postmove follow-up because it is conducted weeks or months after the entire relocation is complete. It is not designed to fix anything related to the relocation, but to assess how well the relocation was conducted.

This chapter discusses the postproject evaluation under three headings:

- Why conduct a postproject evaluation?
- When to conduct the evaluation
- How to conduct the evaluation

10.2   WHY CONDUCT A POSTPROJECT EVALUATION?

The postproject evaluation is conducted for three major reasons:

1. To determine how well the facility is meeting the needs of its workers
2. To determine what parts of the project went well and what parts could be improved and how
3. To gauge the cost-effectiveness of the actions that were taken

10.2.1   Meeting Needs of Workers

If the evaluation is properly designed, it will not only tell the project team how well the facility is meeting the workers' needs, but will also indicate:

- What improvements to the facility should be made in order to satisfy the workers.
- How the effectiveness of the facility compares against that of others. This is termed "benchmarking."

Section 10.4 describes the tools available to satisfy each of the above requirements.

10.2.2   Determining How Well the Project Was Conducted

The postproject evaluation often focuses only on the needs of the users. This process is termed the postoccupancy evaluation (POE). It is also important, however, to examine the *process* of relocating to determine why the resulting facility meets (or does not meet) the needs of the workers and of the management team. In Section 10.4.2 a procedure for evaluating the relocation process is described.

10.2.3   Cost-Effectiveness of the Implementation

Throughout the relocation decisions are being made on hirings, move policies, furniture, and so on. The postproject evaluation provides methods of determining how good those decisions were. The result can be used in future relocations.

10.3   WHEN TO CONDUCT THE POSTPROJECT EVALUATION

Most experts in relocation agree that the postproject evaluation should be conducted after the postmove follow-up has been completed and employees have had an opportunity to become comfortable in their surroundings. This generally occurs 6–12 months after the relocation is complete.

If the evaluation is conducted too soon, the participants may be responding to local, near-term issues, which cloud their opinion of the total process. On the other hand, if the evaluation is left too long, the participants may have relocated once again or may have forgotten some of the major issues

10.4   HOW TO CONDUCT A POSTPROJECT EVALUATION

The postproject evaluation can consist of different processes that are conducted using different groups inside or outside of the organization. The type(s) of evaluations that are conducted are determined by the needs of the organization, the types of information that are required, and the reasons for collecting the data. This section introduces the project team to several different analytical processes that target the three reasons for conducting postproject evaluations:

1. Determining how well the facility meets the needs of the worker
2. Determining how well the relocation process was conducted
3. Evaluating the cost-effectiveness of the decisions that were made during the relocation

Each of the analytical processes stands alone, and each generally focuses on different aspects of the relocation process. A complete postproject evaluation would use several of the analyses to obtain a total picture of the results.

10.4.1   Meeting the Needs of the Worker

Analyses that have been developed to determine whether the facility meets the needs of the workers are termed postoccupancy evaluations (POEs) since they target the office workers. The objectives of a POE are to determine not only how the facility meets the needs of the worker, but what retrofits are required to fix problems. Depending on the analysis conducted, the project team may also obtain information that compares, or benchmarks, the new facility with other facilities. Benchmarking exercises must seek the same information to compare different facilities, so the disadvantage of the POE is the lack of flexibility in its questions. This section describes three types of analytical procedures:

1. Structured interviews
2. Focus group exercises
3. Questionnaires

10.4.1.1.   Structured Interviews
The structured interview is a one-on-one interview of a user by a member of the interview team. The characteristics of the structured interview are:

- Those to be interviewed are sampled from the facility's worker population. In the interest of accuracy, the proportion of workers in the sample from a particular working group, for example, secretaries, should be the same as the proportion of those workers in the workforce.
- The interview team is typically composed of worker representatives, members of the project team, and staff from building services. Interviews are best conducted by pairs of interviewers.
- Structured interviews are conducted by asking standard questions that the interview team has developed as a group.
- Because the questions are targeted at specific activities or results, the interviews will not likely provide data that permit comparison with other facilities.

10.4.1.2. Focus Groups

The focus group is also comprised of a diagonal slice of users in the organization, that is, of representation from different levels and different functions within the organization.

One process that works well with groups of users is brainstorming. During brainstorming, each group member creates as many answers as possible to a structured question. For example, the question might be: "What are the advantages (disadvantages) of your current workspace over the workspace that you had in the previous facility?" Questions like this can provide data with which to compare facilities.

The brainstorming process, to be effective, must encourage spontaneity and the generation of ideas and not be constrained by the makeup of the group. Attendees are encouraged to provide as many answers as possible no matter how outrageous they are. All individual judgment about the responses of others must be suspended.

The ideas that are generated should be grouped into categories of solutions that provide the team with direction for follow-up.

10.4.1.3. Questionnaire

The user questionnaire process is probably the most widely used method for obtaining data about how well the facility meets users' needs. If the questionnaire is designed carefully, it can also be used to benchmark one facility against another. If questionnaires are designed to be completed quickly and are easy to evaluate, the level of effort required to conduct an analysis is manageable, even with a large workforce.

In 1989, the Canadian Ministry of Public Works (Public Works Canada) published an occupant survey that permitted office workers to rate their facility on seven dimensions:

1. Thermal comfort
2. Air quality
3. Office noise control
4. Spatial comfort
5. Privacy: visual and voice
6. Lighting
7. Building noise control

The survey questionnaire consisted of 24 questions that were answered with a rating of 1 to 5 where, 1 = bad and 5 = good. A copy of the questionnaire is reproduced in Table 10.1.

The survey is evaluated by averaging the ratings from each respondent over each of the seven dimensions. The worksheet is reproduced in Table 10.2

In addition to obtaining the average rating to each question, and the average rating on each of the seven dimensions, the survey also provides benchmarking

Table 10.1. Tenant Survey Questionnaire

Date
ID Number

TENANT
SURVEY QUESTIONNAIRE

INSTRUCTIONS: Please rate the following attributes of **your particular desk location** in this building by circling the appropriate number between **1** and **5** that best summarizes your experience of working here.

No.	Attribute	1	2	3	4	5
1.	Temperature comfort	1 BAD	2	3	4	5 GOOD
2.	How cold it gets	1 TOO COLD	2	3	4	5 COMFORTABLE
3.	Temperature shifts	1 TOO FREQUENT	2	3	4	5 CONSTANT
4.	Ventilation comfort	1 BAD	2	3	4	5 GOOD
5.	Air freshness	1 STALE AIR	2	3	4	5 FRESH AIR
6.	Air movement	1 STUFFY	2	3	4	5 CIRCULATING
7.	Noise distractions	1 BAD	2	3	4	5 NOT A PROBLEM
8.	Background office noise level	1 TOO NOISY	2	3	4	5 COMFORTABLE
9.	Specific office noises (voices and equipment)	1 DISTURBING	2	3	4	5 NOT A PROBLEM
10.	Furniture arrangement in your workplace	1 BAD	2	3	4	5 GOOD
11.	Amount of space in your workspace	1 BAD	2	3	4	5 GOOD
12.	Work storage	1 INSUFFICIENT	2	3	4	5 ADEQUATE
13.	Personal storage	1 INSUFFICIENT	2	3	4	5 ADEQUATE
14.	Visual privacy at your desk	1 BAD	2	3	4	5 GOOD
15.	Voice privacy at your desk	1 BAD	2	3	4	5 GOOD
16.	Telephone privacy at your desk	1 BAD	2	3	4	5 GOOD
17.	Electrical lighting	1 BAD	2	3	4	5 GOOD
18.	How bright lights are	1 TOO MUCH LIGHT	2	3	4	5 NOT TOO BRIGHT

Page E1

Table 10.1. (Continued)

19. Glare from lights	**1** HIGH GLARE	2	3	4	**5** NO GLARE
20. Noise from air systems	**1** DISTURBING	2	3	4	**5** NOT A PROBLEM
21. Noise from office lighting	**1** BUZZ / NOISY	2	3	4	**5** NOT A PROBLEM
22. Noise from outside the building	**1** DISTURBING	2	3	4	**5** NOT A PROBLEM
How would you rate your overall satisfaction with your workspace	**1** DISSATISFIED	2	3	4	**5** VERY SATISFIED
Please rate how this space affects your ability to do your work	**1** MAKES IT DIFFICULT	2	3	4	**5** MAKES IT EASY

Comments

Thank you for your cooperation.

For enquiries about the results of this survey, please contact:

Name	Telephone No.

Page E2

Source: Reproduced from Dillon and Vischer (1987), with the permission of Public Services Canada.

information. At the time of publication, Public Works Canada (PWC) had developed a database that contained "normative" ratings of a number of buildings on each of the seven dimensions. The normative ratings varied slightly, depending on the size of the survey sample. Figure 10.1 provides the normative ratings on each of the seven dimensions for a sample size of 70.

Public Works Canada provides the survey free to the public. Their only request is that users submit their data to PWC so they can update their database.

Table 10.2. Tenant Survey Worksheet

 Public Works   Travaux publics
Canada   Canada

	Date of Survey	Total Number of Questionnaires Completed ▷
TENANT SURVEY WORKSHEET	Building Name	
	Address	

Dimension	Sum of attributes for the dimension	Mean scores
1. Thermal Comfort	1 "Temperature comfort": _____ (1) 2 "How cold it gets": _____ (2) 3 "Temperature shifts": _____ (3)	$\dfrac{(\,[1]+[2]+[3]\,)}{(\,3\times[\text{TOT}]\,)}=\boxed{}$
2. Air Quality	4 "Ventilation comfort": _____ (4) 5 "Air freshness": _____ (5) 6 "Air movement": _____ (6)	$\dfrac{(\,[4]+[5]+[6]\,)}{(\,3\times[\text{TOT}]\,)}=\boxed{}$
3. Office Noise Control	7 "Noise distractions": _____ (7) 8 "Background office noise level": _____ (8) 9 "Specific office noises": _____ (9)	$\dfrac{(\,[7]+[8]+[9]\,)}{(\,3\times[\text{TOT}]\,)}=\boxed{}$
4. Spatial Comfort	10 "Furniture arrangement": _____ (10) 11 "Amount of space": _____ (11) 12 "Work storage": _____ (12) 13 "Personal storage": _____ (13)	$\dfrac{(\,[10]+[11]+[12]+[13]\,)}{(\,4\times[\text{TOT}]\,)}=\boxed{}$
5. Privacy	14 "Visual privacy": _____ (14) 15 "Voice privacy": _____ (15) 16 "Telephone privacy": _____ (16)	$\dfrac{(\,[14]+[15]+[16]\,)}{(\,3\times[\text{TOT}]\,)}=\boxed{}$
6. Lighting	17 "Electrical lighting": _____ (17) 18 "How bright lights are": _____ (18) 19 "Glare from lights": _____ (19)	$\dfrac{(\,[17]+[18]+[19]\,)}{(\,3\times[\text{TOT}]\,)}=\boxed{}$
7. Building Noise Control	20 "Noise from air systems": _____ (20) 21 "Noise from office lighting": _____ (21) 22 "Noise from outside the building": _____ (22)	$\dfrac{(\,[20]+[21]+[22]\,)}{(\,3\times[\text{TOT}]\,)}=\boxed{}$

Page F1

Source: Reproduced from Dillon and Vischer (1987), with the permission of Public Services Canada.

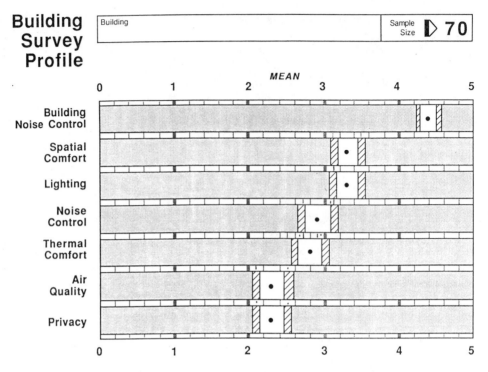

Figure 10.1. Building survey profile. Reproduced from Dillon and Vischer (1987), with the permission of Public Services Canada.

10.4.2   Determining How Well the Relocation Process Was Conducted

The best people to provide information about the good and bad aspects of the relocation process are the ones who took part in it. These might include:

- The project team
- The departmental move coordinators
- The contractors, including the moving company, the interior designers and architects, the general contractors, and specialist consultants
- Building services

There are many techniques available to obtain opinions from the participants, including interviews and questionnaires, but because of the variety of activities involved in each phase of the project, the use of standard techniques may not yield as much good information as other more specialized techniques.

One method that has been observed to work well is a modified brainstorming process that is used in conjunction with clustering and rating techniques. The method can be explained with the help of the following example, which I will call a debriefing exercise.

The purpose of the debriefing is to develop recommendations to improve the relocation process, in other words:

- To identify the constraints that were imposed on each activity
- To learn what must be changed in the future
- To record the activities that went well and should be continued unchanged

The exercise involves conducting parallel sessions (because of the number of people involved), each led by an experienced facilitator.

During each session, opinions are gathered on the three topics identified for improving the relocation process. Further structure can be provided by addressing each of the topics as they apply to the planning, design, preparation, implementation, and follow-up of the project. In other words, each of 3 questions can be posed for each of the 5 phases of the project for a total of 15 different exercises.

After each brainstorming session, the ideas are clustered under topic headings that are suggested by the ideas put forward. At breaks and during lunch, the results of each session can be posted so each of the groups can read what the others have developed.

At the end of the exercise a draft report can be issued to each participant, highlighting the results of the exercise and listing recommendations for improvement. Participants would be invited to comment on the draft. A final report is then presented to the management team.

10.4.3   The Cost-Effectiveness of the Decisions That Were Made During the Relocation

The focus of the follow-up process is the quality of the relocation project that was just completed. So, the judgment about how good the decisions were is best made by an outsider who is experienced in all aspects of facilities relocation.

Cost-effectiveness evaluations are typically limited to what the experts can see, hear, and experience. Data collection is guided by a checklist that is developed by the analyst after being briefed by the relocation team. The opinions generated by expert appraisal should be comparable to those generated from the employee survey, except that the expert's opinions are more precise and provide advice on where to target follow-up improvements.

REFERENCES

Dillon, R. and J. C. Vischer (1987). User manual:tenant questionnaire survey. Public Works Canada, Architectural and Engineering Services Technology, Ottawa, ON, Canada, Catalogue No. FM 4-b.

ADDITIONAL READINGS

Beaker, F. and W. Sibs (1990). Assessing building performance. Chapter 13 in F. Beaker (Ed.), The total workplace. New York: Van Nostrand Reinhold.

Farren, C. E. (1989). Streamlined project management. Tutorial #T-1, International Facilities Management Association '89 Conference, Seattle, WA, November 1.

Owens, D. D. (1993). Facilities planning and relocation. Kingston, MA: R. S. Means Co.

Parshall, S. (1988). Eight good reasons for a post-occupancy evaluation. Proceedings, Canadian Facility Management Conference, Toronto, ON.

Appendix One

User Evaluation of Office Chairs: Procedure and Experimental Design

A1.1 REQUIREMENTS

1. This procedure is meant to be used with the "office chair evaluation" form shown in Table 7.10.
2. Chairs selected for evaluation for a particular employee category should be evaluated by employees in that category. For example, typists' chairs should be evaluated by typists, not managers.
3. Moreover, employees selected to participate in the evaluation should, as a group, perform the full range of jobs for that category of work. In this way, the chair will receive a full functional evaluation.
4. At least six evaluations should be performed on each chair selected for test. This may meam acquiring two or more copies of each chair.
5. In preparing for the evaluation, it is essential to explain to each participant:
   - Why the evaluation is being conducted
   - How it will be conducted
   - What is expected from each participant
   - Exactly how each chair operates
   - Proper methods of adjustment

   Participants should not know which chair they are to evaluate until they are given the chair to evaluate. In addition, each participant should be asked not to discuss his or her opinions about the chairs being evaluated with any of the other participants.

A1.2   EVALUATION PROCEDURE

1. Each participant will be asked to evaluate two chairs.
2. Chairs will be evaluated in sequence: the first chair for two days, then the second chair for two days.
3. Each pair of chairs should be evaluated at least twice; once in one sequence order, once in the reverse order.
4. It is important that the order of presentation assigned to a participant be maintained.
5. Here's how to determine how many pairs of chairs you'll need for one category of chair and how to determine the sequence of test:
   - Let N = number of chairs to be evaluated.
   - The number of different pairs of chairs required is given by:

$$\frac{N(N-1)}{2}$$

   - Since each pair of chairs is to be evaluated twice, once in one sequence order, once in the other, the number of employees needed for the evaluation is at least twice the number of pairs calculated above.
   - Each chair should receive at least six evaluations.
6. Given the above, here's an example of how the evaluation might work:
   - Suppose we have four types (N = 4) of typist chairs to evaluate:
   —Herman Millar (M)
   —Steelcase (S)
   —Hayworth (H)
   —Sit-rite (T)
   - The number of distinct pairs is given by:

$$\frac{4(4-1)}{2} = 6 \text{ pairs}$$

   - The six pairs would be given by all possible pairs:

M–S	M–H	M–T
S–H	S–T	H–T

   - Since each pair must be evaluated twice, once in the original order and again in the reverse order, at least 12 participants need to be selected.
   - The participants would be assigned to chair types as follows:

		Order of Evaluation	
Pair	Participant	First	Second
1	1	M	S
	2	S	M
2	3	M	H
	4	H	M

Pair	Participant	Order of Evaluation	
		First	Second
3	5	M	T
	6	T	M
4	7	S	H
	8	H	S
5	9	S	T
	10	T	S
6	11	H	T
	12	T	H

- Considering the above, each chair would be evaluated six times. But, if any fewer than four different models of chair are to be evaluated, the above design would not result in six evaluations per chair. So, at least two employees would have to be selected for each pair sequence.
- Suppose, for example, you have only three chairs to be evaluated (e.g., M, S, and T). The number of distinct pairs is given by:

$$\frac{3(2)}{2} = 3$$

The pairs would be: M–S, M–T and S–T. If each pair is evaluated twice:

M–S	M–T	S–T
S–M	T–M	T–S

each chair would be evaluated only four times. However, with two employees evaluating each chair sequence, each chair would be evaluated eight times, as follows:

Pair	Participant	Order of Evaluation	
		First	Second
1	1	M	S
	2	S	M
1	3	M	S
	4	S	M
2	5	M	T
	6	T	M
2	7	M	T
	8	T	M
3	9	S	T
	10	T	S
3	11	S	T
	12	T	S

- Each chair will be evaluated by having each employee complete the office chair evaluation form at the end of the two-day evaluation period.
- The score obtained by each chair is determined by summing the individual scores that are assigned in each row of the evaluation form.
- The chair that ranks highest in the evaluation is the one receiving the highest total score; the least preferred is the one receiving the lowest total score.

Appendix Two

Using the Diskette to Access Electronic Files of Tables and Figures

======

A2.1   INTRODUCTION

Many of the tables and figures contained in this book will be useful to the relocation team during their projects. Each of the tables and figures listed in Table A2 below has been copied to the diskette that accompanies this text.

Table A2 is divided into four columns. The first column lists the table or figure number in the text. The format Table *X.Y* means the Table *Y* in Chapter *X*. The second column lists the name of each figure or table as it appears in the text. The third column lists the book page on which each table or figure is located. The fourth column lists the name of the file in which each table and figure is stored in the accompanying diskette.

A2.2   HOW TO USE THE FILES

Each table and figure is stored in a file that is formatted in Microsoft® Word® Version 6.0.

A2.2.1 System Requirements

- IBM PC or compatible computer running Windows 3.1 or later
- 3.5" floppy disk drive

Table and Figures:

- Word version 6.0 or higher or other word processor capable of reading Word 6.0 files.

Table A.2. *Listing of Selected Tables and Figures That Have Been Stored in Word 6.0 Files in the Diskette That Accompanies This Book*

Table or Figure Number	Name of Table or Figure	Page Location in the Text	Filename
Table 2.1	Assigning Project Activities to Project Team Members	21	TBL_2-1.DOC
Table 3.3	Office Location Survey	36	TBL_3-3.DOC
Table 7.1	Advantages and Disadvantages of Conventional and Systems Furniture	119	TBL_7-1.DOC
Table 7.2	When to Provide Continuously or Intermittently Adjustable Furniture	122	TBL_7-2.DOC
Table 7.3	Job Types Corresponding to Office Activities	127	TBL_7-3.DOC
Table 7.4	Furniture that Would Support Selected Office Activities	128	TBL_7-4.DOC
Table 7.5	Preferred Settings for a VDT Workstation Versus Recommended Settings	133	TBL_7-5.DOC
Table 7.6	Workstation Needs Assessment	137	TBL_7-6.DOC
Table 7.7	Selection Criteria for Furniture Systems	142	TBL_7-7.DOC
Table 7.8	Recommended Dimensions and Adjustment Ranges in cm (inches) for Office Chairs (Refer to Figure 7.18 for Dimension Definitions)	150	TBL_7-8.DOC
Table 7.9	Office Chair Evaluation Procedures	152	TBL_7-9.DOC
Table 7.10	Office Chair Evaluation Form	154	TBL_7-10.DOC
Table 7.11	Storage Checklist for Office Workers	159	TBL_7-11.DOC
Table 7.12	Design Recommendations for Keyboard Keepers and Wrist Rests	161	TBL_7-12.DOC
Table 8.1	Checklist Evaluation of the Interior Wayfinding System	168	TBL_8-1.DOC
Table 8.2	Design Considerations for Different Wayfinding Components	173	TBL_8-2.DOC
Table 8.4	Eight Point Plan to Ensure a Barrier-Free Facility After Relocation	179	TBL_8-4.DOC
Table 8.5	Space Recommendations for Meeting/Conference Rooms by Function	180	TBL_8-5.DOC
Table 8.6	Guidance in the Selection of Meeting Room Furniture	181	TBL_8-6.DOC
Table 8.7	Recommendations for the Provision of Services in Meeting Rooms	181	TBL_8-7.DOC
Table 8.8	Recommendations for Wall Surfaces in Meeting/Conference Rooms	182	TBL_8-8.DOC
Table 8.9	Checklist of Human Factors principles in the Design of Restrooms	185	TBL_8-9.DOC

Table A.2. *(Continued)*

Table or Figure Number	Name of Table or Figure	Page Location in the Text	Filename
Table 9.2	Typical Move Schedule for a Phased Relocation Among Several Buildings	199	TBL_9-2.DOC
Table 9.3	Information Required or Entered by the Telecommunications Coordinator	201	TBL_9-3.DOC
Table 9.4	Office Assignments by the Space Planner	202	TBL_9-4.DOC
Table 9.5	Data Provided to the Move Coordinator	203	TBL_9-5.DOC
Table 9.6	Guidelines for Reducing the Risk of Injury During the Move	205	TBL_9-6.DOC
Table 9.7	General Policies on the Relocation of Contents, Furniture, and Equipment	208	TBL_9-7.DOC
Table 9.8	Move-Out Checklist	212	TBL_9-8.DOC
Table 9.9	Moving Your Group	213	TBL_9-9.DOC
Table 9.10	Summary of Topics to Consider when Preparing the Package to Orient Employees to Their New Building.	216	TBL_9-10.DOC
Table 9.11	Moving-In Checklist for Supervisors	218	TBL_9-11.DOC
Table 9.12	Moving-In Checklist for Employees	220	TBL_9-12.DOC
Figure 4.1	An example of a relocation newsletter.	44	FIG_4-1.DOC
Figure 4.2	A "Welcome" card for the newly relocated employee.	48	FIG_4-2.DOC

Evergreen Move Schedule (discussed in depth in Appendix Three):

- Microsoft® Access® version 2.0

A2.2.2 Installing the Diskette

The installation program copies files from the diskette to your hard drive in the default directory **C:\RELOCATE.** To run the installation program do the following:

1. Insert the disk into the floppy drive of your computer.
2. In Windows 3.1, choose File, Run in Program Manager and type **A:\INSTALL.** In Windows 95, choose Run from the Start Menu and type **A:\INSTALL.** Click OK to start the installation program.
3. The default destination drive and directory is **C:\RELOCATE.** If you wish to change the default destination, you may do so now. Follow the instructions on the screen.

4. The installation program will copy all files to your hard drive in the default directory or the user-designated directory.

You should use the files installed on your hard drive in order to keep the original files on the diskette intact. To access each table or figure file:

- Open Word 6.0.
- Insert the diskette that accompanies this book into the a: or b: drive.
- Click on the File in the toolbar to display a menu or command.
- Click on Open (CTRL+O) to display the files in the active disk drive.
- Click on the down arrow in the Drives: window.
- Click on the c: drive and double click on the C:\RELOCATE Directory.
- Double-click on the file name that you select in Column 4 of Table A2.
- Print or Edit the file as desired.

A2.2.3 User Assistance and Information

John Wiley & Sons, Inc. is pleased to provide assistance to users of this disk package. If you have questions or problems, please call our technical support number at (212) 850-6194 between 9AM and 4PM Eastern Standard Time, Monday through Friday.

To place additional orders or to request information about other Wiley products, please call (800) 879-4539.

Appendix Three

Using the Evergreen Move Schedule Template

A3.1 INTRODUCTION

The Evergreen move schedule was developed to solve the communications issue that invariably arises between the members of the project team when they are in the throes of the relocation. The schedule is written as a relational database, which means that the relocation information in a table that is used by one member of the team is 'linked' to the information that is used in another table by another member of the relocation team. Both tables are in the database. The beauty of a relational database is that when you change the information in one table, the same information changes in every other linked table. If, for example, a new office worker is added to a particular move date by the move coordinator, the new worker and all of his or her information will automatically be copied into the table that is used by the departmental coordinator who is responsible for that particular move. No more hand preparation of individual schedules by team members from a "master" schedule controlled by the move coordinator. With the Evergreen schedule, the subschedules are updated immediately and automatically.

The key to the design of a database is the linkages that must be developed between individual tables. When we review the design of the Evergreen schedule, the linkages will become apparent.

The Evergreen schedule that is contained in the enclosed diskette is written using the Microsoft® Access® version 2.0 database, so you need to have Access on your computer and you need to know something about using the software. See Section A2.2.2 for instructions on installing the diskette. Access comes with a tutorial, which can make you a knowledgeable users with a few hours of effort.

The following review will show you how to use the Evergreen schedule that has been developed for this text. The tables and report in the schedule are very rudimentary. I assume that you will want to develop new tables, queries, and reports for your own use. Consequently, the tables in the file have been kept simple on purpose so they can demonstrate a principle rather than serve a particular need.

If you have Access on your computer, you might want to load the file EVRGREEN.MDB from the enclosed disk and follow along with this review.

A3.2   REVIEWING THE EVERGREEN DATABASE

When you open Access, your screen will look like that of any other Microsoft application.

1. Click on File in the toolbar.
2. Click on Open Database.
3. Select c: drive and double click on the C:\RELOCATE directory.
4. Double-click on EVRGREEN.MDB

The screen illustrated in Figure A3.1 will show on your monitor.

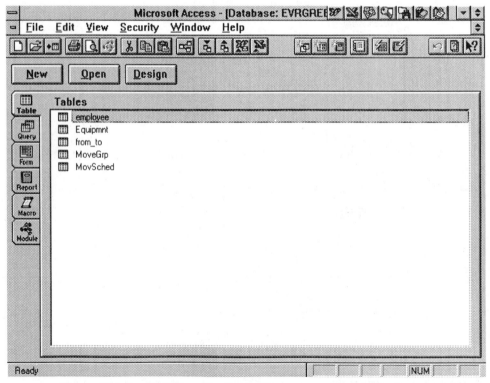

Figure A3.1 Screen listing tables for the Evergreen move schedule database.

Five tables have been developed for use by the relocation team. These may be previewed by double-clicking on any of the five. Each table is reproduced below as Tables A3.1 through A3.5.

Table A3.1 is the main employee information table. It lists the characteristics of each employee, such as his or her location and departmental affiliation.

Table A3.2 lists the equipment that each employee owns. The link between Tables A3.1 and A3.2 is the employee identification (ID) number.

Table A3.3 is the "from-to" list for each employee. It lists the current location of each employee (identified by his or her employee number) and the location to which that employee is scheduled to move.

Table A3.1. Building the List of Employees for the Move Schedule

Employee ID#	Last Name	Initials	Common	Electronic	Relocation	Depart	Division	Group	Buil	Room	Company
12345	empl_1	m.a.	Marie	MAEMP1	Coor_1	TECH	ELECT	business	B1	228	555-6301
23456	empl_2	n.j.	Neil	NJEMP2	Coor_2	Bus	I.H.	Field	C	917	555-6008
34567	empl_3	J.L.	John	JLEMP3	Coor_3	Bus	Mgmt	--	A	214	555-6292
45678	empl_4	D.J.	David	DJEMP4	Coor_4	TECH	MECH	field	C	1057	555-6316
5678	empl_5	D.E.	Delf	DEEMP5	Coor_5	Bus	I.H.	Lab	B2	142	555-6034

Table A3.2. Building the List of Equipment for the Move Schedule

Employee ID #	Workstation (Y/N)	Chair (Y/N)	Other furniture	Phone (Y/N)	Files (Y/N)
12345	y	y	n	n	y
23456	y	y	y	y	n
34567	n	y	y	n	y
45678	y	y	y	n	y
56789	n	y	y	y	n

Table A3.3. Building the "From-To" List for Each Employee

Employee Id #	From Building	From Room	To Building	To Room	From Telephone	To Telephone	From Computer	To Computer
12345	B	228	C	180	6301	6005	CC1	CD1
23456	C	917	A	614	6008	6602	CD6	BC3
34567	B	214	B	223	6292	6664	BC4	AA9
45678	C	1057	C	667	6316	6060	CC5	DD3
56789	B	142	A	222	6034	6118	AD3	CC7

Table A3.4. Assigning Employees to "Move Groups"

Employee ID #	Move Group #
12345	1
23456	2
34567	1
45678	3
56789	2

Table A3.5. Move Schedule List Developed by Access

Move Group	Move Date	Move Time
1	23-Jul-95	4:30 pm
2	05-Aug-95	3:30 pm
3	04-Aug-95	5:00pm

Employees are generally moved in groups at the same time. So, each member in the same "move group" would have the same move date and, with minor exceptions, the same move time. Table A3.4 assigns a move group to each employee, and Table A3.5 assigns the time and date of the relocation of each "move group."

Figure A3.2 shows the queries lists. Queries are items that any user can design to look at particular information in the database. In this case, only one query was entered. Double-clicking on "schedmove" gives you Table A3.6, which provides the move dates and times of selected employees.

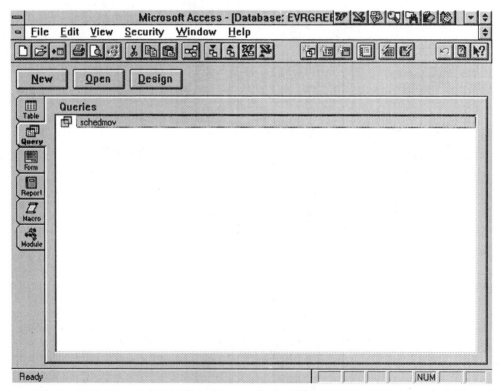

Figure A3.2. Screen showing list of queries designed for the Evergreen move schedule database.

Table A3.6. Building a Master Move Schedule Under "Queries"

Move Group #	Last Name	Initials	Move Date	Move Time
1	empl_3	J.L.	23-Jul-95	4:30 pm
1	empl_1	m.a.	23-Jul-95	4:30 pm
2	empl_2	n.j.	05-Aug-95	3:30 pm
3	empl_4	D.J.	04-Aug-95	5:00pm

Figure A3.3 lists the individual forms that have been developed to provide information for the database. The five forms listed are shown in Figures A3.4 through A3.8.

Figure A3.9 lists the reports that have been custom designed for this relocation. Individual reports would be designed for each member of the relocation team. These would provide the team members with only the information that they need to outline their part in the relocation. In fact, reports could be developed for each employee who is relocating. These could be sent to the employee one week before the move. In this example, one report titled "Equipment" (Figure A3.10) has been designed.

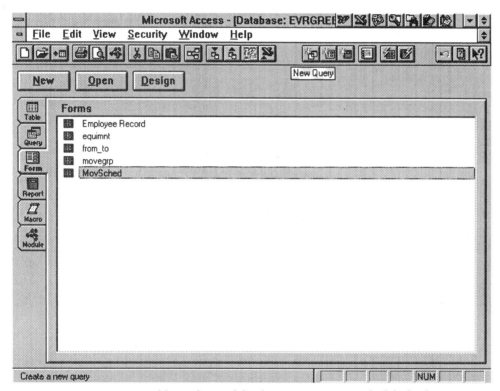

Figure A3.3. List of forms designed for the Evergreen move schedule database.

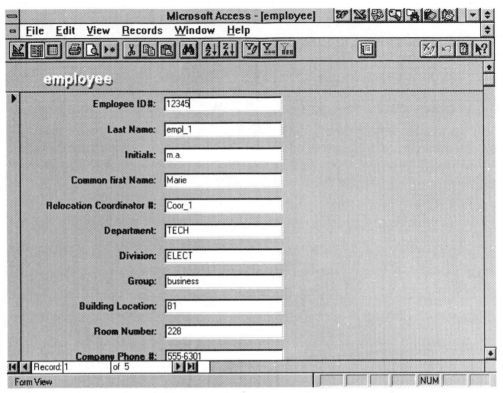

Figure A3.4. Employee data form.

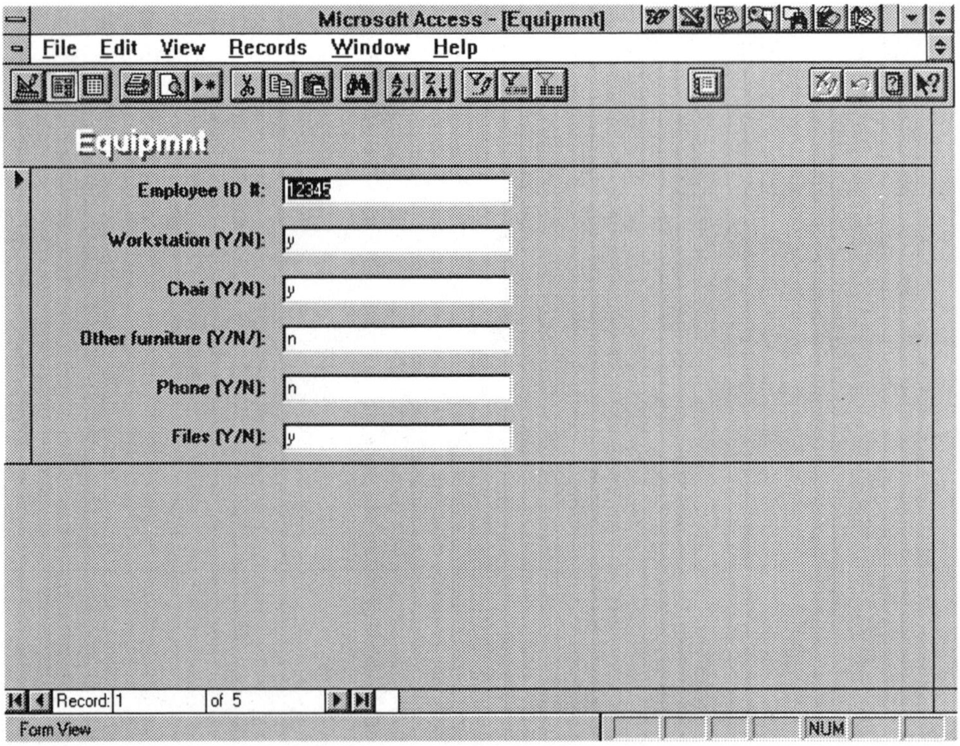

Figure A3.5. Equipment listing for each employee.

246

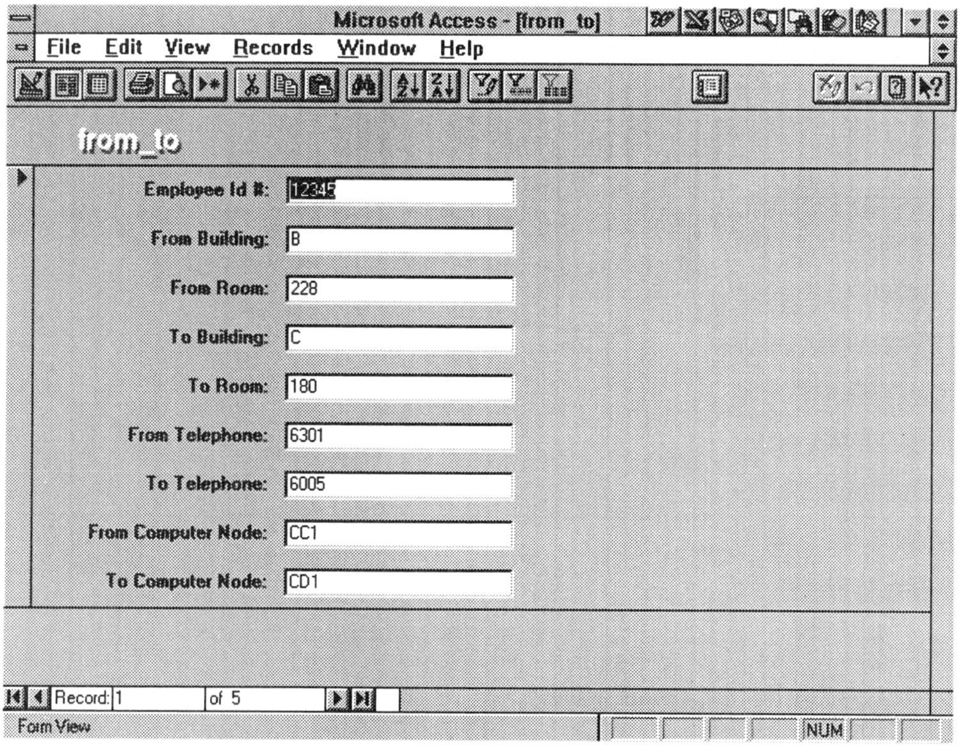

Figure A3.6. "From-to" information for each employee.

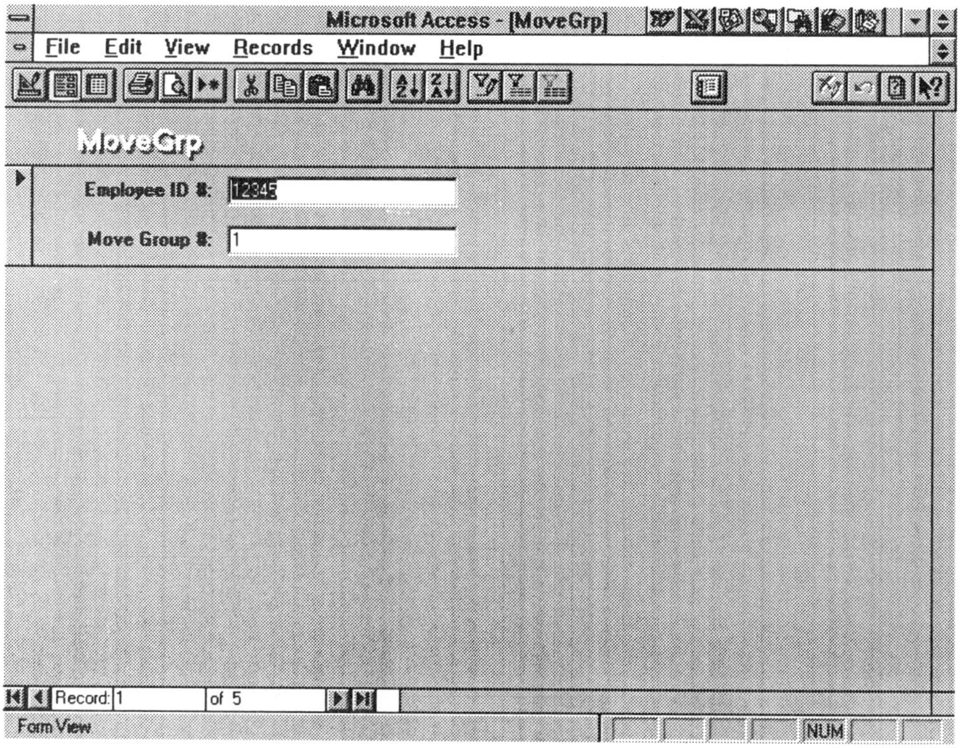

Figure A3.7 Move group form for each employee.

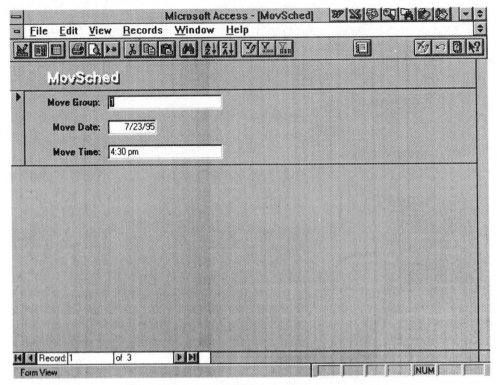

Figure A3.8 Move schedule for each move group.

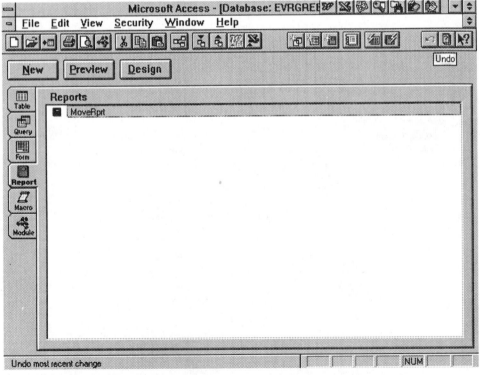

Figure A3.9. Reports list built for the Evergreen move schedule database.

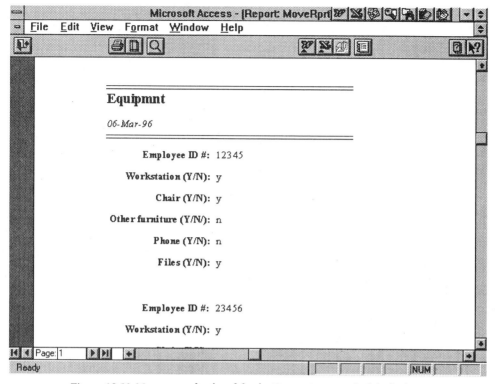

Figure A3.10 Move report developed for the Evergreen move schedule database.

A3.3   CONCLUSION

The above tables and figures illustrate the use of the Evergreen move schedule. You may want to modify the figures and tables provided or customize materials for your own use.

Clearly, the most flexible implementation of a database like the Evergreen move schedule is to load it onto a LAN so each member of the team can access the information from his or her own workstation. Otherwise the burden of updating the database and distributing reports falls on the person who "owns" the database.

Glossary

Accommodation: The ability of the eyes to adjust to or "accommodate" different viewing distances.

Acuity: See Visual acuity.

Adaptation: The ability of the eyes to adapt to changes in the luminance (brightness) of the surroundings.

Alternative workplace strategies (AWS): Strategies that use workplace designs, flexible work schedules, and modified furniture standards to increase the number of work locations that can be used by a worker.

Ambient illumination: General lighting supplied by artificial or natural sources that illuminates specific tasks or general surroundings.

Americans with Disabilities Act (ADA): Legislation enacted in the United States in 1992 to protect the rights of people with disabilities.

Anthropometry: The study of human body size and range of movement as a function of age, gender and other demographic variables.

Articulation index: The percentage of words or sentences that can be understood by a listener.

Asset management: A system consisting of computers, specialized software, and data logging equipment that codes and inventories individual pieces of furniture and equipment and tracks the movement and disposition of the asset over time.

Auditory map: Auditory description of a building layout or complex space provided to help people find their way in buildings.

Blocking: The process of assigning a "block" of space on a floor to a team, a group, or a department.

Braille: A method of writing words by means of dots arranged in cells, for the use of blind persons. The dots are read by touch.

Candelas per square meter: In the SI measurement system, a measure of *luminance* (emitted or reflected light) obtained by means of a photometer.

Carpal tunnel syndrome: A repetitive injury to the median nerve, which is compressed by inflamed tendons in the carpal tunnel of the wrist. Symptoms are tingling and numbness in the fingers.

Case goods (conventional furniture): Individual pieces of office furniture.

Centimeter: A metric measure of distance: 1 cm = 1/100 meter, the standard measure of length in the SI system.

Churn rate(%): The total annual number of office moves as a proportion of the average number of employees in the facility for the year multiplied by 100.

Closed-plan office: An office system consisting of floor-to-ceiling partitions that separate building floor space into private or semiprivate compartments. These may be offices, conference or reception rooms, work or support areas.

Color rendering index (CRI): A number between 1 and 100 that describes the effect of a light source on the color appearance of objects, compared with the effect produced by a reference light source of comparable color temperature.

Communication: The transmission and reception of a message that travels between two or more points.

Contrast: A measure of how well an object stands out from the background. The contrast between an object and its background is specified by the following equation:

$$\text{Contrast } (C) = \frac{L_o - L_b}{L_b} \times 100\%$$

$$L_o = \text{Luminance of the object}$$
$$L_b = \text{Luminance of the background}$$

Contrast glare: A visual effect caused by large luminance differences between adjacent surfaces. Contrast glare makes details on the darker surface, such as characters, difficult to make out.

Coping strategies: Individual strategies designed to identify and deal with causes of stress in order to reduce their effects.

Cumulative trauma disorder (CTD): Injury to the soft tissues of the body due to repetitive trauma.

Decibel (dB): The unit of sound pressure level. The dB refers to the ratio of sound pressure levels as follows:

$$dB = 20 \, \text{Log}_{10} \, (P_1 / P_0)$$

where: P_0 is the standard reference pressure, defined as the lowest level that the average human observer can hear (absolute threshold) when the signal is a 1000 Hz pure tone, and P_1 is the sound pressure being measured.

Degree: A unit of angular measure. A circle is composed of 360 degrees.

Direct glare: Glare that is caused by a bright source of light that shines directly into the eyes.

Direct lighting: Ambient lighting that radiates directly from the light source.

Disability: A reduction in the efficiency of one or more body systems, making it difficult to carry out major activities such as moving, walking, seeing, hearing, speaking, breathing, learning, or understanding.

Efficacy: A measure of how effectively the electrical energy that is provided to a lamp is converted to light.

Flexible workspace concept: A workspace design that permits the reconfiguration of an office space quickly and easily to meet a functional need.

Foot-candle (ft-c): A measure of illuminance in the English system. It is measured with an illumination meter held against the surface of interest. 1 ft-c = 10.76 lux.

Footrest: A foot support used primarily in seated workplaces to help accommodate workers who are unable to rest their feet comfortably on the floor and to relieve postural stresses.

Free address: Work space shared on a first come, first served basis, usually in large open-office space with many workstations.

Full spectrum lighting: A lighting system that attempts to reproduce the spectral power distribution of natural daylight.

Glare: A sensation caused by light within the visual field that is brighter than the level of light to which the eyes are adapted.

Hertz (Hz): The unit for frequency, in cycles per second, in the SI system. Relates to pitch at the subjective level.

Homework: An alternative work strategy where employees link their offices and home using telecommunications equipment and work out of their home one or more days a week. Homes are provided with proper furniture, telecommunications, and computer equipment to permit employees to work in an environment similar to what they would have in the office.

Hoteling: Work quarters for employees who normally work in the field. Office space is reserved on a first call basis and is not assigned to any worker beyond a specified occupation time.

Human factors (ergonomics): The process of designing for human use through the systematic application of our knowledge about humans to the equipment and management systems that they use and the environment in which they operate.

Illuminance: The amount of light falling on a surface. Illuminance is expressed in units of foot-candles or lux, where: 1 foot-candle = 10.76 lux.

Indirect glare: Glare that is caused by light reflected from a highly reflective surface.

Indirect lighting: General lighting produced by light that is reflected from ceilings or walls.

Integrated common plan: Open-plan offices, dedicated to a workgroup or team and surrounding closed spaces that are used for team meetings, personnel matters, and noise-generating equipment.

Just-in-time concept (JIT): An alternative workspace concept that is much the same as hoteling and nonterritorial offices—build offices for only 20% of the employees. The difference between the JIT concept and others is that employees do not reserve space. Employees "drop-in" and occupy workstations on a first-come, first-served basis.

Legibility: The ease with which a label, document, or display can be read and understood. The design and size of characters, contrast, illumination, color of characters and background, and construction of textual information all affect legibility.

Lumbar: Adjective referring to the five vertebrae of the lower back (between the thorax and sacrum).

Luminaire: An assembly consisting of lamps, housing, and lens (or louver) used to distribute light.

Luminance: The amount of light emitted by or reflected from a surface, expressed in units of candelas per square meter (cd/m^2) or foot-lamberts (ft-L), where: 1 ft-L = 3.43 cd/m^2. Luminance is related to the perception of brightness.

Luminance ratio: The ratio of the brightest surface in the visual field to the least bright surface. The luminance ratio should not exceed 10:1.

Lux: A measure of illuminance in the SI measurement system.

Masking: The amount by which a sound's threshold of audibility is raised by the presence of another (masking) sound. It is measured in decibels.

Matte: A surface or finish that causes light to be diffused or reflected in many directions. Contrast with "glossy."

Musculoskeletal system: Includes the bones and muscles of the body.

Neighborhood concept: Open-plan offices designed around small workgroups or teams that are separated from other teams by closed offices, meeting rooms, equipment rooms, and so on.

Noise: Unwanted sound that interferes with the detection of an auditory signal.

Noise reduction coefficient (NRC): The ability of a barrier to absorb sound. The NRC is usually expressed as an arithmetic average of the sound absorption characteristics of the barrier at frequencies of 250, 500, 1000, and 2000 Hz.

Nonterritorial offices: The term given to a group of workplace strategies whose objective is to eliminate assigned offices in order to reduce office space and office costs.

Office automation: The process of simplifying administrative or clerical work and procedures by using electronic devices. The objective is to increase efficiency by means of carefully focused capital investments in equipment to support and enhance the capabilities of work at all levels.

Open-plan office: An office system that is configured with varying height partitions that are freestanding.

Optimal visual field: The field of vision that provides optimal visual performance. It is usually defined as the area bounded by the horizontal line of sight, lines that are +/– 45 degrees laterally of the center line of vision and the line that is 45 degrees below the horizon.

Parabolic deflectors: A plastic or glass device fitted over the housing of a fluorescent fixture that focuses the light produced.

Privacy: The ability of individuals or groups to satisfactorily regulate their accessibility to others.

Postoccupancy evaluation: As part of the postproject evaluation, a survey of the office workers in a facility after the project has been completed to determine how well the facility meets their needs.

Postproject evaluation: An evaluation of the performance of the facility and the work of the project team that is usually performed several weeks or months after the relocation has been completed.

Readability: Ability of a reader to comprehend or understand the message that is being displayed. (See also Legibility.)

Reflectance factor: A number between 0 and 100 that describes the percentage of incident light reflected from a surface.

Retina: The innermost surface on the back part of the eyeball on which the image is formed by the lens of the eye. The retina is composed of cells that are sensitive to light intensity and color.

Satellite offices: An alternative workplace strategy that locates employees in office centers that provide technology and administrative support and are located close to the employees' homes.

Seat pan: The surface of a chair that supports the buttocks and most of the weight of the body.

Seat reference point (SRP): The seat reference point is the point at which the centerline of the seat back surface and the centerline of the seat pan intersect.

Sick building syndrome: When airborne contaminants reach the point where 10 % of the building occupants complain of symptoms such as headache, dizziness, or nausea.

SI units: Abbreviation for Le Systeme Internationale d'Unites (International System of Units). It is a coherent measurement system based on the metric unit of 10. An international committee recommended its use for worldwide scientific and commercial designations of measurements, such as distance, weight, force, illumination, noise, and volume.

Sound masking: The controlled use of noise to mask conversations, thus increasing the privacy of speech between two or more people.

Sound transmission class (STC): The effectiveness of a barrier in blocking the transmission of sound in the voice range of frequencies (125–4000 Hz).

Space plan: A plan created by a space planner, interior designer, or architect showing the utilization of the space by the occupants and the layout of furnishings and equipment.

Speech intelligibility: A measure of the percent of words, phrases, or sentences correctly understood over a specific speech communication system in a specific noise situation.

Stacking: A process whereby groups of people are assigned to floors of a multifloor building.

Stress: A physical, chemical, or emotional factor that causes tension in the body or the mind and that may be a factor in disease causation.

Systems furniture: Modular furniture that may be freestanding or panel hung, and that can be assembled to support the needs of the office worker.

Task analysis: A formal analysis of a worker's task that is conducted by breaking the job into its component parts or activities in order to be able to determine the human factors issues involved with the task.

Task lighting: Supplementary lighting provided for tasks requiring more light than that provided by general room lighting. Task lighting illuminates only the specific area where more light is required.

Team environments: Flexible work areas designed to meet the needs of project teams as they expand and shrink.

Telecommuting: See Homework.

Teleconferencing: Transmitting both voice and visual signals between two individual locations.

Thermal comfort: The temperature at which an individual desires neither further warmth nor further cooling.

Usability testing: Testing how well a system or a piece of equipment or a facility meets the needs of the user.

Veiling luminance: A uniform increase in the brightness of the background of a VDT screen that reduces the character/background contrast.

Viewing distance: The distance between the eye and the object being viewed.

Virtual offices: The capability for an employee to work anywhere through the use of telecommuncations and computer technology.

Visual acuity: The ability of the eye to discriminate or resolve fine detail. One of the best measures of legibility.

Visual angle: The angle subtended at the eye by the object being viewed.

Visual display terminal (VDT): A device that displays visual information that an operator uses to communicate with a computer.

Wayfinding: Ability of a visitor to arrive with ease at his or her destination.

Workspace: The physical area in which a person performs work. It is defined by partitions, furniture, and equipment.

Workstation: The furniture and equipment that occupy the workspace. The workstation may or may not be used by the occupant of the workspace.

Index